The politics of constitutional nationalism in Northern Ireland, 1932–70

MANCHESTER
1824

Manchester University Press

For Francesca and Patrick

The politics of constitutional nationalism in Northern Ireland, 1932–70

Between grievance and reconciliation

Christopher Norton

Manchester University Press
Manchester and New York
distributed in the United States exclusively
by Palgrave Macmillan

Published by Manchester University Press
Oxford Road, Manchester M13 9NR, UK
and Room 400, 175 Fifth Avenue, New York, NY 10010, USA
www.manchesteruniversitypress.co.uk

Distributed in the United States exclusively by
Palgrave Macmillan, 175 Fifth Avenue, New York,
NY 10010, USA

Distributed in Canada exclusively by
UBC Press, University of British Columbia, 2029 West Mall,
Vancouver, BC, Canada V6T 1Z2

British Library Cataloguing-in-Publication Data
A catalogue record for this book is available from the British Library

Library of Congress Cataloging-in-Publication Data applied for

ISBN 978 0 7190 5903 2 hardback

First published 2014

Edited and typeset
by Frances Hackeson Freelance Publishing Services, Brinscall, Lancs
Printed in Great Britain
by CPI Antony Rowe Ltd, Chippenham, Wiltshire

Contents

Contents

Acknowledgements

I am particularly indebted to my colleagues Michael Cunningham, Eamonn O'Kane and Hildegard Norton-Uhl who were generous enough to read earlier drafts of this book and whose comments and suggestions proved immensely helpful. In this regard my thanks also go to Manchester University Press's anonymous reader. My good friend, Francis McCaffrey, originally put the idea of writing this book into my head and has maintained a supportive and encouraging interest in its development ever since. Much welcome hospitality and friendship was provided by Paul and Jane McGowan in Belfast. I would like to thank the staff of the Public Record Office of Northern Ireland, the National Archive of Ireland and the Linen Hall Library, Belfast for their courteous help. The staff of Manchester University Press have shown great patience and professionalism for which I am extremely grateful.

Finally, my warmest thanks go to my children Francesca and Patrick for their support, good humour and the sheer joy of their company.

Abbreviations

DEA	Department of External Affairs
FOI	Friends of Ireland
GAA	Gaelic Athletic Association
IAPL	Irish Anti-Partition League
IRA	Irish Republican Army
IrLP	Irish Labour Party
IUA	Irish Union Association
LDF	Local Defence Force
NCU	National Council for Unity
NDP	National Democratic Party
NICRA	Northern Ireland Civil Rights Association
NILP	Northern Ireland Labour Party
NPF	National Political Front
NU	National Unity
RLP	Republican Labour Party
RUC	Royal Ulster Constabulary
S-CMA	Six-Counties Men's Association
SDLP	Social Democratic and Labour Party
UUC	Ulster Union Club
UVF	Ulster Volunteer Force

Introduction

This book considers the constitutional nationalist tradition in Northern Ireland, its articulation and representation of Catholic interests, and the political outcomes and consequences of its attempts to achieve its goal of Irish unity by constitutional and peaceful political means. It is a work that focuses on the strategic considerations and decisions of constitutional nationalist political leaders, activists and political organisations in the years 1932–70. As such it does not rehearse the Catholic experience of discrimination and disadvantage in Northern Ireland during this period; an area already well documented and subject to serious and balanced scholarly enquiry.[1] The memory of that experience was undoubtedly a poignant one for many, and, as we shall see, memories were consistently invoked in nationalist discourse to rationalise and legitimise political action or, quite often, inaction. I make no attempt here to recount memories, for in Ireland memory has long been an instrument of politics and memories are frequently called upon, often to defend entrenched political positions and nearly always to present a fatalistic vision of the past. This book attempts to move beyond the restraints of memory, it is a work of history, and, as the philosopher Pascal Bruckner has pointed out, the advantages of history are many, for whereas 'memory intimidates, condemns, blasts; history desacralizes, explains, details. One divides, the other reconciles'.[2]

To set the historical background of this study let us turn to the question of strategy and strategic considerations prior to 1932. In 1921 some 430,000 northern Catholics[3] found themselves a reluctant minority in the recently established Northern Ireland state; an outcome that neither they, nor the political leadership of Irish constitutional nationalism, had initially envisaged. Indeed, following the 1910 British general election, the dominant political party of nationalist Ireland, the moderate and constitutional Irish Party, under the leadership of John Redmond, was left holding the balance of power at Westminster and expectations were high that a Home Rule settlement, encompassing the whole island of Ireland, was within reach. The introduction of the Third Home

Rule Bill at Westminster by the Liberal Prime Minister Herbert Asquith in April 1912 was met, however, with an immediate and strident response from Ulster Protestant unionists of all social classes, who feared that Home Rule constituted a real threat to their religious liberties, economic and social advance and British cultural identity; fears which some of the unionists' pro-Home Rule opponents thought had some substance.[4] Ulster unionist resistance against inclusion into a Home Rule Ireland without their consent was resolute. In September 1912, in a significant display of constitutional militancy, a quarter of a million people signed the Ulster Covenant solemnly pledging their opposition to Home Rule. More ominously, in 1913, the formation of the Ulster Volunteer Force, a 100,000-strong militia – and the consequent establishment of an Irish nationalist militia (the National Volunteers) – signalled a dangerous militarisation of politics in Ireland. As the Home Rule Bill continued its stormy passage through both Houses of Parliament, events in Ireland, particularly the arming of the respective militias in 1914, revealed that the prospects of reconciling the divergent aspirations of Irish nationalism and Ulster unionism were becoming ever more remote, and the probability of some form of exclusion from Home Rule for part of the northern province of Ulster, where most Protestant unionists were located, ever more likely.

The question now arose as to what shape or form such exclusion would take: how many counties in Ulster were to be potentially excluded from Home Rule and would such exclusion be a temporary expedient or a permanent fixture? This was clearly an issue that fixed the minds of Catholics in the eastern Ulster counties who were faced with the prospect of permanent minority status. Redmond, politically and temperamentally inclined to seek an accommodation rather than a confrontation with Ulster unionists, proposed the temporary exclusion of those Ulster counties with Protestant majorities as a compromise, and his northern lieutenant, the West Belfast MP Joe Devlin, while at first hostile to this proposal, gradually came to accept the necessity of a conciliation strategy.[5] For their part, and in an attempt to assuage unionist fears, the government introduced an amendment to the Home Rule Bill, in March 1914, which facilitated the temporary exclusion of Ulster counties (for a period of six years) by enabling each county to vote itself in or out of the Home Rule settlement. This proposal was rejected as unacceptable by the Ulster Unionist leader Sir Edward Carson who insisted on the permanent exclusion of six north-eastern Ulster counties. By the time the Home Rule Bill received royal assent, in September 1914, a compromise between the two sides had not been reached.

The mounting sense of crisis in Ireland was, at this point, temporarily suspended by Britain's entry into World War I and by the government's decision to delay the implementation of Home Rule until war's end. Both Redmond and Devlin threw their support behind the British war effort, hoping that a demonstration of nationalist Ireland's wartime reliability would allay unionist misgivings; but in this they were to be disappointed and the years 1914–18 were to see a major reconfiguration of nationalist politics in Ireland which seriously undermined Redmond's party. The apparent interminable duration of the war, its increasing unpopularity throughout nationalist Ireland, the non-delivery of Home Rule and the political fall-out of the 1916 Easter Rising all culminated, at the 1918 general election, in the Irish Party's electoral demise and Sinn Féin's political ascendancy: Sinn Féin secured seventy-three seats to the Irish Party's six. Of the Irish Party's six seats it is significant that five were gained in the north of the country. One of these one was secured by Joe Devlin who convincingly held his West Belfast constituency against a challenge mounted by the sole surviving commandant of the 1916 Rising, Eamon de Valera. Electoral success in the other four, however, came primarily as a result of a pre-election agreement between Sinn Féin and the Irish Party not to stand against each other in marginal constituencies where a split nationalist vote would hand the seat to a Unionist candidate. Devlin had assented to this pact in the belief that without it his party's prospects of returning candidates to Westminster would have been even worse than they turned out to be.[6] The pact clearly represented a coming to terms with the new political realities in Ireland, and yet, despite the Irish Party's overall paucity of seats, constitutional nationalism remained much more resilient in Ulster compared to the rest of the country. In fact, support for the Irish Party in the Ulster counties held up and in contests in Unionist majority non-pact constituencies it outperformed Sinn Féin.[7]

Constitutional nationalism in the north-east may have shown itself to be politically robust, but as Sinn Féin carried out its abstentionist programme – withdrawing from Westminster in early 1919 to convene a parliament of the Irish Republic in Dublin – Devlin found himself in the unenviable position of leading a tiny and inchoate Irish Party presence at Westminster. The Irish Party had earlier entertained hopes that, in the event of an exclusion settlement for Ulster, a safeguard for northern nationalists would be provided by the dual pressure of an Irish Home Rule parliament within the UK and the continued influence of Irish MPs sitting at Westminster. These hopes were now dashed.[8] Additionally, the weight of constitutional nationalist input into the British government's ongoing attempts to reconcile increasingly incompatible positions within Ireland was greatly reduced. These attempts were to culminate in the Government of Ireland Act, 1920, a measure which superseded the provisions of the 1914 Home Rule Act and provided for the creation of two jurisdictions in Ireland (a six-county Northern Ireland and a twenty-six county Southern Ireland) each with its own home rule parliament, one in Belfast and one in

Dublin. While the partition of Ireland was an integral part of the 1920 Act, it did allow for the future reunion of Ireland based on the principle of consent, but this was premised on the development of amicable relations between the two Irish parliaments and on conditions of stability and democratic accord within their respective territories. The intensification of the IRA's violent campaign (under way since 1919) determined that this was not to be. Between 1920 and 1922 the IRA embarked on a concerted and violent effort to destabilise the new Northern Ireland state; the ferocity of their endeavours being matched by an equally ferocious response. The social and political effects of this violence, in which over 600 people lost their lives, were unquestionably negative: sectarian tensions and hostilities increased exponentially while those of moderate disposition, who advocated rapprochement and tolerance, were sidelined.[9]

The gravity of the situation inevitably impacted on the strategic choices taken by Devlin and the Irish Party. At the time of the first Northern Ireland general election, in May 1921, pressure to present a united front against partition appeared irresistible and Devlin entered into yet another election pact with Sinn Féin. As with the earlier pact, this did not signal a thawing in relations between constitutional nationalists and republicans; on the contrary, de Valera actually hoped that the pact would see off Devlin's Irish Party.[10] In this he did not succeed, but as a condition of the pact, de Valera had insisted upon (and secured) Irish Party acceptance of Sinn Féin's policy of refusing to enter the Northern Ireland parliament. Devlin thus reluctantly contested the election on an abstentionist platform which he did not support. The election outcome resulted in both parties returning six seats each (the Unionists returned forty seats), however, in percentage terms Sinn Féin's 20 per cent of the vote compared to the Irish Party's 12 per cent represented a considerable swing in political fortunes between the two parties.[11]

The scale of the Unionist victory at the 1921 election was undoubtedly formidable, but even so, there remained a prevailing mood of optimism among northern nationalists that the situation in which they found themselves would be one of relatively short-lived duration. The grounds for this optimism were the terms of the Anglo-Irish Treaty, signed in London by representatives of Sinn Féin and the British government in December 1921, which appeared to hold out the possible transfer of predominantly Catholic-populated northern border counties from Northern Ireland to the Irish Free State. The Treaty – a compromise settlement between the British government and Irish republicans following the latter's rejection of the Government of Ireland Act, 1920 – was, in 1922, to ignite a bitter civil war in the South between pro and anti-Treaty factions of Irish republicanism. However, at the time of its signing, attention in the North focused on article 12 of the Treaty which allowed for the establishment of a

Boundary Commission to adjudicate on the final contours of the border between the Irish Free State and Northern Ireland. Republican plenipotentiaries
at the Treaty negotiations with the British government assumed that the work-
ings of the Boundary Commission would result in the transfer of substantial
tracts of northern territory to the South; it was also believed that a physically smaller Northern Ireland would prove unviable in the long term and that
therefore unionists would come to accept the inevitability of their inclusion
into a unitary state. These beliefs were to prove erroneous, but their effect at
the time was to strengthen a northern nationalist position of abstention from,
and non-recognition of, the governing institutions of the Northern Ireland
state. There was intra-nationalist division over this; Devlin's preference was to
reconstitute a new united constitutional nationalist movement which would
recognise and engage with the Northern Ireland parliament, but in this he
faced stern opposition from border nationalists who remained convinced that
the Free State government and the Boundary Commission would secure their
deliverance.[12]

This political dissonance produced a dilemma at the 1924 Westminster
election when de Valera unilaterally announced that anti-Treaty Sinn Féin candidates would contest Northern Ireland parliamentary seats on an abstentionist
ticket. In its response pro-Treaty Sinn Féin dithered on whether to stand,
before eventually deciding not to put forward candidates; this was much to
the chagrin of Devlin and his supporters who had little choice but to follow
suit.[13] The result for anti-Treaty Sinn Féin proved disastrous; the Catholic electorate rejected de Valera's radical republican alternative and stayed away from
the polls, the nationalist vote duly collapsed and two previously held seats (in
Fermanagh-Tyrone) were lost. The experience did, however, provide the impetus for the formation of a loose political coalition – made up of the remnants of
Devlin's Irish Party and pro-Treaty Sinn Féin – which was in place by the time
of the next Northern Ireland general election in 1925. This coalition, its candidates contesting constituencies as Nationalists, registered an impressive reversal
in the political balance between constitutionalists and republicans: Nationalist
candidates were returned in ten seats with 24 per cent of the vote, abstentionist Republicans took two seats and 5 per cent of the vote.[14] Devlin, who had
more stridently voiced his rejection of parliamentary abstentionism during the
course of the election, entered the Northern Ireland parliament within weeks
of his election in West Belfast. His example was not, however, followed by all
elected Nationalist representatives, some of whom continued to look towards
the Irish government for guidance and leadership, and it was not until 1927 –
when all hopes of territorial transference had faded – that the rest his colleagues
joined him.

By 1928 Devlin managed to form this electoral coalition into a political party of sorts (the National League of the North), but the unity of this new formation was fragile and the diverse political and ideological backgrounds of National League MPs ensured there was little agreement on where their immediate priorities should lie: Devlin looked towards a vigorous campaign highlighting the need for improvements in the social and economic conditions of Catholics and working-class Protestants as a means of breaking down sectarian barriers, others emphasised anti-partitionism above all else and showed little appetite for parliamentary attendance.

These differences remained unresolved by the time Devlin led his party out of the Northern Ireland parliament in 1932, which is the starting point of this study. The history of constitutional nationalism after this time is one coloured by a legacy of ideological diversity; a diversity further supplemented by a variety of labourist-orientated anti-partitionist organisations which, by the mid-1940s, had emerged as the principal representatives of political opinion in many Catholic working-class districts in Belfast. Given the complexity of constitutional nationalist politics it was perhaps inevitable that strategic coherence, or agreement, would be difficult to achieve. The following chapters address a series of questions which continued to be hotly contested among constitutional anti-partitionists across a broad left–right political spectrum: questions of whether to participate in, or abstain from, Northern Ireland's parliament; of whether fidelity to the Irish government in Dublin should remain the pre-eminent political strategy above all others; of whether the immediacy of anti-partitionism outweighed all other socio-economic concerns; and of whether northern unionists were to be courted and convinced of the desirability of a united Ireland, or ignored and coerced. They will also consider the ways in which constitutional nationalism confronted the challenge posed by militant republicanism both in its violent and electoral guises.

Notes

1 John Whyte, *Interpreting Northern Ireland* (Oxford, Clarendon Press, 1991); Mary Harris, 'Religious Divisions, Discrimination and the Struggle for Dominance in Northern Ireland', in G. Hálfdanarson (ed.), *Racial Discrimination and Ethnicity in European History* (Pisa, Pisa University Press, 2003); M. Mulholland, 'Why Did Unionists Discriminate?', in Sabine Wichert (ed.), *From the United Irishmen to Twentieth-Century Unionism: Essays in Honour of A.T.Q. Stewart* (Dublin, Four Courts Press, 2004).
2 Pascal Bruckner, *The Tyranny of Guilt: An Essay on Western Masochism* (Princeton University Press, Princeton, NJ, 2010), pp. 158–159.

3   John Darby, *Northern Ireland: The Background to the Conflict* (Belfast, The Appletree Press, 1983), p. 20.
4   Paul Bew, *Ireland: The Politics of Emnity 1789–2006* (Oxford, Oxford University Press, 2007), p. 368.
5   A.C. Hepburn, *Catholic Belfast and Nationalist Ireland in the Era of Joe Devlin 1871–1934* (Oxford, Oxford University Press, 2008), p. 150.
6   Eamonn Phoenix, *Northern Nationalism: Nationalist Politics, Partition and the Catholic Minority in Northern Ireland 1890–1940* (Belfast, Ulster Historical Foundation, 1994), p. 50.
7   Hepburn, *Catholic Belfast*, p. 199.
8   Bew, *Ireland*, p. 383.
9   See Robert Lynch, *The Northern IRA and the Early Years of Partition, 1920–1922* (Dublin, Irish Academic Press, 2006) for a meticulously informed treatment of this.
10   Tom Hennessey, *A History of Northern Ireland 1920–1996* (Dublin, Gill & Macmillan, 1997), p. 16.
11   Lynch, *The Northern IRA*, p. 78.
12   Phoenix, *Northern Nationalism*, p. 287.
13   *Ibid.*, p. 309.
14   Hepburn, *Catholic Belfast*, p. 257.

1

The politics of abstentionism, 1932–39

In May 1932, the veteran northern nationalist leader, Joe Devlin, led his party (the National League of the North, formed in 1928) out of the Northern Ireland parliament proclaiming his frustration with the Unionist government's refusal to cooperate with National League politicians who wished to offer a constructive opposition within Northern Ireland's political system. For much of his political career Devlin had espoused a 'non-sectarian social radicalism'[1] that had emphasised themes of fair play and justice for northern nationalists alongside broader and more generalised demands for greater economic and social improvement for the working class, both Catholic and Protestant. This was a policy underpinned by a principled but conciliatory nationalism. Devlin was strongly committed to Irish national unity under a Dublin parliament, but this objective was to be achieved only by constitutional, non-violent means.[2] However, by the time of Devlin's walk-out the National League found itself perceived in the most malign way possible by significant sections of unionist political and popular opinion. In the words of the main Unionist daily newspaper, the *Belfast Telegraph*, the National League sought nothing less than 'the destruction of the parliament of Northern Ireland'.[3] This harsh judgement was rooted in the still recent memories of the violent and costly (in human terms) early years of the Northern Ireland state; a period which saw Unionist and Nationalist conciliatory gestures scuppered by a concerted, but ultimately futile, republican attempt to destabilise the newly established political institutions, and a vicious loyalist response to this.[4] Moderate and accommodating tendencies within unionism, which had been in evidence in the early 1920s,[5] were now replaced by more implacably defensive (if not outwardly sectarian) positions, the effects of which were to strengthen deepening mutual suspicion and hostility between unionism and nationalism.

Devlin's walkout was dramatic but not intemperate. Never in command of a united party, and challenged by more militant republican voices outside his organisation,[6] Devlin's action sought, in part, to limit damage to the National

League's credibility in view of the failure of his parliamentary strategy to achieve tangible results for northern Catholics. As such it was premised on, and a response to, wider developments within nationalist Ireland: namely, the election to office in 1932 of Eamon de Valera's Fianna Fail party in the Irish Free State and the upsurge of physical force republicanism on both sides of the border.[7] During the 1932 election campaign the IRA had thrown its support behind de Valera[8] and, once in power, the Fianna Fail government rewarded this support by reversing the restrictions that had earlier been imposed on militant republicans by the outgoing Cumann na nGaedheal government: IRA prisoners were now released, the proscription of the IRA rescinded and the ban on the IRA newspaper, *An Phoblacht*, lifted.[9] In the North this apparent accommodation of the IRA was to boost republican ranks with those who assumed, quite wrongly as it turned out, that de Valera 'was going to do something' about partition.[10]

Some of Devlin's colleagues in the National League certainly appear to have seen in de Valera's victory the possibility of the opening-up of an alternative militantly constitutionalist strategy for northern nationalist representatives – this was the prospect of elected National League MPs turning their back on the North's unwelcoming parliamentary institutions and instead taking seats in the Dáil. So confident were certain National Leaguers that this eventuality would come to pass that even those whose political origins lay in the pro-Treaty wing of Sinn Féin, most notably Cahir Healy MP (a former close associate of Arthur Griffith and Michael Collins), readily abandoned their support for William Cosgrave's outgoing Cumann naGaedheal government (the successor of Griffith's and Collins's pro-Treaty Sinn Féin) to embrace de Valera's Fianna Fail party (the successor of anti-Treaty Sinn Féin).[11] It is highly unlikely that Devlin, mindful of the need to conciliate unionist opinion, entertained the benign outcome anticipated by some of his colleagues. In fact, de Valera downplayed the border question during the 1932 general election and whatever hopes were held that he would prioritise the grievances of northern nationalists, and the whole partition issue, in a constructive and interventionist manner proved remarkably short-lived. At a meeting in Dublin in February 1933 de Valera disabused Devlin and Healy of any likelihood that the Dáil would open its doors to the Northern League representatives. De Valera pointed to northern weakness – in effect nationalist political fragmentation and the absence of a strong united party – as the reason for his refusal to grant Dáil entry. Fianna Fail, he argued, could not be seen to intervene in a way that could be interpreted as favouring one nationalist faction over another.[12] Faced with this rebuff Devlin and his colleagues decided, at a party meeting in May 1933, to return to the northern parliament after the summer recess. However, this was not to be in the capacity as official opposition but rather, in the words of Healy (MP for both the Northern Ireland parliamentary seat of South Fermanagh and the Westminster seat of Fermanagh-Tyrone), 'to attend on occasion when we had something special to talk about or some statement to make'.[13]

This vacillating partial abstentionist position left the League vulnerable to electoral competition and at the Northern Ireland parliamentary general election of November 1933, republican candidates, standing on an unambiguously abstentionist platform, challenged the National League in four constituencies: Belfast Central, Foyle, South Armagh and South Down. In South Armagh, where there was a three-way split of the nationalist vote, the republican candidate took the seat. In Belfast Central and Foyle the League won comfortably (Devlin taking the Belfast Central seat), however, the republican candidates in these constituencies fared credibly well – the political context of their vote being one of raised expectations among the North's Catholic electorate that Fianna Fail's entry into office would mean a reopening of the border issue. Only in the fourth contested constituency of South Down did the republicans poll poorly. Here their opponent was Eamon de Valera who had reluctantly accepted his nomination as an abstentionist candidate following the failure of the local constituency organisation to select an agreed nationalist nominee. As Eamon Phoenix has pointed out de Valera's selection (and subsequent election) was significant, indicating as it did the start of a discernible shift in constitutional nationalist strategy away from Devlin's earlier emphasis on the Catholic minority looking 'to its own resources'[14] in order to redress their grievances, towards one that held that the Dublin government was the only agency that could deliver nationalist salvation. This shift was to have major repercussions on future nationalist political developments.

Devlin's death in January 1934 (he was terminally ill at the time 1933 election) was a major blow to the National League. With his passing Northern nationalism lost its most able and experienced politician and tactician; effectively the National League was left both leaderless and rudderless.

Devlin's successor T.J. Campbell, a lawyer and former editor of the North's main nationalist daily newspaper, the *Irish News*, was an ardent Devlinite and noted moderate. Described by the writer, poet and former senior Stormont civil servant, G.C. Duggan, as 'a gentle and cultured man, little fitted for the rough and tumble of political life',[15] Campbell lacked the élan and command of his predecessor and was rivalled by Cahir Healy for the effective leadership of the League. Indeed, strong leadership was noticeably absent following Devlin's departure: there was to be no review of National League strategy or tactics and the ad hoc policy of partial abstentionism, despite the indications of its weaknesses, remained in place.

In terms of electoral advancement the League was marginally disadvantaged by the Unionist government's decision, in 1929, to abolish the proportional representation electoral system to the Northern parliament and replace it with a first-past-the-post system. This measure was not intended as a deliberate action to curtail nationalist political representation, rather it was a response to successful challenges to the Unionist Party by Northern Ireland Labour Party (NILP) and Independent Unionist candidates in Protestant working-class districts of Belfast during a period of severe economic recession and high unemployment.[16] However, although the new electoral constituencies were drawn up in such a way as to return the same number of nationalist representatives as under the PR system (twelve in total), a miscalculation of the National League's strength in Belfast by the Parliamentary Draftsman resulted in a reduction of the League's Belfast seats from three to two, thus cutting overall nationalist representation in the Northern parliament by one seat.[17] The reduced presence of NILP and Independent Unionist parliamentary representatives in the city also moved the National League further from Devlin's social radicalism and non-sectarian preparedness to cooperate with labourist parties and closer to what A.C. Hepburn has called 'the cocoon of a minority sectarian party'.[18] The introduction of the electoral changes thus ultimately worked to the detriment of nationalists, even if, from the Unionist Party's point of view, it successfully reduced inter-class Unionist competition in Belfast and refocused political divisions to a more manageable Nationalist/Unionist axis.[19]

It was not electoral performance, however, but a general deterioration in the political climate in Northern Ireland that was to impact quite markedly on nationalist politics. This was linked not only to continuing nationalist frustrations but also to a growing sense of unionist vulnerability. De Valera's triumph in the Free State, resurgent IRA activism on both sides of the border, and economic uncertainty in the North, together fuelled the development, in the early and mid-1930s, of a militant Protestant critique of the Unionist government's alleged laxity in pandering to 'disloyal' Catholics; a critique articulated by the stridently sectarian Ulster Protestant League (UPL).[20] The activities of the UPL undoubtedly exacerbated communal tensions, but so too did a series of highly provocative statements and speeches by Unionist Party politicians and government members, which appeared to justify, and support, the portrayal of Catholics as disloyal, untrustworthy and seditious.[21] Perhaps the most infamous of these was a speech delivered by Basil Brooke, then a junior government whip, at Newtownbutler on 12 July 1933. Addressing an Orange Order gathering Brooke resorted to the use of highly emotive and sectarian language in order to alert his audience to what he saw as a real and incipient danger:

a great number of protestants ... employed Roman catholics ... He felt that he could speak freely on this subject as he had not a Roman catholic about his own place ... He would point out that the Roman catholics were endeavouring to get in everywhere and were out with all their force and might to destroy the power and constitution of Ulster. There was a definite plot to overpower the vote of Unionists in the North. He would appeal to loyalists, therefore, wherever possible, to employ protestant lads and lassies (cheers) ... Roman catholics ... had got too many appointments for men who were really out to cut their throats if opportunity arose.[22]

Brooke was to repeat the same hard-line sentiments in a number of subsequent speeches over the coming months, much to the outrage of the nationalist parliamentary representatives. Criticism of Brooke did come from moderate unionists but he was supported, rather than rebuked, in his comments by the Prime Minister, Sir James Craig, and by other members of the government. This, understandably, served to infuriate nationalist opinion. The speech was to earn Brooke the lasting enmity of Catholics who saw in his words the very epitome of Unionist triumphalism, sectarianism and backwardness. It was also a speech that was to haunt him for the rest of his political career.

The wholly disagreeable and offensive nature of Brooke's speech was indeed depressingly stark. The resultant caricature of Brooke as an unrepentant sectarian bigot, however, must be weighed against the knowledge that he did not keep to his own advice regarding the employment of Catholics and indeed, in June 1940, was prepared to contemplate Northern Ireland's inclusion into a united Ireland if that was the price to be paid for the Southern state's entry into the war against Nazi Germany.[23] Furthermore, not only was he later to express regret that he ever made such controversial comments[24] he was also (in 1951) to repudiate the very sentiments that underpinned them.[25] In recent times historians have situated Brooke's extreme views and intemperate language firmly in the political context of unionist insecurity in the Fermanagh of the early 1930s; a time when it was feared that unionist disunity and lack of vigilance was jeopardising its supposedly precarious hold on that county.[26] The belief that Fermanagh's finely balanced political demographic could be upset (in favour of nationalists) by the inflow of large numbers of migrant farm labourers from the Free State was of particular concern to the Unionist political leadership, especially as many of these migrant labourers were allegedly employed by Protestants.[27] Brooke's speeches were a wholly excessive response to this perceived threat and his widely publicised comments undoubtedly impacted on community relations in a most damaging way; not only encouraging the prejudices of Protestant ultra-loyalists but also reinforcing a wider popular Protestant perception of Catholicism as being implacable hostility to the state: a perception no doubt strengthened in the minds of many Protestant unionists by the high-profile attacks on the Northern Ireland state frequently delivered by the then head of the Catholic Church in Ireland, Cardinal Joseph MacRory.[28]

Parliamentary exchanges (the parliament now relocated in Stormont on the outskirts of Belfast) between the National League and Unionists now became increasingly fractious and bitter as the League attempted to force a retraction of Brooke's calls for sanctions on the employment of Catholics and the government stubbornly defended discrimination, not against Catholics but against 'disloyalists'.[29] The eruption of widespread sectarian rioting in Belfast in July 1935, the worst outbreak of violence the city had experienced since 1922, further added to the nationalist sense of political alienation.[30] The League's attendance policy to the Northern Ireland parliament now became increasingly sporadic. Of the nine National League MPs who held Stormont seats two were effectively abstentionist (Hugh McAleer, Mid Tyrone; Alex Donnelly, West Tyrone), five were infrequently attending partial abstentionists (Cahir Healy, South Fermanagh; Joe Stewart, East Tyrone; J.J. McCarroll, Foyle; Patrick O'Neill, Mourne; George Leeke, Mid Londonderry) and only two were in regular attendance (T.J. Campbell, Belfast Central; Richard Byrne, Falls).[31]

Against this background the League's electoral vulnerability, evident in the 1933 election, resurfaced at the Westminster general election in November 1935 when republicans put forward abstentionist candidates in four of Northern Ireland's Westminster constituencies – West Belfast, Armagh, Co. Down and Fermanagh and Tyrone.[32] The challenge in the latter constituency was particularly significant; the National League held the dual seats of Fermanagh and Tyrone – the outgoing MPs being Cahir Healy and Joe Stewart[33]- and a contest here carried with it the distinct possibility of a split nationalist vote and the loss of both seats to Unionist Party candidates. The republicans' election manifesto, taking advantage of the League's discrepancy in attendance policy towards the Stormont and Westminster parliaments (they favoured attendance at Westminster), emphasised their own 'principled' abstentionism in contrast to the allegedly unprincipled position of the National League: 'It is particularly deplorable that citizens styling themselves "Irish Nationalists", should sit, in defiance of the wishes of the Irish nation in the Parliament of the conqueror. Representation in the Parliament is a symbol of Ireland's slavery and subjection.'[34] In a rather unnerved response the League's Tyrone–Fermanagh nationalist convention manoeuvred to retain the seats by nominating Healy and Stewart as abstentionist candidates. However, their candidature still proved to be unacceptable to republicans and a contest between them was only avoided by a last minute compromise that saw the nomination of two non-party abstentionist candidates: Anthony Mulvey, the editor of the provincial nationalist newspaper the *Ulster Herald*; and Patrick Cunningham, a wealthy farmer. Both men came with impeccable republican credentials.[35] Enda Staunton, in his valuable study, has suggested that Mulvey and Cunningham's subsequent election, and the sizeable votes received by republican candidates in Armagh, Down and Belfast can be read as a vindication of republican strategy.[36] Certainly the strategy paid off, but the significance of the election outcome may not be as transparent as the results suggest. It is notable that Armagh and Down (at this time both safe Unionist seats) had not been contested by a nationalist candidate of any description since 1924 and so the 1935 election was the first opportunity in eleven years that the sizeable nationalist minorities in these constituencies had to cast their vote for a non-unionist candidate. Considering this, the atmosphere of heightened sectarianism resulting from the recent riots *and* the failure of the National League to put forward candidates, it was hardly surprising that the nationalist electorate registered an anti-Unionist vote by casting their ballots for republican candidates. Interestingly, in West Belfast, a seat frequently contested by nationalist candidates,[37] the republican contender, Charles Leddy, saw his share of the vote fall.[38] Meanwhile, in Fermanagh and Tyrone the successful abstentionist candidates, Mulvey and Cunningham, with the advantage of campaigning to prevent a Unionist gain, together registered a slight drop in the nationalist share of the vote from the previous election in 1931.[39] The election of Mulvey and Cunningham, and the credible performance of the republicans,[40] may well be viewed more as an expression of Catholic communal solidarity reflecting unease with the existing state of affairs rather than conclusive evidence of a widespread shift in Catholic political attitudes towards more radicalised positions. Indeed, in Fermanagh and Tyrone the complete absence of any discernible policy other than abstentionism did not stand in the way of success. After the election Mulvey admitted, 'We held no election campaign. We simply issued a statement saying that if elected we would not go to Westminster' while Cunningham brusquely declared, 'I'm a farmer … being an MP doesn't interest me.'[41] And yet unionists were to interpret the National League's decision to concede the election to republicans in the most malign way possible. In advance of the election John Andrews, the Minister of Labour, anticipated that the republican's candidature would show, 'how many downright disloyalists exist in the parts of our area where they are standing for election',[42] while following on from the election an appeal by the unionist moderate, Major-General Hugh Montgomery, for unionists to differentiate between constitutional nationalists and republicans was summarily dismissed by the Secretary of the Ulster Unionist Council, Sir Wilson Hungerford: 'I am afraid that I cannot share the view that "constitutional" Nationalists, if treated in a different way would not unite themselves with Republicans and others who are trying to "down" the Northern government. No doubt their tactics may not be so violent but their object is the same.'[43] For unionists the election outcome merely served to confirm their view of nationalist politics as a threat incapable of conciliation. Their response to this threat was to gerrymander local government electoral boundaries to ensure Unionist Party domination.

The 1935 Westminster election was a watershed for constitutional nationalists in the North. In its wake the National League, after the loss of Devlin always more a loose and unstable coalition of politicians than a political party, ceased to function as a coherent organisation. Its decline was the occasion, in early 1936, for Anthony Mulvey to attempt the launch of a united front organisation – the Reunion of Ireland Organisation – designed to bring together the Fermanagh-Tyrone abstentionist MPs and republicans. This venture was however short-lived, collapsing at the first hurdle when, at a delegate Convention held in Belfast in June, republican insistence that the new body should reject both parliaments in Ireland led to a walkout by Mulvey and his supporters.[44]

Attempts were also made to reconstitute a broad umbrella constitutional nationalist political grouping in the mould of the League. The first such endeavour, the Irish Union Association (IUA) in September 1936, brought together a number of former National League MPs, including, most prominently, Cahir Healy. The IUA, whose constitution declared its first objective to be 'the national unity and independence of Ireland',[45] did secure the support of the Catholic clergy but left broader issues of leadership, strategy and tactics unresolved. It also failed to re-integrate all representatives formerly associated with the National League. The two Belfast MPs T.J. Campbell and Richard Byrne, who attended the founding convention of the IUA, chose to remain outside its ranks, disagreeing with both the new organisation's pro-Fianna Fail bias and its informal, but active, policy of abstention from the Stormont parliament: Campbell and Byrne were now the only elected nationalist representatives who were in regular attendance at Stormont.[46] Somewhat ironically it was the informality of the IUA's abstentionist policy that ruled Mulvey and Cunningham out of the organisation. They insisted on a strict, and permanent, adherence to parliamentary abstentionism whereas Healy's more experienced political instincts led him to regard abstention as a political tactic not a hallowed principle. Healy felt that rigidity on this issue could be fraught with problems, and these he raised in a letter to Eamon Donnelly (the Northern-born Fianna Fail TD for Leix-Offaly who in 1933 advocated Northern Nationalist incorporation into Fianna Fail)[47] in October 1936. There were, Healy wrote, potential political, legal and financial difficulties associated with the nomination of abstentionist candidates to the Northern Ireland parliament – they faced the financial penalty of forfeited election deposits and the prospect of the likely loss of seats in by-elections which would be called once unoccupied seats had been declared vacant. Healy warned that other Catholic, or worse still socialist, candidates would put themselves forward in such a situation. Citing republican orthodoxy – 'Arthur Griffith, the sponsor of Abstention, only intended it for a definite period and to meet a certain situation' – Healy signalled his belief that the policy could operate only within a limited timeframe and suggested that a suitable alternative strategy would be for elected nationalist candidates to, 'take their seats formally, make a considered protest and then leave'.[48] This suggestion of a moderated abstentionism was poorly received by Donnelly. Buoyed by resolutions submitted to the forthcoming Fianna Fail Ard Fheis, which called for northern elected representatives to be permitted to sit and vote in the Dáil,[49] Donnelly saw little to be gained from even limited nationalist political involvement in the parliaments at Stormont or Westminster. The question of partition, he believed, would be resolved by Dublin and London, not by political engagement with, 'deluded ignorant Orangemen'. His advice to Healy was to, 'demand your seat in the Dáil'.[50]

While Healy's position appeared to be more reflective of the views of nationalist opinion in the North (subsequent Nationalist Conventions in Fermanagh, Tyrone, Derry and Belfast produced majorities in support of the retention of seats in Stormont while South Down and Armagh opted for total abstention)[51] events in the Irish Free State were soon to undermine both the IUA and any reappraisal of the abstentionist tactic.

The acceptance of de Valera's new Constitution by a majority (albeit not an overwhelming one)[52] of the Free State electorate in the referendum of 1937, and Fianna Fail's return to office, as a minority government, in the simultaneous general election of that year brought heart to that section of northern political nationalism most favourable to Donnelly's standpoint. Nationalists north of the border warmly welcomed the strong Catholic ethos of the Constitution and its irredentist claim (in articles 2 and 3) to the territory of Northern Ireland. However, even though the inclusion of articles 2 and 3 was designed more to placate Fianna Fail's republican wing and win over IRA militants in the South to constitutionalism rather than to signal a major initiative on re-unification,[53] de Valera's anti-partitionist rhetoric, and his public and private assurances to his republican wing that 'the next move forward must be to get within that Constitution the whole of the thirty-two counties of Ireland',[54] received an enthusiastic reception particularly among nationalists in the border counties of Northern Ireland. It also encouraged the emergence, in December 1937, of a new organisation under the leadership of the abstentionist Westminster MP for Fermanagh and Tyrone, Anthony Mulvey, which enjoyed substantial support among the Catholic clergy: the Northern Council for Unity (NCU).[55] For the

NCU the prospect of applying the Constitution to the thirty-two counties of Ireland raised expectations that northern Nationalist MPs would be admitted to the Dáil thus legitimising its core policy of abstention from Stormont and Westminster. In comparison to the parliamentary procrastination and relative inactivity of the IUA, Mulvey's group, which was enthusiastically supported by Eamon Donnelly, must have appeared more in tune with the apparent dynamics of Irish political developments; certainly the defection of the IUA's joint secretary (the Omagh cleric Dr McShane) to the NCU would suggest this.[56] By the end of the year the IUA, could no longer muster sufficient resources, or interest, to hold its annual conference.[57]

All eyes now turned to de Valera who, in 1938, was about to embark on a major diplomatic rapprochement with Britain. Anxious to preserve Irish neutrality as the prospect of imminent war in Europe loomed, and faced with economic stagnation at home, de Valera sought to negotiate with the British government the return of the Treaty ports (which under the 1921 Anglo-Irish Treaty remained under British military control for the purpose of British defence) and the termination of economic sanctions imposed by Britain on Ireland during the protracted dispute between the two governments over the repayment of land annuities to the British Exchequer (the so called 'Economic War' of 1932–38).[58] Facing a British prime minister, Neville Chamberlain, wedded, in a deteriorating European political climate, to a policy of appeasement and anxious to avoid 'the strategic consequences of having an unfriendly Irish neighbour'[59] de Valera fared remarkably well in the negotiations, regaining the Treaty ports and settling the economic war on terms highly favourable to the Irish government. He did not, however, enter the negotiations secure in the knowledge that such an outcome was likely and from the outset de Valera's negotiating strategy was one that elevated the ending of partition as his major priority. This 'partition ploy', in the words of Tim Pat Coogan,[60] served a dual purpose; it placated Fianna Fail's republican wing,[61] for whom the 'betrayal' by the Republican negotiating team at the 1921 Anglo-Irish Treaty negotiations was an abiding memory, and it put pressure on the British to accommodate de Valera by making concessions in the more deliverable areas of defence, trade and the economy.[62] De Valera's strategy, while galvanising nationalist opinion in the North, was privately criticised at the time by a member of the Irish negotiating team; the Belfast-born Sean MacEntee. In a letter to de Valera, MacEntee warned that playing the partition card ran the risk of 'subordinating reason to prejudice' and intensifying 'the distrust of the [Unionist] people in the North whose confidence we wish to win'. His view was that 'the Partition problem cannot be solved except with the consent of the majority of the Northern non-Catholic population'.[63]

McEntee's misgivings were prescient. Shortly after the Anglo-Irish negoti-ations were under way in January 1938, Craigavon, having been alerted by newspaper reports that de Valera would raise the question of partition, took the opportunity to call a snap general election in Northern Ireland. Presenting the election, which took place in February, as a plebiscite on the border, Craigavon, faced with increasing criticism from within unionism over his government's in-action on social and economic issues, found himself in the fortuitous position of seeing off a challenge to the dominance of the Unionist Party from a group of dynamic, and moderate, unionist rebels who had formed the Progressive Unionist Party. Craigavon's success was such that he actually increased the number of Unionist Party seats in Stormont.[64] On the nationalist side, raised expectations that partition was to be a substantive issue in the negotiations reinforced both the NCU's total abstentionism and the Healyites qualified ab-stentionism. The NCU's refusal even to nominate candidates for the election – calling instead for 'a straight referendum on the question of unity'[65] – result-ed in a net loss of nationalist seats at Stormont.[66] In the border region, three constituencies that had formerly returned Nationalists went uncontested; of these, two (Mourne and South Down) were lost to Unionists while the third (South Armagh) went to Patrick Agnew of the Northern Ireland Labour Party. Meanwhile, those elected representatives associated with Healy's IUA took their seats in Stormont, but, upon signing the obligatory oath of state, with-drew pending the outcome of the British-Irish negotiations in London. This once again left the Belfast MPs, Campbell and Byrne – much to the opprobri-um of their Nationalist colleagues – as the sole representatives of the nationalist minority in Stormont.

Nationalist rejection of Stormont and reliance on Dublin to 'solve' the par-tition problem was a precarious strategy: quite simply Dublin could fail to deliver, as it had in the past. At the onset of the London talks Campbell and Byrne, the IUA, and Mulvey and Cunningham all sent telegrams to the Irish delegation emphasising the primacy of the partition issue.[67] Healy, alive to the danger that de Valera might conclude a deal on defence and trade at the expense of partition, personally led a delegation of his colleagues to London during the course of the negotiations, determined to stiffen de Valera's resolve on the issue. After a day spent petitioning the Irish government's negotiating team Healy emerged to announce that nationalists would regard any outcome that left par-tition unresolved 'as a betrayal of all our interests', but he concluded, 'we think he [de Valera] has no intention of doing such a thing'.[68] Despite this note of optimism Healy's past experience must have prepared him for the 'betrayal' he feared. The negotiations culminated in April with the signing of trade, financial and defence agreements but with partition left unresolved. The outcome (the

Anglo-Irish Agreement), followed by a snap election in June which returned Fianna Fail to the Dáil with a working majority, was a personal triumph for de Valera, a man now at the 'height of his political power'.[69] It was also, as Richard Dunphy has argued, the culmination of Fianna Fail's 'development strategy' to extend its electoral support beyond its traditional, and declining, small farmer social basis to encompass the South's entrepreneurial and working classes. The signing of the Anglo-Irish Agreement in 1938, and the promise of an improved economic climate that it heralded, enabled Fianna Fail to offer itself to these social classes as a party capable of delivering strong and decisive government.[70] However, this hegemonic strategy, which successfully propelled the party to a position of unprecedented political dominance in southern Irish politics, was premised on an attitude to the North that was 'distinctly cool'.[71]

Other than the employment of a verbose republican rhetoric, designed to placate Fianna Fail's unreconstructed republican wing, no concrete steps were taken to ensure that northern Catholic grievances were addressed, nor was there any offer to assist or coordinate the nationalist opposition in the North. Even the improved terms for Irish trade secured under the Anglo-Irish Agreement meant little for Catholics living in Northern Ireland. Although encouraged by the British prime minister to make a conciliatory gesture to the Unionist government, de Valera's refusal to countenance the inclusion in the Agreement of trade concessions that would improve cross-border trading relationships – on the grounds that Catholics were being oppressed in the North – precluded any prospect for material improvement in the conditions of the more disadvantaged sections of Northern Ireland society.[72] With northern unemployment rates in the late 1930s averaging 27 per cent[73] and levels of absolute poverty registering 36 per cent in certain working-class districts of Belfast, the growth in the activities of Catholic voluntary societies – the Society of St Vincent de Paul, the Ladies of Charity, the Catholic Young Men's Society[74] – indicated the severity of the situation facing the Catholic poor.

In the Dáil debate on the Anglo-Irish Agreement, de Valera's bargaining tactics, and in particular his flagging up of the partition question, was roundly criticised by the deputy leader of Fine Gael, James Dillon:

> We knew, when he went to London, that he could not abolish Partition in the course of these negotiations. We never expected he would be able to abolish Partition. No reasonable man who understood the situation ever dreamt he would abolish Partition, but he did commit the wrong against the people of Ulster in leading them into the belief that he was going to abolish Partition in the course of these negotiations. That was a cruel mean thing to do … there is nothing more contemptible, nothing meaner than to make capital out of the natural anxiety of Northern Nationalists to get back into Ireland and to hold yourself out as a knight in shining armour who is

going to surrender everything unless he succeeds in abolishing the Border, which he knows in his heart and soul he is not able to abolish.[75]

And yet the clarity of Dillon's observation, and the intensity of his critique, was largely absent in the North where the response of nationalist political organisations to the Anglo-Irish Agreement was publicly uncritical. The NCU, at a meeting held in Belfast at the end of April, congratulated the Irish government on the outcome. The return of the Treaty ports was described as an 'instalment of the full recognition of Irish sovereignty', while the trade and finance settlement was regarded as 'favourable to the Irish nation'. An NCU request to the Irish government to take steps to safeguard 'old established' northern industries pending their integration into Ireland's national economy – a proposal considered a 'new departure' in 'constructive patriotism' by an *Irish Times* leader[76] – was ironically something which de Valera had just flatly refused to do. Overall the NCU expressed itself satisfied that de Valera had done everything possible to secure Irish unity and confident that there would be 'no relaxation' in the efforts of his government to achieve this.[77] There were dissenting voices, the nationalist Senator John McHugh considered de Valera to be 'only using us for his own purposes'[78] while Cahir Healy, in correspondence with Eamon Donnelly, noted his disappointment with the outcome of the Anglo-Irish negotiations: de Valera, he wrote, had 'concluded another good deal for the twenty-six counties!'[79] Healy's disenchantment with de Valera led him to consider a more ambitious strategy to unite northern nationalists and abolish partition, a strategy based on the traditional republican dictum that 'England's danger is Ireland's opportunity'. Writing to Peter Murney, the Secretary of the NCU, in September 1938, Healy counselled that with 'a world war threatening' the time was ripe for 'Six County Nationalists' to decide upon a course of united and determined action.[80] Healy's suggested course of action was a plan to undermine Britain's strategic defence interests by thwarting British attempts to win American support to its side in any future war with Nazi Germany. This could be achieved, he claimed, through the organisation of a propaganda campaign by the 'most influential people in the United States, viz., the Irish, Germans and Italians'.[81] Healy's grandiose plan, however, encountered the obstacle of nationalist factionalism.[82] Murney, on behalf of the NCU, refused to participate in any united front against partition until Healy and his associates publicly announced their 'intention not to enter the present Belfast Parliament again during its lifetime'.[83] Healy's plan, though it came to nothing, was based on a wholly unrealistic assessment of the resourcefulness that even a united nationalist political body could muster.[84] The proposal, indicative of an absence of feasible strategic alternatives, also demonstrated a profoundly conservative reading of the unfolding international political conjuncture.

While there were tactical differences between Healy's IUA and the NCU there was little that divided the two main groups in terms of objectives and outlook; both emphasised the urgency and immediacy of Irish unity and both underplayed, or ignored, the North's internal divisions. They also both looked to exogenous forces to resolve the partition issue. This reliance on outside agencies (the Irish and British governments) or international pressures, which called into question the need for an efficient and representative nationalist political machine within Northern Ireland, constrained the development of their respective organisations. Political activism was the preserve of their small, mainly middle-class membership, assisted by the Catholic clergy. Political success was premised neither on popular mass support nor on a campaign of concerted political activity within Northern Ireland.

That this lack of political organisation was not without problems became evident towards the end of 1938 when the NCU conducted a series of public meetings in an attempt to consolidate its support among northern Catholics. At a rally in Newry on 2 October the audience, of about 1,000, listened to a series of passionate speeches calling for the ending of partition and denouncing the sectarianism of the northern state. The audience were not, however, called upon to vote for the NCU, nor even, on this occasion, to join the organisation. Instead they were set the more amorphous task, in the words of the Chairman, the Very Rev. P.T. McComisky, to 'never cease in your efforts … never rest until Ireland is one and undivided'.[85] In a similar vein Peter Murney, expounding on the benefits of the 1937 Irish Constitution, called on 'all sections of our race to direct their energies towards bringing about its immediate and effective application to all Ireland'.[86] Precisely how the 'energies' of the Catholic minority were to be directed was left deliberately vague. The only certainty, for the audience, was that the NCU demand for Irish unity was more radical than that of the Northern League in that it precluded all recognition of, or involvement in, the Northern parliament, a position clearly enunciated at the rally by Hugh Corvin, a prominent member of the NCU and the Secretary of the Ulster Gaelic League in Belfast:

> For some years past the people have to some extent been misled by their appointed spokesmen. To judge by the actions of some of our leaders, one would have thought that all the Nationalist people of the North wanted was, to pick up some of the crumbs the ascendancy party allowed to fall from their table. I think a change and a very definite change has come. We are now proving that we will not be satisfied with the crumbs that fall from the Imperial Agents in this Country. We will cry like Sean MacDermott[87] 'To hell with your concessions, we want our Country.'[88]

And yet, despite the strident militancy of Corvin's rhetoric, his statement was not a call for Catholics to partake in any discernible political action, quite the reverse, it was a rationalisation for the NCU's abstentionism and their non-activity in formal politics. This was further reinforced by the keynote speaker, Anthony Mulvey MP, who spoke eloquently on Ulster's historic role 'in the van of the fight for sovereign independence' but was decidedly less impressive on the current situation and future prospects. Suggesting to his audience that events were in train that would result in the desired goal of Irish unity, his claim that, 'a large proportion of our Protestant Countrymen in this area united with us in our demands' appeared specious and entirely unsupported by any evidence; meanwhile his references to an allegedly advantageous international situation and to de Valera's continuing support for northern nationalists were brief and irresolute in tone: 'Our movement is being started at a time when the rights of the minorities are being brought to light elsewhere, and *I hope* the people of the North will stand united on this question … The Government of the South of Ireland *should* raise its voice on this question on the unity of this nation.'[89] (Emphasis added.)

The NCU stance of calling on Catholics to 'stand firm' and await their imminent delivery into a united Ireland was not, however, guaranteed a favourable reception. At a rally in Armagh, on 9 October, Anthony Mulvey and Aodh de Blacam, one of de Valera's political advisors, encountered a rather sceptical audience. Following on from the largely courteous reception of the platform speakers,[90] questions from the audience focused on whether the same conditions enjoyed by workers and the unemployed in Northern Ireland would be maintained in a united Ireland. The inability of any of the platform party to provide a satisfactory answer was met with a caustic outburst of jeering and laughter.[91] At a larger demonstration in Downpatrick on 30 October, which attracted around 1,500 people marching behind three bands, a very mixed response was again visible. On this occasion the customary policy of appointing a prominent member of the Catholic clergy to officiate as Chairman at such gatherings exposed an ad hoc and amateurish organisation. The priest who had been invited to act as Chairman failed to turn up and the Revd P. McKillop, parish priest of Portaferry, was quickly drafted as a replacement. Father McKillop, who had attended as a spectator, delivered an opening address that was clearly unrehearsed ('I have very little to say to you … There are a number of resolutions to go before you but I know nothing about them') but staunchly in keeping with nationalist sentiment ('The object of this meeting is to re-unite Ireland … A country can do nothing if it is divided up into two parts. I think that all true Irishmen would like to see Ireland united and that is the reason of this meeting protesting against Partition.') While he may have lacked political acumen Father McKillop was, however, an astute observer of human nature and he cannily implied that the presence of marching bands on the day, and the spectacle of the demonstration itself, accounted for at least part of the turn-out: 'We are here to protest against Partition I hope. There are some here I am sure who are not protesting against Partition, but I hope they are.'[92] Father McKillop's intuition was probably correct. The audience's response to the keynote address by Anthony Mulvey, who spoke of the fight against partition 'entering on the last round' and who identified the opponent in the fight as not 'Britain's tools in Belfast' but 'British duplicity and hypocrisy',[93] was subdued.[94] It was only when Patrick McCann, a speaker from Dublin, launched an attack on 'Craigavon and his clique'[95] and denounced the treatment of Catholics in Northern Ireland that the audience became animated.[96] At the conclusion of the meeting a request by Father McKillop for those assembled to show their approval of the speeches made, and resolutions passed, by 'a good hearty cheer' failed to inspire the audience, police observers reporting that his request was supported by only one-third of those present.[97]

The varied and often lukewarm reception shown to the NCU showed little sign of abatement as the campaign of rallies continued. It was again evident at a meeting held at the gates of Burren Catholic Church, Warrenpoint, on 20 November. Timed to coincide with the end of Sunday Mass to maximise attendance, the congregation (though not the parish priest) were addressed by Eamon Donnelly and Peter Murney who announced that the purpose of the meeting was to enlist support for the establishment of a branch of the NCU in Burren. The contributions of the two speakers were characteristically optimistic in their assessment of likely political developments but vague regarding future NCU activities. Donnelly, who spoke favourably of the German minorities of Hungary, Poland and the Sudetenland being 'rescued' from the domination of governments they had no allegiance to by the 'power of Germany', assured his audience 'that they could likewise count on the support of Mr. de Valera and forty-million Irishmen all over the world'. With this support, the audience were told, Partition would end 'sooner than they thought'.[98] This prospect did not, however, inspire the audience who dispersed rapidly at the conclusion of the meeting without any attempt being made to set up an NCU branch. [99]

That these signs of Catholic apathy did not appear to have been a cause for immediate concern is hardly surprising given that Mulvey and Cunningham's election in 1935 had demonstrated that electoral success was not conditional on the maintenance of a party machine. Indeed, for some considerable time nationalist politics in the North had lacked the structures of a formal political party. The nationalist political machine, where it existed, was parish-based and loosely organised around the local parliamentary candidate and a handful of supporters amongst whom the local clergy were particularly prominent. Its function, principally to ensure the registration of voters, did not require a large membership, or even an active one outside of election time. Even the fulfilment of this role was hardly pressing, the vast majority of local government council seats in Northern Ireland went uncontested between 1923 and 1939[100] and the policy of parliamentary abstentionism relieved nationalist politics of many of the pressures of normal party political activity.

However, there was always the danger of demoralisation and despair if political goals appeared to be unrealisable. In this respect it was the anti-partitionist gestures of de Valera's government which cushioned the northern nationalist political groups from the more unpalatable realities of their immediate political situation and encouraged them in their belief that they were on the cusp of major political developments. De Valera's launch, in October 1938, of the Irish Anti-Partition League (a propaganda body set to popularise the anti-partition message in Britain), his instruction to Fianna Fáil deputies and senators to speak on nationalist platforms in the North and his continued use of a vociferous anti-partitionist rhetoric in public statements,[101] all combined to create the illusion of momentum. Even the seasoned, and sceptical, Cahir Healy, could, at an IUA rally in Derry in October 1938, speak in terms of it being 'zero hour' for northern nationalists. The rally, which included members of the Irish Senate and the Dáil on the platform, [102] started with the reading of a message from de Valera sent by 'special courier' from Dublin. While de Valera's message, stating that he regarded the ending of partition as 'a matter of vital concern', was relatively anodyne, the comments and tone of the platform speakers, draped in a millenarian rhetoric that was all too familiar of nationalist political spokesmen at the time, conveyed a sense of urgency and impatience certain to arouse the most negative of unionist fears and prejudices. In his address to the rally, George Leeke, one of the two local nationalist MPs present, suggested a scheme of population transfer – of Irish émigrés back to Ireland and Ulster unionists to mainland Britain – as a solution to partition. This radical proposal in fact echoed de Valera's own position: de Valera had advocated population exchange from as early as 1934 and continued to do so until 1943.[103] Leeke's colleague and fellow parliamentarian, Paddy Maxwell, on the other hand, spoke approvingly of Hitler's more resolute solution for the Sudeten Germans and hinted at the possibility of physical force when he referred to the people of Derry securing their rights by 'unconstitutional means if necessary'.[104]

The resort to this kind of increasingly militant rhetoric, by men who were after all committed to constitutional methods, was not unfamiliar in the North's polarised politics. Throughout 1938 unionist fears that the return of the Treaty ports represented a disquieting act of appeasement by the British government towards the Southern state, their concerns over de Valera's anti-partition posturing, and their ongoing suspicions of the 'disloyalty' of the Catholic minority all ensured a prevalence of combative 'No Surrender' politics on Unionist Party and Orange platforms. To a degree nationalist rhetorical excess was a mirrored response to the tactlessness of unionist political oratory. However, if the political context of unionist discourse was one of insecurity and a 'siege mentality', that which encouraged constitutional nationalists to exaggerate their commitment to a nationalism that appeared more militant and threatening than it was, was one coloured by competition from more radical elements within the nationalist bloc, and by the frustrations and disappointments that resulted from both the fruitless tactic of abstentionism and the continued unrealistic expectation that the Dublin government was poised to intervene on their behalf to end partition. Faced with this situation was there any possibility that northern nationalist politicians could forge a united and coherent strategy that would effectively prioritise and tackle Catholic grievances in the North? In fact the whole political situation on the island of Ireland was about to undergo momentous changes as a result of the outbreak of World War II and this challenge was to present itself to the nationalist political class.

Notes

1 A.C. Hepburn, *Catholic Belfast and Nationalist Ireland in the Era of Joe Devlin 1871–1934* (Oxford, Oxford University Press, 2008), p. 264.
2 Although not all Devlin's colleagues subscribed to his parliamentary strategy. See E. Phoenix, *Northern Nationalism: Nationalist Politics, Partition and the Catholic Minority in Northern Ireland 1890–1940* (Belfast, Ulster Historical Foundation, 1994), p. 371.
3 *Belfast Telegraph*, 29 May 1928 cited in D. Harkness, *Northern Ireland Since 1920* (Dublin, Criterion Press, 1983), p. 75.
4 For a graphic account of the wholly negative impact of republican and loyalist violence at this time see A.F. Parkinson, *Belfast's Unholy War: The Troubles of the 1920s* (Dublin, Four Courts Press, 2004).
5 See C. Norton, 'An Earnest Endeavour for Peace? Unionist Opinion and the Craig/Collins Peace Pact of 30 March 1922', *Études Irlandaises* 32: 1 (2007), pp. 91–108.
6 Hepburn, *Catholic Belfast*, pp. 260–264.
7 Phoenix, *Northern Nationalism*, p. 369.
8 Some members of the IRA had joined Fianna Fail following de Valera's split from Sinn Féin in 1926. P. Bew, *Ireland: The Politics of Emnity 1789–2006* (Oxford, Oxford University Press, 2007), p. 449.
9 T.P. Coogan, *De Valera: Long Fellow, Long Shadow* (London, Hutchinson, 1993), p. 463.
10 R. Munck and B. Rolston, *Belfast in the Thirties: An Oral History* (Belfast, Blackstaff Press, 1987), p. 174.
11 When de Valera called a snap general election in January 1933 Healy along with other former pro-Treatyite members of the National League, Joseph Connellan MP (South

Armagh), Joseph Stewart MP (East Tyrone) and J.H. Collins MP (South Down) crossed the border to campaign for Fianna Fail. See E. Staunton, *The Nationalists of Northern Ireland 1918–1973* (Dublin, Columba Press, 2001), p. 110.

12 J. Bowman, *De Valera and the Ulster Question 1917–1973* (Oxford, Oxford University Press, 1982), p. 132.

13 Cahir Healy was later to remind de Valera of the February encounter, recalling not only de Valera's rejection of the National League's request to enter the Dáil but also reminding him of his reluctance to, 'give us any direction as to what we ought to do regarding attendance here' [i.e. in Northern Ireland]. PRONI D2991/B/1398, Cahir Healy papers, Healy to de Valera 10 June 1956.

14 Phoenix, *Northern Nationalism*, p. 373.

15 G.C. Duggan, *Northern Ireland: Success or Failure* (Dublin, Irish Times, 1950), p. 26.

16 J.L. McCracken, 'The Political Scene in Northern Ireland, 1926–1937', in F. McManus (ed.), *The Years of the Great Test 1926–39* (Dublin, Mercier Press, 1978), p. 158. See also Christopher Norton, 'The Left in Northern Ireland 1921–1932', *Labour History Review* 60: 1 (Spring 1995), pp. 3–20.

17 P. Buckland, *The Factory of Grievances: Devolved Government in Northern Ireland 1921–3* (Dublin, Gill & Macmillan, 1979), p. 241.

18 Hepburn, *Catholic Belfast*, p. 264.

19 Of the 16 Belfast seats in the 1925 parliamentary election, Independent Unionists took 3 seats, Labour 3, Nationalists 1 and Unionists 9. By 1929 this was changed to 2 Independent Unionist, 1 Labour, 2 Nationalists and Unionists 11. In the 1933 Northern Ireland parliamentary election the Unionists took 10 seats, Independent Unionists 2, Labour 2 and Nationalists 2. See A.C. Hepburn, *A Past Apart: Studies in the History of Catholic Belfast 1850–1950* (Belfast, Ulster Historical Foundation, 1996), p. 176.

20 See G. Walker, '"Protestantism before Party!": The Ulster Protestant League in the 1930s', *Historical Journal* 28:4 (1985) for a discussion of this organisation.

21 G. Walker, *A History of the Ulster Unionist Party: Protest, Pragmatism and Pessimism* (Manchester, Manchester University Press, 2004), p. 72.

22 Quoted in B. Barton, *Brookborough: The Making of a Prime Minister* (Belfast, Institute of Irish Studies, 1988), p. 78.

23 Bew, *Ireland*, pp. 459, 469.

24 Barton, *Brookborough*, p. 89.

25 H. Patterson, 'Party versus Order: Ulster Unionism and the Flags and Emblems Act', *Contemporary British History* 13: 4 (Winter 1999), p. 113.

26 See Barton, *Brookborough* also S. Prince, *Northern Ireland's '68: Civil Rights, Global Revolt and the Origins of the Troubles* (Dublin, Irish Academic Press, 2007), pp. 15–16.

27 Concerns over the ethnic/political demographic of Fermanagh were to continue to exercise the minds of the Unionist leadership for the next three decades. See M. Mulholland, 'Why Did Unionists Discriminate?', in Sabine Wichert (ed.), *From the United Irishmen to Twentieth-Century Unionism: Essays in Honour of A.T.Q. Stewart* (Dublin, Four Courts Press, 2004).

28 Cardinal MacRory's controversial and widely publicised questioning, in 1931, of the right of the protestant churches to be considered part of the 'Church of Christ', a

statement that provoked inevitable outrage, ensured his lasting unpopularity among Protestants. See O. Rafferty, *Catholicism in Ulster 1603–1983: An Interpretative History* (Dublin, Gill & Macmillan, 1994), pp. 229–230.

29 T. Hennessey, *A History of Northern Ireland 1920–1996* (Dublin, Gill & Macmillan, 1997), pp. 66–67; Harkness, *Northern Ireland*, p. 76.

30 On the impact of the Belfast riots of 1935 see A.C. Hepburn, *A Past Apart: Studies in the History of Catholic Belfast 1850–1950* (Belfast, Ulster Historical Foundation, 1996), Chapter 10.

31 M. Farrell, *Northern Ireland: The Orange State* (London, Pluto Press, 1978), p. 144; Phoenix, *Northern Nationalism*, p. 377; Staunton, *The Nationalists*, p. 120. Of the other two seats occupied by nationalist candidates de Valera held South Down as an abstentionist while P.J. McLogan held South Armagh as a Republican abstentionist.

32 A change in the law in 1934 requiring all candidates to declare their intention of taking their seats if elected to the Northern parliament prevented the nomination of abstentionist candidates. This effectively prohibited republicans from contesting Northern Ireland parliamentary elections. There was no such restriction on contesting Westminster seats.

33 Stewart had succeeded Joe Devlin as MP.

34 Quoted in Hennessey, *A History*, p. 71.

35 On this see Brendan Lynn, *Holding the Ground: The Nationalist Party in Northern Ireland, 1945–72* (Aldershot, Asgate, 1997), p. 248. However, it should be noted that Mulvey, a former member of the IRB and a participant in 1916, was also a man of moderate disposition who enjoyed the friendship of Unionist companions. The author and broadcaster Benedict Kiely was later to recount how, as a secondary school boy, which would have been in the mid-1930s, he had sought out Mulvey in the hope that the latter would publish the young Kiely's recently penned tribute to a friend and fellow pupil who had tragically died. Kiely described the scene: 'I went … looking for Mr. Anthony Mulvey, M.P., editor of The Ulster Herald, The Fermanagh Herald, the Nationalist newspapers. I was told: "Mr Mulvey isn't here. He's down at Mr. Parks," who was editor of The Tyrone Constitution, the Unionist paper. So I went down and found Parks and Mulvey (dear friends and political opponents) having tea and drank tea with them and presented my copy. That was the first thing of mine that was ever printed'. See Franck Kersnowski, 'Benedict Kiely – b. 1919', *Journal of the Short Story in English* 41 (Autumn 2003), p. 3.

36 Staunton, *The Nationalists*, p. 124.

37 Most recently in both the 1929 and 1931 Westminster elections.

38 The share of Catholic votes in the previous two Westminster elections when the constituency was contested by Nationalist candidates was as follows: 1929 – Frank McDermot (Nat) 42.08 per cent; 1931 – Thomas Campbell (Nat) 41.43 per cent. In contrast in 1935 the Republican candidate, Charles Leddy, received 37.36 per cent.

39 From 52.89 per cent in 1931 to 52.29 per cent in 1935 and this was despite having the advantage of a slightly increased electorate.

40 In 1924 Michael Murney (SF) received 8,941 votes in Down while James McKee (SF) received 11,756 votes in Armagh. In the 1935 election Patrick O'Hagan (Rep)

received 20,236 votes in Down while Charles McGleenan received 16,284 votes in Armagh.

41 D. Kennedy, 'Catholics in Northern Ireland 1926–1939', in F. McManus (ed.), *The Years of the Great Test 1926–39* (Dublin, Mercier Press, 1978), pp. 144–145.

42 Andrews to Montgomery, 6 November 1935, quoted in P. Bew, K. Darwin, G. Gillespie, *Passion and Prejudice: Nationalist-Unionist Conflict in Ulster in the 1930s and the Founding of the Irish Association* (Belfast, Institute of Irish Studies, 1993), p. 19.

43 Hungerford to Montgomery, December 1935, *Ibid.*, p. 39.

44 *Belfast Newsletter*, 15 June 1936.

45 *Irish Times*, 3 October 1936.

46 Staunton, *The Nationalists*, pp. 129–131; Phoenix, *Northern Nationalism*, p. 382; T. Hennessey, *A History*, pp. 72–73.

47 Bowman, *De Valera*, p. 133. Born in Middletown, Co. Armagh, Donnelly had been involved in the republican movement since 1916. Following his release from internment he became Sinn Féin Organiser for Ulster. During the Treaty split he sided with de Valera. In the years 1925–29 he held the Stormont seat for South Armagh as an abstentionist MP. Donnelly was a founder member of Fianna Fail and in 1932 was the Director of Elections for the party. He was elected to the Dáil in 1933 as TD for Leix-Offaly, a seat he held until 1937. See also Anthony J. Carroll, 'Eamon Donnelly Remembered', *Newry Journal*, www.newryjournal.co.uk/content/view/1890/31/.

48 Public Record Office of Northern Ireland (hereafter PRONI), D2991/B/10/1, Cahir Healy papers, Healy to Donnelly, 25 October 1936.

49 Bowman, *De Valera*, p. 135.

50 PRONI, D2991/B/10/6, Cahir Healy papers, Donnelly to Healy, 30 October 1936.

51 PRONI, D2991/B/19/11, Cahir Healy papers, Healy to Murney, 21 September 1938.

52 With 10 per cent of voting papers spoiled, out of an effective turnout of 68.3 per cent, the Yes vote came to only 38.6 per cent. Protestants in the Free State voted strongly against the constitution. See R. Sinnott, *Irish Voters Decide: Voting Behaviour in Elections and Referendums Since 1918* (Manchester, Manchester University Press, 1995), p. 220. See also J. Lee, *Ireland 1912–1985* (Cambridge, Cambridge University Press, 1989), pp. 210–211.

53 Bowman, *De Valera*, p. 150. See also the discussion in M. Kennedy, *Division and Consensus: The Politics of Cross-Border Relations in Ireland, 1925–1969* (Dublin, Institute of Public Administration, 2000), p. 59.

54 Coogan, *De Valera*, p. 491. See also Bowman, *De Valera*, p. 156.

55 *Irish Times*, 9 December 1937.

56 Staunton, *The Nationalists*, p. 130.

57 Phoenix, *Northern Nationalism*, p. 382.

58 See the discussion of the 'Economic War', in K. Kennedy, T. Giblin and D. McHugh, *The Economic Development of Ireland in the Twentieth Century* (London, Routledge, 1989), pp. 41–43.

59 A. Jackson, *Ireland 1798–1998: Politics and War* (Oxford, Blackwell, 1999), p. 298.

60 Coogan, *De Valera*, p. 516.

61 De Valera's government at this time was a minority government dependent on the support of Labour Party TDs in the Dail. It was therefore imperative to preserve party solidarity.
62 See the discussion in Kennedy, *Division*, pp. 59–69.
63 See 'Did de Valera get it wrong in his handling of partition?', *Irish Examiner*, 6 January 2007.
64 Buckland, *Factory*, p. 72.
65 *Irish Times*, 15 January 1938.
66 It has been claimed that the NCU's boycott tactic was taken at the behest of de Valera, however the evidence for this is inconclusive. Staunton, *Nationalists* (p. 134) states 'Mulvey's son told a Belfast historian in 1978 that the boycott tactic was De Valera's idea', Staunton's reference for this is Phoenix, *Northern Nationalism* (p. 384) who in turn references Farrell, *Orange State* (pp. 145–146). Farrell, however, does not appear to make this claim.
67 *Irish Times*, 18 January 1938.
68 *Irish Press*, 26 January 1938 quoted in T. Hennessey, *History*, p. 79.
69 D. Keogh, *Twentieth-Century Ireland: Nation and State* (Dublin, Gill & Macmillan, 1994), p. 104.
70 R. Dunphy, *The Making of Fianna Fail Power in Ireland 1923–1948* (Oxford, Oxford University Press, 1995), pp. 210–213.
71 *Ibid.*
72 Kenny, *Division*, p. 68–69. The adverse balance of exports between Northern Ireland and the South in the first year of the Agreements operation (a 25 per cent increase in exports from South to North and a slight 4 per cent increase from North to South) also served to reinforce Unionist suspicions of an irredentist neighbour wielding economic sanctions to destabilise the Northern State.
73 D.S. Johnson, 'The Northern Ireland Economy, 1914–39', in L. Kennedy and P. Ollerenshaw (eds), *An Economic History of Ulster 1820–1939* (Manchester, Manchester University Press, 1985), p. 191.
74 D. Ferriter, *The Transformation of Ireland 1900–2000* (London, Profile Books, 2004), p. 438.
75 Dáil Éireann Debates, vol. 71, 28 April 1938, pp. 187.
76 *Irish Times*, 5 May 1938.
77 *Irish News*, 30 April 1938.
78 *Irish News*, 28 April 1938, cited in Hennessey, *A History*, p. 82.
79 Healy to Donnelly, 18 February 1939, cited in Phoenix, *Northern Nationalism*, p. 386.
80 PRONI, D2991/B/19/9, Cahir Healy papers, Healy to Murney, 11 September 1938.
81 *Ibid.*
82 PRONI, D2991/B/19/11, Cahir Healy papers, Healy to Murney, 21 September 1938.
83 PRONI, D2991/B/19/10, Cahir Healy papers, Murney to Healy, 19 September 1938.
84 Healy's plan involved the setting up staffed offices in America and London. PRONI, D2991/B/19/9, Cahir Healy papers, Healy to Murney, 11 September 1938.
85 PRONI, HA32/1/634, Ministry of Home Affairs papers, RUC, Crime Special Department report on NCU meeting, 2 October 1938.
86 *Ibid.*

87 Sean MacDermott (1884–1916) Leitrim-born, but Belfast-based, member of the Irish Republican Brotherhood. A participant in the Easter Rising and signatory of the Proclamation, he was executed in 1916.

88 PRONI, HA32/1/634, Ministry of Home Affairs papers, RUC, Crime Special Department report on NCU meeting 2 October 1938.

89 *Ibid.*

90 The exception was the hostile response that greeted Joseph Connellan, the editor of the Newry-based *Frontier Sentinel*. Connellan had earlier voted against the Armagh Gaelic Football Club when they lodged a complaint against the referee's decisions in the Ulster Final between Armagh and Monaghan; as a consequence he was considered persona non grata in Armagh. PRONI, Inspector General's Office, RUC, report on NCU meeting, 11 October 1938.

91 *Ibid.*

92 PRONI, HA/32/1/634, Ministry of Home Affairs papers, RUC, Crime Special Department report on NCU meeting, 4 November 1938.

93 *Ibid.*

94 PRONI, Ministry of Home Affairs papers, Inspector General's Office, RUC, Report on NCU meeting at Downpatrick, 4 November 1938.

95 PRONI, Ministry of Home Affairs papers, RUC, Crime Special Department report on NCU meeting, 4 November 1938.

96 PRONI, Ministry of Home Affairs papers, Inspector General's Office, RUC, Report on NCU meeting at Downpatrick, 4 November 1938.

97 *Ibid.*

98 PRONI, HA/32/1/634 Ministry of Home Affairs papers, Inspector General's Office, RUC, Report on NCU meeting at Burren, Warrenpoint, 23 November 1938.

99 *Ibid.*

100 D. Fitzpatrick, *The Two Irelands 1912–1939* (Oxford, Oxford University Press, 1998), p. 179.

101 See R. Fisk, *In Time of War: Ireland, Ulster and the Price of Neutrality 1939–45* (Dublin, Gill & Macmillan, 1983), p. 82; Bowman, *De Valera*, p. 191; Phoenix, *Northern Nationalism*, p. 387.

102 Respectively, Henry McDevitt and Neil Blaney.

103 'De Valera advocated forcefully moving one million Protestants', *Irish Examiner*, 4 January 2003; Bowman, *De Valera*, p. 209; Bew, *Ireland*, p. 471.

104 *Belfast Newsletter*, 17 October 1938; PRONI, HA/32/1/634, Ministry of Home Affairs papers, Inspector General's Office, RUC, Report on Irish Union Association meeting, 20 October 1938. Despite Maxwell's approval of Hitler's Sudeten policy at this time he was to prove far more circumspect in his thoughts on Nazi Germany than certain of his colleagues in the early 1940s. See Maxwell to Healy, 5 June 1949, cited in Staunton, *The Nationalists*, p. 119 and the discussion presented in Chapter 3 of this work.

2

The outbreak of war, 1939–40

The calamitous deterioration in international politics in the late 1930s was concomitant with the re-emergence in Ireland of the IRA's violent, physical-force republicanism, and this, as we shall see, was to have a considerable effect on the strategic considerations of constitutional nationalists. Some thought that the IRA campaign would provide them, albeit indirectly, with an opportunity to strengthen their relationship with the Dublin government; but in this they were to be mistaken. Depleted in strength and increasingly marginalised in the South[1] the IRA had nonetheless maintained a low level of activity in the North, and, even though much of the northern leadership of the IRA had been apprehended during an RUC raid in Belfast in 1936,[2] the organisation was still capable of sporadic bouts of violence. Thus in 1937 a number of customs huts along the border were destroyed by explosions while in 1938 the IRA launched an attack on Maghera RUC station and detonated four bombs in Belfast.[3] These latter actions were intended as a precursor to what was envisaged as a major bombing campaign (the so-called S-Plan) on mainland Britain, an operation planned by Sean Russell, the right-wing leader of the IRA, who was at the time actively seeking collaboration with Nazi Germany.[4] In January 1939 the IRA Army Council – styling itself the 'Government of the Irish Republic' – issued an ultimatum to the British government giving it four days to withdraw from Northern Ireland; this was followed, on the expiry of the four days, by an IRA 'Declaration of War' and the commencement of the S-Plan campaign in Britain, which, resulting in the deaths of seven innocent civilians and injury to almost 200,[5] served only to alienate British public opinion and scupper the activities of de Valera's recently created Irish Anti-Partition League.

The response of the Northern government to the upsurge in IRA activity in Northern Ireland was to make use of the powers available to it under the Special Powers Act (1922) to re-introduce internment without trial and subdue the republicans. This placed constitutional nationalists in somewhat of a predicament; they did not support physical force solutions to resolve partition

– politically coercive solutions were perhaps another matter – but neither could they support the actions taken by a State they held to be discriminatory, sectarian, and even despotic, to deal with the perpetrators of violence. There was also a danger that the Northern government's actions might inflame Catholic opinion and propel republicans to public prominence[6] at a time when the political campaigns of the various nationalist groups were noticeably running out of steam. At least this is how the NCU presented the situation to the Irish government in 1939. Writing in November to Joseph Connolly,[7] a Belfast-born senior member of Fianna Fail, Peter Murney warned of the possible consequences of Dublin's continued failure to offer northern nationalists 'practical direction': 'In the absence of even vocal leadership, our people feel deserted and are tempted to listen to the dangerous counsels of those who have less responsibility.' Murney suggested that there were 'practical things' that de Valera's government could do to 'correct bad impressions', and he cautioned that the 'imprudent military movement is apt to take the lead away from us if the Constitutional movement becomes a dead letter through lack of active measures … in the partitioned area'.[8] There was of course a certain irony here; the NCU's attempt to consolidate its support among the Catholic population entailed a deliberate rising of expectations, which, if unfulfilled, could lead to frustrations that radical organisations like the IRA would be only too ready to exploit.

In fact there was little possibility of constitutional politicians being eclipsed by the IRA which had limited support within the Catholic community in Northern Ireland. In West Belfast the local populace received the IRA's 'Declaration of War', which was posted on walls throughout the district, with incredulity.[9] Furthermore, the state of IRA organisation was, according to Paddy Devlin (an IRA member at the time), 'ramshackle' and 'heavily penetrated by police on both sides of the border'.[10] Indeed, it would appear that the effectiveness of the Northern government's internment measure[11] was in large part a result of the steady stream of reliable information on IRA personnel and activities that was passed by members of the Catholic community to the RUC;[12] a problem so incapacitating for the IRA that they resorted to a policy of 'executing' suspected informers to stem the flow of information.[13] However, Murney's appeal to Connolly for de Valera to receive a 'representative deputation' from the North to discuss the situation was successful and a deputation, including Murney and Healy, met with de Valera in early 1940.

The deputation arrived in Dublin resolute in their belief that the onus for action to improve the plight of the North's Catholic minority lay not in their own hands but with Dublin. This was a view extensively held in northern nationalist circles (despite de Valera's earlier rebuttals) and strongly supported by the hierarchy of the Catholic Church. Speaking in Derry in January 1940 the newly appointed Bishop of Derry, the Most Revd Dr Farren, admonished 'those leaders and Parties in the Twenty-Six Counties who, to judge by events, seem to be more concerned with domestic affairs than with the best means whereby one-third of the Irish people may be delivered out of Imperialist shackles and re-united with their Motherland'.[14] Dr Farren was particularly critical of what he saw as the 'deplorable tendency' of the Southern government to acquiesce in the 'scandal of Partition' by treating the northern State as a 'next-door neighbour, with whom good relations were essential'.[15]

Whatever their expectations, on their arrival in Dublin the deputation were to discover that the political landscape in the South was now changed completely by the declaration of war between Britain and Nazi Germany (in September 1939) and the Irish government's subsequent declaration of Irish neutrality. De Valera made it abundantly clear to the northern delegation that protecting Irish neutrality and Irish independence (in the twenty-six counties) took precedence over all else, including anti-partitionism; moreover, he announced to the deputation that he was not prepared to undertake any action to 'reintegrate the country' that would imperil Irish neutrality.[16]

The disappointment of the deputation must have been considerable. The northern political groupings strongly supported de Valera's neutrality policy but they believed that it was only feasible if Ireland was a strategic unit; partition and continued British 'occupation' of the North, they argued, threatened to embroil all of Ireland in the European war.[17] To this end the whole thrust of the NCU's political strategy had only recently been reaffirmed following a two-day meeting of NCU representatives in Newry, in late January 1940. This called for a settlement of partition ('this supreme grievance of the Irish race') and appealed to the 'Government of the liberated area' to ensure that this demand was met with the utmost urgency.[18]

That this setback with de Valera did not result in a period of critical self-reflection among the northern groupings is partly explained by structural factors: there was no united nationalist opposition, there was no centralised party executive capable of formulating policy to respond to changing political circumstances, the existing political groupings did not hold annual delegate conferences to discuss and review policy, and there was a distinct shortage of up-and-coming ambitious young political activists armed with new ideas and prepared to step into the shoes of their ageing chiefs. But, in addition to this, northern nationalism's small and insular political class was also imbued with a debilitating weakness: their political outlook, determined as it was by an overwhelming sense of the intrinsic moral correctness of their position and an overriding belief that the injustices and indignities faced by the Catholic minority in the North could only be rectified by the establishment of a unitary state dominated by Irish nationalism, prevented any consideration of the interests and calculations of other political actors. Thus, if there was any acknowledgement of failure at all it was invariably seen as a failure of de Valera's government – or rather by elements within that government, de Valera himself being, at least publicly, exempted from blame. De Valera's latest rejection of their request for 'assistance' therefore did little to damper their resilient fatalism: the belief that Dublin should, and could, be persuaded to come to their rescue remained paramount.

In this belief the nationalist political groupings had the continued support of the Catholic Church, an institution which held a position of influence in the Catholic community that the political groups had never come close to supplanting. While the absence of a formalised party system in the North meant that the majority of Catholics had little involvement or contact with the nationalist political groupings, their relationship to the Church was, in contrast, comprehensive and meaningful. In the early 1940s, as general unemployment levels rose,[19] the Church's welfare agencies provided a vital lifeline for the most economically disadvantaged in the Catholic community; but a much broader spectrum of the Catholic community also experienced significant aspects of their daily lives – religious and educational but also social and recreational[20] – through the multifarious institutions and organisations of the Church. And, unlike the political groups, the Church had developed a highly effective series of parish-based integrative mechanisms – often concerned with fund-raising – which ensured that Catholic parishioners were kept in constant contact with their church, that these contacts were continually renewed (often on a daily basis) and that levels of commitment were high.[21] The Church also had a significant 'political' profile. It had opposed the establishment of the northern state in 1921 in the belief that it would prove incompatible to the granting of Catholic rights. From the outset the Church was concerned with the danger of its functions being usurped by secular state institutions – Catholic education was an important issue – and although there was, in the mid-1920s, a desire to seek rapprochement with the Unionist administration[22] the intervening years had hardened the belief that this was not possible.[23] The head of the Catholic Church in Ireland, Cardinal Joseph MacRory, had (as Bishop of Down and Connor) been a vociferous critic of partition back in 1916 when John Redmond, the leader of the constitutional Home Rule Party, consulted the hierarchy over the possible exclusion of the North-east from a Home Rule settlement.[24] Now that Catholic social doctrine was enshrined in de Valera's 1937 Constitution, which reserved a 'special role' for the Church, the contrast between the elevated status of the Catholic Church in the South and its position in the North was more sharply defined and MacRory remained vehemently opposed to partition and resolute in his belief that anti-Catholicism was endemic in, and an integral part of, the northern state. Speaking at Maynooth College in June 1940 MacRory ruefully contrasted the gains and advantages of Independence in the twenty-six counties with the situation in the six counties, where, he dolefully reported, 'there was neither freedom nor justice for Catholics'.[25] For the Cardinal the resolution to this injustice was to see the border 'wiped away and … unity restored to the country' (although, despite the vehemence of his language MacRory was in no way advocating physical coercion).[26] It was the much reported and publicised 'political' public statements such as these,[27] alongside the pastoral pronouncements of the hierarchy – most notably the annual Lenten pastorals of the Catholic Bishops which identified, defined and gave guidance on major moral issues faced by Catholics – that both reinforced the authority of the Church and provided the nationalist political class with its agenda.

The outbreak of war in 1939 engendered little enthusiasm among northern nationalists. There had been early indication of this in April 1939 when Craig attempted to have conscription apply to the North; his suggestion elicited a hostile and defensive response. The issue of conscription into the British army had, of course, a significant historical resonance for Irish nationalists. When, in 1918, the British government had considered introducing conscription in Ireland the consequences had been dramatic – its political repercussions contributing to the eclipse of the constitutional Irish Parliamentary Party by Sinn Féin in the 1918 general election. 1939 was not 1918, nonetheless, any suggestion of involuntary compulsion to enlist in military service was enough to elicit strong feelings from Catholics whose reaction to the conscription issue took the form of a brief but emphatic campaign of protest against its introduction – led by Cardinal MacRory – which quickly convinced the British government that any attempt to introduce the measure would be resisted by the Catholic community and would not meet its intended purpose.[28] Craig had no choice but to acquiesce to the British government's decision that conscription would not apply in Northern Ireland. It was clear that nationalists did not look upon the war as *their* war. In fact the period of 'phoney war' between 1939–40, which saw an influx of military personnel into Northern Ireland (but also a complete absence of threat from German aggression)[29] appears, if anything, to have reaffirmed nationalist positions. The British government's fears that Northern Ireland's defences could be imperilled by IRA activities, which intelligence reports indicated would precede a German invasion attempt, translated into a cool and cautious attitude towards the Catholic community by the incoming troops: Catholics were invariably identified as being sympathetic to the IRA. As the first tranche of troops arriving in the North consisted entirely of British soldiers whose initial task was to secure the border, their defensive preparations – the mining of cross-border bridges, the barricading of cross-border roads and the garrisoning of border towns – tended to be viewed by border nationalists as punitive actions directed at them by their historic oppressor. An Irish police report from mid-1940 speaks of the Catholic population being in 'a state bordering panic' and of British troop enmity towards them for being allegedly pro-German.[30] The sheer volume of troop arrivals (70,000 by the end of 1940)[31] added to the general sense of apprehension and unease felt by border Catholics. Additionally, Craig's decision, in May 1940, to depart from the British model of civilian recruitment to a home guard under military command and instead base the force (the Local Defence Force) on the exclusively Protestant Special Constabulary – ostensibly to offset any attempt by republicans to infiltrate the new force[32] – further added to Catholic alienation from the war effort. It was left to Independent Unionist MPs, in the Stormont parliament, to criticise the sectarian basis of the new force after evidence came to light that 'B' Special Commandants were refusing to accept Catholic ex-servicemen into the Local Defence Force (LDF).[33] However, given the partisan reputation of the 'B' Specials it is questionable if a more equitable recruitment policy would have succeeded in attracting many Catholics into the LDF.

The nationalist political groupings did not view the outbreak of war as a reason to be deflected from their maximalist objective. The NCU for its part, calling on nationalists to regroup under a single 'well-organised cohesive party', clearly saw the occasion as an opportunity to consolidate nationalist opinion under its banner of abstentionism and the demand that the British invite de Valera 'to negotiate a settlement of the dispute between the two nations'.[34] As far as local defence initiatives were concerned nationalist MPs and Senators made clear, in July 1940, that while they were willing 'to assist in schemes to evacuate children and other humanitarian measures' they were quite definitely not prepared to co-operate with any defence plan until there was 'a unified National Defence for the whole country'.[35] This partial engagement with the war effort was not confined to the Catholic community; there was initially a general apathy amongst both Catholics and Protestants regarding the war and little apparent consideration of its potential consequences. In comparison to the 1914–18 war there was a noticeable reluctance by Protestant males to volunteer for the armed forces and the initial poor response by Protestants to enlist in the LDF puzzled observers south of the border.[36] In fact there is evidence that as a result of high levels of unemployment and limited employment prospects in Northern Ireland, more Catholic males than Protestant enlisted in the British armed forces at this time.[37]

Although the Belfast-based Catholic daily newspaper, the *Irish News*, was pro-Allies in its war coverage, discussion of the war in the provincial press was generally geared towards highlighting both the inequities of partition and the defects of the northern regime. Thus, the references made by Leslie Burgin, the British Minister of Supply, during a speech in Belfast in April 1940, to 'resistance to tyranny' and 'freedom and liberty' were seized upon in the editorial of the Newry-based *Frontier Sentinel* as examples of rank British duplicity which ignored the oppressive conditions faced by the Catholic minority,[38] while the announcement by Sir Joseph Davison, the Grand Master of the Orange Order, in June 1940, of the decision to cancel the forthcoming annual 'Twelfth' parades in July was portrayed as the epitome of Unionist shallowness and hypocrisy. It was alleged that the cancellation was called so that 'the Allies may not be disheartened by the spectacle of stay-at-home armies parading on the Six-County front'.[39]

The outbreak of war hostilities, however, provided the occasion for certain members of the nationalist political class to consider the question of the war and its outcome in a more instrumental way. In August 1940 two Newry-based members of the NCU, Peader Murney and John Southwell, accompanied by Senator Thomas McLaughlin[40] from Armagh, met with the German minister, Edouard Hempel, in Dublin, and took it upon themselves to 'place the catholic minority in the north under the protection of the Axis powers'.[41] Murney's senior position in the NCU suggests that both he and Southwell were representing their organisation. McLaughlin was not a member of the NCU but he was a close associate of Cardinal MacRory, whom Hempel believed to have pro-Axis sympathies.[42] A further approach to senior German and Italian officials in Dublin, this time by Eamon Donnelly, occurred in November 1940. On this occasion the Axis representatives made Donnelly promises of support for what he announced was 'a new organisation which would be more virile than the present Council of Unity'.[43] They also offered to have 'the case of Partition of the Six Counties broadcast in the German and Italian controlled radio stations'.[44] Whether these contacts were part of a concerted and coordinated effort is unclear; we cannot assume that all these men, politically conservative and anti-British though they may have been, were unambiguously sympathetic to fascism. Certainly, prior to the outbreak of war, as we have seen, it was not unknown for speakers on nationalist political platforms to draw approvingly upon the example of Hitler's 'solution' for the Sudeten Germans as a suitable model for achieving a united Ireland; it was also the case that some nationalists compared the alleged authoritarian facets of Unionist rule with those of Nazi Germany and Stalinist Russia, regimes which were regarded in an entirely unfavourable light.[45] There was ambiguity here. It was the case, however, that in

1940 nationalist politicians and activists in Northern Ireland found themselves in a position of increasing isolation. De Valera's refusal to take a more decisive and interventionist role at the start of the year was quickly followed by a failed attempt to engage American government interest in Catholic grievances when a request by Cahir Healy for a meeting with the US Under Secretary for Foreign Affairs, Sumner Welles, during his visit to London in March, was refused.[46] It was in this situation, with no feasible strategy for advancing nationalist political objectives, and with widespread belief in Ireland that Britain was losing the war,[47] that some nationalist representatives contemplated a scenario of British defeat and entertained the possibility of achieving national unity in an Ireland occupied by Nazi Germany.[48] Healy was one of those who voiced such sentiments. Speaking in Enniskillen in July 1940, and clearly alluding to the likelihood of an imminent German victory, he expressed the opinion, 'At all events we (Nationalists) have the consolation that we cannot be much worse off politically than we are. We have nothing to lose.'[49] This was a very different position from the IRA, who sought to actively support German military designs on Ireland and assist in Britain's defeat, but it was nonetheless a policy that envisaged possible collaboration with a victorious Nazi Germany. It also went against the emphatic advice given by de Valera that northern nationalists should not seek 'the intercession of outside forces'.[50]

There was now a very real gap between de Valera's vision of nationalist advancement in the twenty-six counties and the northerners' unrealistic expectations of what de Valera could deliver for them. However, so pervasive were the essentials of the northern nationalist *weltanschauung* that they operated as a constraint preventing the leaderships of the nationalist political groupings from any consideration of the wider political context in which they found themselves. There was a yawning gulf between their political outlook and the *realpolitik* that determined de Valera's (highly popular) policy of twenty-six county neutrality;[51] a policy he refused to abandon even when a British offer of Irish unity was on the table.[52] Cognizance of this gulf was not immediately obvious to the leading members of the northern nationalist political groups and, as the war progressed, tensions with Dublin were to continually resurface.

For its part the Southern government called on the nationalist groups in the North to show 'unity of purpose', a call which contained an implied criticism of the northerners' factionalism and ineffectiveness. However, the internal dynamics of northern politics had a tendency to unite nationalists around issues that found little favour with Dublin, and it was to be the issue of the welfare of IRA prisoners and internees, coordinated by the Green Cross Fund, that was to unite the disparate nationalist opposition in one of their more sustained campaigns of the war years. The Green Cross Fund was initially set up in October 1940 for the purpose of raising money 'for relief of distress among dependents of Republican prisoners'. Dublin-based, its President was Caitlín Clarke, Lord Mayor of Dublin and the widow of the executed 1916 hero Thomas J. Clarke. The timing of the appearance of the organisation suggests that it was the welfare of republican internees and prisoners in the South, rather than the North, which was the primary focus of its activities. Internment of IRA suspects had been introduced by de Valera in January 1940, a response to the IRA's increasingly audacious unlawful activities in the South[53] and the threat that these activities posed to Ireland's neutral status. De Valera feared that the appearance of a revived republican movement, prepared to challenge the authority of his government and launch armed attacks on Britain, would encourage German support for the IRA and ultimately provoke British intervention in Ireland.[54] The Dublin government's response towards the Green Cross Fund was, therefore, inevitably cautious. A request to be allowed to raise funds, made by the Green Cross organising committee to the Minister of Justice, Gerry Boland, in October 1940, elicited a report on the organisation by Steven Roche, the Secretary of Justice, which left no doubt as to the concerns held regarding the whole raison d'être of the Fund:

> it seems to me that the Committee's appeal to the public must be essentially on the basis that the men in Mountjoy, Arbour Hill, and the Curragh Internment Camp are patriots suffering undeserved punishment … The root idea is *not* the relief of poverty and suffering, as such: the root idea is the support of the militant "Republican" movement by guaranteeing for the 'Army' activists a certain security for their families, and the honest title for the proposed Fund would be 'The Irish Republican Army Dependants Fund'. Some of the promoters might deny this and might believe that they were honest in their denial but in my view they are only deceiving themselves.[55]

Boland, who was appalled by the 'wanton murder' of the IRA's bombing campaign in Britain, was not prepared to turn a blind eye to its activities in Ireland.[56] Although the Fund was allowed to raise money privately Boland ensured it was subject to strict press censorship laws which prevented its activities being publicised thus reducing its effectiveness.

In the North constitutional nationalists were unanimously uncritical of de Valera's actions against the IRA; the need for 'national discipline' and the unquestioning acceptance of the authority of the Irish state were seen as essential to the maintenance of Irish democracy.[57] However, while little interest was shown in the plight of IRA prisoners and their dependents in the South, concerns expressed by senior members of the Catholic hierarchy that the Unionist government's internment policy was not just a wholly unwarranted measure against their political opponents but also an attack on Catholic homes and the institution of the Catholic family[58] lent considerable weight to a campaign to provide for the welfare of the dependants of convicted republican prisoners and internees in Northern Ireland.[59] The Church's sponsorship of the campaign ensured the active involvement of all of the nationalist political groupings. By 1941 the Green Cross Fund had the public support of Cardinal MacRory and other senior members of the clergy, Eamon Donnelly was appointed Secretary of the Fund and a new Belfast-based committee representing all of the northern nationalist factions was in existence. It would appear that there was now a feeling in certain sections of the Southern administration that the northern bias of the Fund allowed for the adoption of a more relaxed attitude towards it. A memo from the Department of Posts and Telegraphs, drawn up in August 1941, considered an application from the Fund's Belfast Committee to make a broadcast appeal on RTE, the Irish radio channel. On the basis that Dublin 'will be accused of showing no interest in the people of the North if we decline', the memo concluded that 'a very carefully worded appeal on humanitarian grounds should be allowed'.[60] De Valera, however, while vigorously suppressing the IRA in the South, was unlikely to be impressed with the 'humanitarian grounds' for supporting their comrades in the North. Granting northerners a platform on which to condemn what were palpably the more restrained policies of the Unionist government was hardly politic. A meeting of the Irish Cabinet in September duly rejected the proposal.[61] By 1942 the northern organisers of Green Cross, complaining bitterly of the 'ungenerous response from the twenty-six counties',[62] were faced with the reality that their campaign had failed to achieve popular support in the South.

If the results of the prisoner campaign were less than auspicious south of the border, involvement in the Green Cross did have certain attractions for nationalist groupings in the North. The prisoner issue was one that could unite all northern factions irrespective of their position on abstentionism; it also offered the potential of raising the political profile of constitutional nationalists in a key republican constituency i.e. the families and dependants of IRA prisoners and internees. Furthermore, it offered a more tangible range of activities with which nationalist activists and supporters in the North could engage. The establishment of Green Cross support groups in nationalist districts, towns and villages and the collection of monies to support the dependants of the prisoners were conducted with enthusiasm and with a high level of support. The charitable basis of the campaign was clear enough; the incarceration of adult or adolescent males placed families in dire economic straits, often with no financial support and with no recourse other than to depend on charitable sustenance. But just as the humanitarian aspect of the campaign was lost on the Dublin government, so too the Unionist government saw constitutional nationalist involvement in the IRA prisoner issue not as a charitable enterprise but as something distinctly political and subversive – a view reinforced by the tendency of nationalist spokespersons to refer to convicted IRA members (and not just internees) as 'political prisoners'.[63] There was a grey area here. Support for the Green Cross did not involve condoning the violent activities of the IRA, but for some time past senior nationalist politicians had adopted a position on the motivations of those involved in IRA violence which appeared to absolve IRA members of responsibility for the consequences of their violent actions. This was evident in the protests made by northern nationalist politicians following the trial and execution in England (in February 1940) of two IRA men, Peter Barnes and John McCormack, for their part in an IRA bomb attack in Coventry (in 1939) which had resulted in the deaths of five civilians. In one such protest Cahir Healy and a number of his fellow Nationalist MPs and Senators[64] sent an open letter to Sir John Anderson, the British Home Secretary, deploring his refusal to show clemency to the two men. The letter, which did not presume the innocence of the pair, acknowledged that the bombing was 'misguided' and its effects 'regrettable', but it also held that the bombing was 'designed primarily to draw attention to the hypocritical action of the British government in making a war in Europe for principles which it so shamelessly outrages at home'. As such the IRA operation, which 'inadvertently' killed the innocent civilians, was 'endeavouring mainly to arouse the conscience' of the British people to the iniquities of partition.[65] The nationalist hyperbole of the letter is best understood in the context of the highly charged circumstances of the men's death. The execution of Irish republicans in English prisons had long proved to be a sensitive issue that drew the sympathies of the Irish public and the Barnes/McCormack case proved no different. In southern Ireland there were displays of national mourning following the deaths of the two men: flags were flown at half-mast, sporting and entertainment events were cancelled and masses held.[66] In the North masses were said in many Catholic churches and messages of sympathy to the relatives of the executed men were issued by the NCU, the Irish National Foresters and by Nationalist members of local government councils.[67] And yet Healy's letter while reflecting public sympathy for the executed men also appeared to exhibit ambivalence towards IRA violence; an ambivalence that was absent from de Valera's condemnation of the IRA's bombing campaign.[68] As long as Healy and his colleagues spoke publicly of IRA volunteers as idealistic, if somewhat misguided, young men who found themselves outside the law as a result of injustices perpetrated by the Unionist government and the British State then there was a danger that Unionists would see a correspondence between the actions of the IRA and the impassioned rhetoric of constitutional nationalists. The tone of Healy's letter to Anderson was indeed distinctly empathetic towards the two IRA men and casually dispassionate on the fate of the unfortunate victims of the attack; but the letter formed part of an emotional wave of protest that reflected historic and deep-rooted concerns within the Irish nationalist psyche over perceived past British injustices, it was not a considered statement of intent or policy. However, for unionists the line between condoning IRA violence and its rationalisation must, at times, have appeared imperceptibly thin. In fact the Unionist administration regarded Healy's letter as proof of his implacable and bitter hostility to both the Stormont and British governments.

There must be little doubt that the opprobrium of the Unionist government mattered little to nationalist representatives. What was important, however, was winning the support and sympathy of the Dublin government. This was an immediate priority, but it was one in which an effective strategy was sorely lacking. Indeed, support for republican prisoners in the North, combined with a sullen anti-partitionism that spoke of having been forgotten, let down or abandoned by Dublin, could impact on southern politics in a way wholly unintended by northern nationalists. This is demonstrated by the case of the Six-Counties Men's Association (S-CMA), a new anti-partition group set up by Eamon Donnelly in September 1940. Initially intended by Donnelly to be a united and more virile replacement for the existing northern groupings, the S-CMA rapidly developed instead into a southern-based anti-partition umbrella organisation, providing northern nationalists with a platform on which to rally the support of the Irish public. In the course of a series of well attended S-CMA meetings held in the Mansion House, Dublin, between September and November 1940, northern politicians and activists took the opportunity to reveal the full extent of their 'persecution' in Northern Ireland[69] and admonish their audience, in the words of Anthony Mulvey MP, for 'the unconscious development of a mentality in the South that regards the Irish nation as extending no further North than the Border'.[70] While northern speakers on S-CMA platforms were careful to express their support for de Valera, the general tenor of the meetings was critical of the Irish government's approach to the partition question which, it was felt, lacked a requisite sense of urgency. In the North such expressions of discontent were a staple feature of nationalist discourse; however, in the South these kinds of sentiment inadvertently positioned the northern nationalists alongside de Valera's more vociferous republican critics. This is evident from the police report on an S-CMA 'monster meeting' that took place in the Mansion House on 19 November. Those in attendance included a veritable array of republican radicals from across the political spectrum: Peadar O'Donnell, Sean McBride, Con Lehane; the Irish fascist leader General Eoin O'Duffy; veteran anti-Treaty republicans Maude Gonne McBride and Moria Broderick; Roger McHugh and Sean Dowling of the new radical republican party Córas na Poblachta;[71] and members of the communist Unemployed Workers Movement. There was much that divided this diverse collection of political factions and republican notables, but what united them was the demand that, in relation to the North, de Valera should adopt a more proactive republican anti-partitionism. Also present in the Mansion House, on this occasion, was Karl Peterson, the press attaché at the German Legation. What is clear from the Garda report of the meeting is that while northern nationalists could attract large gatherings under the auspices of the S-CMA they could not control the proceedings of these meetings. Attempts by speakers from the North to condemn the Unionists' internment policy without reference to the situation in the South proved impossible. From the northerners' perspective there was nothing contradictory about condemning the 'inhuman barbarity'[72] of the Unionist government's internment policy while concurrently observing a stony silence on de Valera's domestic security policies, even when those policies resulted in the execution of IRA prisoners, the deaths of IRA men on hunger strike in Irish prisons and the generally poor treatment of IRA internees.[73] However, when Eamon Donnelly referred to the death of an IRA internee in the North he was instantly interrupted by a member of the audience who shouted 'What about the murder of Patrick Harte'- an IRA prisoner recently executed in Dublin's Mountjoy prison. Donnelly chose to ignore his heckler but the 'great applause' that greeted this interjection was indicative of the sympathies of the audience. Another northern speaker, the Derry MP Patrick Maxwell, was even less assured in handling the increasingly emotive mood of the meeting. Always something of a loose cannon, Maxwell's response to interruptions from pro-IRA elements in the audience was to emphasise his own militancy: 'he was not one of those people who say that only peaceful means should be used to bring about the abolition of Partition'. But, it was the contribution from the Córas na Poblachta representative, Roger McHugh, that 'a lot of time was wasted in this country talking about "Unity of Hearts"' when what they wanted 'was "Unity of arms"', a comment received with 'uproarious applause', that left little doubt as to the accuracy of the police observation that the whole event had a 'distinct Republican atmosphere' and was 'definitely of a revolutionary character'.[74]

As it was, the lack of interest in the republican prisoner/internee issue (and in the North generally) determined that the S-CMA had a limited shelf life as an active organisation in the twenty-six counties. There appear to have been no further Mansion House meetings after November and the S-CMA's last hurrah seems to have been a meeting held in College Green, Dublin (in May 1941) to protest against a second failed attempt by the Unionist government to have military conscription introduced in Northern Ireland. However, this very public association with some of the wilder elements on the fringes of southern politics, who continually harped about the Dublin government's republican apostasy, was guaranteed only to reconfirm de Valera's scepticism towards the northern groupings.

The strategy of constitutional nationalists had been far from successful; however, the war-time period was to present them with yet more opportunities, and challenges.

Notes

1 H. Patterson, *The Politics of Illusion: A Political History of the IRA* (London, Serif, 1997), p. 80.

2 P. Devlin, *Straight Left: An Autobiography* (Belfast, Blackstaff, 1993), p. 27.

3 Farrell, *Northern Ireland: Orange State* (London, Pluto Press, 1978), pp. 150–151; R. English, *Armed Struggle: A History of the IRA* (London, Macmillan, 2003), p. 67. A less successful operation in Donegal saw the deaths of three IRA members killed by the premature explosion of the bomb they were constructing. See J. Bowyer Bell, *The Secret Army: The IRA 1916–1979* (Dublin, Academic Press, 1983), p. 153.

4 Divisions within the IRA revolved around the question of targeting, not collaboration with the Nazis. Tom Barry, Russell's predecessor as Chief of Staff, favoured military operations in Northern Ireland and not on mainland Britain. Barry had travelled to Germany in 1939 to discuss the IRA's future action in the event of a European war only to find, on his return, that Russell, the author of the S-Plan, had replaced him as IRA Chief of Staff. UK National Archives, HO/KV/3/120, Report on Barry's visit to Germany. On Barry's visit see also F.H. Hinsley and C.A.G. Simpkins, *British Intelligence in the Second World* War (Cambridge, Cambridge University Press, 1990), p. 17. Russell was later to die on board a German U-boat in August 1940 while returning to Ireland from Berlin. On IRA collaboration with Nazi Germany during this period see D. O'Donoghue, *The Devil's Deal: the IRA, Nazi Germany and the Double Life of Jim O'Donovan* (Dublin, New Island Books, 2010); see also B. Hanley, '"Oh Here's to Adolph Hitler": The IRA and the Nazis', *History Ireland* 13: 3 (May/June 2005), pp. 31–35; J. Duggan, *Neutral Ireland and the Third Reich* (Dublin, Lilliput Press, 1989), pp. 58–59; Patterson, *Illusion*, p. 84.

5 J. Lee, *Ireland 1912–1985* (Cambridge, Cambridge University Press, 1989), p. 220.

6 A series of press statements condemning the arrests of IRA men and attacking 'British imperialism', which were issued in the name of the Anti-Partition Council of Northern Ireland certainly bear the hallmarks of a republican front organisation. See *Irish Times*, 24 December 1938; *Irish Times*, 10 January 1939.

7 Connolly, a businessman and former Irish Minister, who had a reputation as an Anglophobe, was strongly associated with the republican wing of Fianna Fail. See R. Fisk, *In Time of War: Ireland, Ulster and the Price of Neutrality 1939–45* (Dublin, Gill & Macmillan, 1983), p. 167; A. Dolan, *Commemorating the Irish Civil War: History and Memory, 1923–2000* (Cambridge, Cambridge University Press, 2006), p. 48.

8 PRONI, D2991/B/19/5 Murney to Connolly, 20 November 1939.

9 J. Kelly, *Bonfires on the Hillside: An Eyewitness Account of Political Upheaval in Northern Ireland* (Belfast, Fountain Publishing, 1995), pp. 105–106.

10 Devlin, *Straight Left*, p. 26.

11 All the principal officers of the IRA's Belfast Battalion were apprehended and interned in November 1938. See B. Barton, *Northern Ireland in the Second World War* (Belfast, Ulster Historical Foundation, 1995), p. 31.

12 Devlin, *Straight Left*, p. 29.

13 E. Staunton, *The Nationalists of Northern Ireland 1918–1975* (Dublin, Columba Press, 2001), p. 154.

14 *Frontier Sentinel*, 20 January 1940.

15 *Ibid.* Interestingly Dr Farren exonerated de Valera of any implication in this acquiesce; the culprits were 'other members of his Cabinet' who had become preoccupied with 'the cares, responsibilities, delights and fruits of office in the Twenty-Six Counties' at the expense of blotting out 'all thought of responsibility to the people who have yet to be freed.'

16 E. Phoenix, *Northern Nationalism: Nationalist Politics, Partition and the Catholic Minority in Northern Ireland 1890–1940* (Belfast, Ulster Historical Foundation, 1994), p. 389.

17 *Irish Times*, 15 April 1939, see also T. Hennessey, *A History of Northern Ireland 1920–1996* (Dublin, Gill & Macmillan, 1997), p. 85.

18 *Frontier Sentinel*, 20 January 1940.

19 In contrast to the rest of Britain where unemployment was halved, in Northern Ireland it had increased to 71,633 by November 1940. See Barton, *Northern Ireland*, p. 14.

20 Among the social and recreational organisations that proliferated in the period were the Catholic Arts Guild, the Catholic Young Men's Society, the Legion of Mary, the Catholic Boy Scouts, and the Holy Childhood Society. See O. Rafferty, *Catholicism in Ulster: An Interpretative History* (Dublin, Gill & Macmillan, 1994), p. 228.

21 See for example E. McCann, *War and an Irish Town* (Middlesex, Penguin Books, 1974), p. 18

22 Rafferty, *Catholicism in Ulster*, p. 228

23 M. Harris, 'The Catholic Church, Minority Rights and the Founding of the Northern Irish State', in D. Keogh and M. Haltzel (eds), *Northern Ireland and the Politics of Reconciliation* (Cambridge, Cambridge University Press, 1994), pp. 62–83.

24 M. Harris, *The Catholic Church and the Foundation of the Northern Irish State* (Cork, Cork University Press, 1993), pp. 51–52.

25 *Frontier Sentinel*, 29 June 1940.

26 *Ibid.*

27 The views of the hierarchy were also cascaded through the clergy to the laity at religious, cultural and sporting events.

28 Barton, *Northern Ireland*, pp. 16–17.

29 *Ibid.*, pp. 9–13.

30 National Archive of Ireland (hereafter NAI), S.698/40, An Garda Siochana report on Northern Ireland Activities, 2 July 1940.

31 Barton, *Northern Ireland*, p. 7.

32 *Ibid.* p. 33.

33 Col. R.G. Berry (of Newcastle, Co. Down) had brought to the attention of Independent Unionist MP Beattie the case of Alex Stafford a Catholic ex-serviceman with twelve years military service whose application to join the home guard was rejected by the local Commandant on the grounds that 'he did not want ex-servicemen nor Papishes'. *Frontier Sentinel*, 27 July 1940. The sectarian recruitment policy of the LDF was also the subject of a memorial sent to the British prime minister by a group of prominent protestants (including the Earl of Antrim and General Sir Hubert Gough) who protested that the new force 'incurred the odium attaching to a political police force of a type familiar on the Continent of Europe, rather than the general popularity and respect possessed in full measure by the Home Guard throughout the remainder of the United Kingdom'. *Frontier Sentinel*, 19 October 1940.

34 *Frontier Sentinel*, 20 January 1940.

35 *Frontier Sentinel*, 6 July 1940.

36 NAI, S.698/40, An Garda Sìochàna report on Northern Ireland Activities, 2 July 1940.

37 See H. Patterson, *Ireland Since 1939: The Persistence of Conflict* (Dublin, Penguin Ireland, 2006), p. 33.

38 *Frontier Sentinel*, 6 April 1940.

39 *Frontier Sentinel*, 1 June 1940. The belief that Northern Ireland citizens shirked their responsibility by refusing to volunteer for military service is convincingly challenged by Dr Brian Girvin who estimates a figure of 60,000 volunteering from Northern Ireland, see his *The Emergency: Neutral Ireland 1939–45* (London, Pan Books, 2007), pp. 274–275.

40 McLaughlin had been elected to the Northern Ireland Senate in 1933 and continued to hold the position until his death in April 1944. An opponent of abstentionism, McLaughlin dutifully fulfilled his role as Senator. His death notice refers to his activities in the Senate 'where he championed the rights of the minority fearlessly'. See *Frontier Sentinel*, 8 April 1944.

41 See accounts of this meeting in Staunton, *Nationalists* pp. 144–145 and Barton, *Northern* Ireland, p. 123.

42 Duggan, *Neutral Ireland*, p. 125. On MacRory's ambivalence regarding a German victory see Girvin, *The Emergency*, p. 286.

43 NAI, S1104/40, An Garda Sìochàna report, 19 November 1940. The 'more virile' anti-partitionist organisation referred to was the Six-Counties Men's Association (S-CMA) which had in fact been established by Donnelly in September 1940. Details of this meeting appear to have been passed to the police by a 'John Joe Murray of Lurgan' in whom Donnelly had confided.

44 *Ibid.*

45 See for example 'Ultach', 'The Persecution of Catholics in Northern Ireland', *Capuchin Annual*, 1945 (reprinted Athol Books, Belfast, 1998).

46 *Frontier Sentinel*, 16 March 1940.

47 Lee, *Ireland*, p. 247.

48 As Paul Bew has pointed out even de Valera thought at this time that 'a majority of the Irish wanted Germany to prevail'. P. Bew, *The Memoir of David Gray: A Yankee in De Valera's Ireland* (Dublin, Royal Irish Academy, 2012).

49 *Impartial Reporter*, 4 July 1940, cited in P. Livingstone, *The Fermanagh Story* (Enniskillen, Cumann Seanchais Chlochair, 1969) p. 341.

50 Phoenix, *Northern Nationalism*, p. 389.

51 Bowman, *De Valera and the Ulster Question 1917–1973* (Oxford, Oxford University Press, 1982), pp. 207–208; D. Keogh, *Twentieth Century Ireland: Nation and State* (Dublin, Gill & Macmillan, 1994), p. 109.

52 The offer to accept the principle of Irish unity if de Valera abandoned neutrality was made following the fall of Dunkirk; de Valera's refusal was based on the not unreasonable assumption that Britain would lose the war and thus be unable to deliver on their undertaking. Bowman, *De Valera*, p. 237; Keogh, *Twentieth Century Ireland*, p. 114. However, even under more auspicious circumstances the Northerners' intransigent positions would have likely stymied any rapprochement between the Irish and British governments. When, in the summer of 1940, rumours of a deal between de Valera and Churchill over the North leaked out, the instinctive and negative reaction of the Nationalist groups was to protest that 'certain less vital matters' (i.e. entering the war against Nazi Germany) had been allowed to 'eclipse the National issue of the Partition of this country' and to point to a historical parallel with the situation in Ireland between 1914–18, warning the Irish government of the 'disastrous results' that then befell the leadership of Irish Nationalism when it assisted the British war effort in the hope of securing Home Rule. *Frontier Sentinel*, 29 June 1940.

53 In December 1939 about fifty members of the IRA using thirteen lorries carried away the bulk of the Irish Army's ammunition reserves following a successful raid on the Magazine Fort in Phoenix Park, Dublin. The matériel was recovered some short time later. See T.P. Coogan, *The IRA* (London, Palgrave Macmillan, 2002), pp. 135–136; English, *Armed Struggle*, p. 54.

54 See Lee, *Ireland*, p. 221.

55 NAI, S1069/40 Roche to Boland, 17 October 1940.

56 Fisk, *In Time of War*, pp. 87–88.

57 *Frontier Sentinel*, 30 March 1940.

58 This was the position of Bishop Mageegan in 1940/41. See Rafferty, *Catholicism in Ulster*, p. 242; P. McKeever, 'The Discourse of Nationalists in Northern Ireland 1921–1991', unpublished Ph.D. thesis, Queen's University Belfast, p. 165.

59 This did not, however, imply any sympathy with, or condoning of, the IRA's violent activities. In February 1940 Cardinal MacRory, along with his fellow Catholic bishops, issued a pastoral letter condemning IRA violence and declaring membership of the organisation a sin.

60 NAI, S1069/40 Memo, Department of Posts and Telegraphs, 11 August 1941.

61 NAI, S1069/40 Maurice Moynihan to Department of Posts and Telegraphs, 4 September 1941.

62 *Irish Times*, 25 May 1942. By June it was revealed that Northern contributions amounted to between £10,000 and £11,000 while Southern contributions were less than £300. See *Irish* Times, 30 June 1942.

63 See communiqué issued by the NCU. *Irish Times*, 14 January 1939.

64 The other signatories were Joseph Stewart MP, Patrick Maxwell MP, Alex Donnelly MP, Senator John McHugh and Senator T. McLaughlin.

65 PRO, HO144/22162 249815, Cahir Healy open letter to Sir John Anderson, January 1940. This generous depiction of the motivations of the alleged bombers is not supported by Tim Pat Coogan's book *The IRA*, first published in 1971. In this, and in later editions of the book, Coogan's generally sympathetic approach to republicans does not stretch to the man who actually planted the fateful bomb. Coogan, who appears to have discovered the identity of the man, describes him as a known 'psychopath'. See Coogan, *The IRA*, p. 167.

66 Bowyer Bell, *The Secret Army*, p. 175.

67 *Frontier Sentinel*, 17 January 1940.

68 T.P. Coogan, *De Valera: Long Fellow, Long Shadow* (London, Hutchinson, 1993), p. 523.

69 Which, according to Joseph Stewart MP, speaking at the Mansion House on 19 November, had 'reached a greater pitch than at any time within the past 150 years'. *Frontier Sentinel*, 23 November 1940.

70 *Frontier Sentinel*, 14 September 1940.

71 Córas na Poblachta was a pan-republican front organisation that had attracted into its ranks pro-German and ultra-rightist elements. See R.M. Douglas, 'The Pro-Axis Underground in Ireland, 1939–1943', *The Historical Journal* 49: 4 (2006), pp. 173–175.

72 *Frontier Sentinel*, 14 September 1940.

73 In December 1940, following disturbances in the Curragh internment camp after IRA internees protested against the reduction of their butter ration, the Irish army opened fire wounding three and killing one. *Frontier Sentinel*, 21 December 1940.

74 NAI, S1104/40, Garda report on Six County Men's Association, Mansion House, 19 November 1940.

3

The war years, 1940–45

The death of Craigavon, in November 1940, was not the occasion for a thawing of relations between unionism and nationalism in Northern Ireland. In the early turbulent years of the new state Craigavon had shown a willingness to reconcile the North's Catholic minority to their new political situation. He had responded positively to the British government's attempt at a rapprochement between the Unionist government and their counterparts in the Irish Free State – the ill-fated Craig/Collins Peace Pacts of January and March 1922 which held out the prospect of an accommodation between Protestants and Catholics in Northern Ireland.[1] He also had the capacity to maintain amiable personal relationships with several nationalist politicians, most notably Joe Devlin whom he clearly held in some regard.[2] After 1922, however, Craigavon's long period in office was marked by an unhealthy readiness to appease the most unattractive of Orange and loyalist sectarian prejudices and an active promotion of discrimination in the public services. His replacement, John Andrews, who had been a member of the government since 1921, displayed the same flaws as his predecessor: a preoccupation with the numbers of Catholics employed in government departments and an over-responsiveness to Protestant sectarian concerns.[3]

Despite his pedigree the new premier's honeymoon period was brief and he swiftly came under mounting criticism from within his own unionist constituency – voices were raised against his lackadaisical approach to necessary wartime preparations (with accusations that his administration lacked the dynamism, efficiency and foresight required) while more populist protestant elements, alarmed by allegations that Catholics from the Free State were heavily employed in Northern Ireland's war industries, questioned whether Andrews was sufficiently vigilantly robust.[4] The loss of Craigavon's parliamentary seat in North Down to an Independent Unionist candidate in a by-election in March 1941 was a clear indication of unionist discontent.[5] Response to Andrews' setback from the more considered quarters of nationalist opinion was cautious but optimistic. Joseph Connellan, the editor of the Newry-based nationalist newspaper the *Frontier Sentinel*, observed that it would be 'foolish to profess to see in the result a general swing-over from the Unionist camp'. But he nonetheless regarded the failure of the Unionist Party's traditional clarion call to loyally support the Unionist establishment, and the unionist electorate's independence of mind, as highly significant; holding out at least the potential of 'the end of purely Party government in the North-East'.[6] However, Andrews' call for the introduction of conscription in Northern Ireland, in May 1941, ensured that there would be little opportunity for a reconsideration of traditional political positions. It is true that Andrews' request to the British government, a request fully supported by his Cabinet, was in a context in which Britain's fortunes in the war appeared increasingly precarious. It also followed on from the devastation wrought by the Luftwaffe's bombing of Belfast in April and early May. Nonetheless, the Catholic response to his request must have been anticipated – it certainly had been by Charles Wickham, the Inspector General of the RUC, who informed the British Home Secretary, Herbert Morrison, that the likely outcome would be 'massive resistance' and possibly street disturbances and violence.[7] Catholic mobilisation in opposition to Andrews' announcement was indeed swift and uncompromising. On 22 May, Cardinal MacRory issued a strongly worded statement, denouncing conscription, and warning that its enactment would rouse Catholics 'to indignation and resistance'. His colleague Dr Farren, the Bishop of Derry, considered conscription to be a deliberate 'provocation' intended to destroy the good relations between Catholics and Protestants that had arisen from the common suffering inflicted by the Luftwaffe's attack on Belfast. Referring to the 'conscription crisis' of 1918, which saw 'the formation of a political unity amongst Nationalists and Catholics never before achieved in Ireland' (and which provided an electoral boon for Sinn Féin), Dr Farren expressed his hope that that unity could be revisited.[8] Taking their lead from the Catholic hierarchy, nationalist representatives Cahir Healy, Senator McLaughlin, Anthony Mulvey and Alex Donnelly (MP for West Tyrone) all publicly declared both their opposition to conscription and their determination to resist it.[9] On 23 May nationalist representatives gathered for an indignation meeting in St Mary's Hall, Belfast, and on 25 May large protest rallies were held across Northern Ireland (10,000 reportedly attending in Belfast and 8,000 in Newry).[10]

Andrews withdrew his conscription request to London shortly afterwards, partly in response to Catholic opposition but also in the knowledge that there were fears within his own cabinet that the conscription of Protestant workers could lead to resultant vacancies being filled by workers coming from Southern Ireland.[11] In the aftermath of the conscription fiasco Andrews' attempt at a statesman-like plea for a 'better spirit of goodwill throughout the whole country' and his call on the nationalist minority to 'recognise the authority of the Constitution under which it lives', delivered in an address to the Fermanagh Unionist Council in June, was greeted in the *Frontier Sentinel* with a scornful and excoriating attack on his administration for having 'made the lot of the Nationalist people in the Six Counties a hell on earth'.[12] Nor did the episode reverse Andrews' reputation for ineptitude and inefficiency among the unionist electorate. That the timely display of Catholic 'disloyalty' failed to restore unionist discipline was reconfirmed by yet another emphatic defeat for the Unionist Party at a by-election in December, this time at the hands of the Northern Ireland Labour Party in the staunchly unionist East Belfast constituency of Willowfield.[13] Significantly, for Joseph Connellan those glimpses of an alternative scenario of political development that he recognised following the North Down result in March, which hinted at some sort of reconfiguration of the Unionist/Nationalist divide, were now replaced by a more triumphalist assessment of unionist division that invoked traditional nationalist strategies of political disengagement,

> Nationalists take no interest in the result other than to observe with more than passing satisfaction the emergence of the Unionist masses from the trance into which, until now, appeals to history (and incorrect history at that), bigoted utterances and incitements of the grossest kind have been sufficient to throw them. In a contest between two Partitionists it matters little to the Nationalist minority which of them tops the poll, but there is some satisfaction ... in seeing official Unionism steadily shorn of its electoral monopoly.[14]

This political retroflexion by Connellan was clearly presaged in his editorial leader in September,

> The foremost responsibility of all classes of Nationalists is to stand fast by the cause of Irish unity. Without the re-unification of the country there can be no permanent peace, no agricultural progress, no industrial prosperity ... Ireland's most important national concern is the abolition of Partition. Everything else comes after that.[15]

The conscription affair had undoubtedly reinforced this viewpoint but there were other concurrent events that also influenced the pessimistic mood of nationalist spokesmen; most notably the arrest, and subsequent internment, of Northern Ireland's most senior nationalist political figure, Cahir Healy, MP for the Stormont constituency of South Fermanagh. Officers of the Royal Ulster Constabulary (RUC) had arrested Healy at his home in Enniskillen early in the morning on 11 July 1941. On that same evening he was transported out of Northern Ireland en route to Brixton prison where he was interned without trial, in the company of many of Britain's most notable suspect fascist 'fellow travellers', until his eventual release in December 1942.[16] The reaction to Healy's detention among his political colleagues was, understandably, one of outrage. The timing of his arrest, the day before the annual 12 July parades, was seen as deliberately provocative. The fact that the British Home Secretary, Herbert Morrison, signed his detention order on 8 July, the day after he returned from a visit to the province (during which he had publicly demonstrated the British government's solidarity with their Northern Ireland counterpart) further fuelled suspicion that his detention had been orchestrated by the Unionist government. Indeed, this suspicion was well founded; the Unionist government had placed Healy under surveillance shortly after the outbreak of war and this surveillance involved the monitoring of Healy's private correspondence by the RUC. It was arising from this that a letter, posted by Healy on 13 June 1941 to the Newtownbutler-based parish priest and ardent anti-partitionist propagandist, Father Thomas Maguire, was intercepted and the following passage copied by the censor:

> I think we may have a peace at November, or else a long war. In the first eventuality we ought to be sure that Dublin will stand firm. Do you think we should, thro' the Six Counties-Men, make our own approach to Germany in Dublin? We cannot do it publicly. We ought to leave them in no doubt as to our wishes and help in case the opportunity arises. I should like your views before publishing the matter.[17]

Charles Wickham, the Inspector General of the RUC, interpreted this passage as indicating Healy's desire to 'communicate directly or indirectly with the German Legation in Dublin with a view to entering into negotiations with the German government in order to discuss the conditions under which he and his associates would be prepared to give assistance to the Germans in the event of invasion or the defeat of England'. Sir Alexander Maxwell, Permanent Under-Secretary at the Home Office, the British Director of Public Prosecutions and Herbert Morrison, shared Wickham's reading of the letter, which had been rapidly communicated to Whitehall. As a result Healy was detained under Defence Regulation 18B, legislation introduced by the British government in 1939 specifically designed to deal with those deemed to have been engaged in acts 'prejudicial to the … defence of the realm'.[18] Healy firmly denied that he was engaged in any such enterprise, but he was initially unwilling to provide an explanation of the contents of his letter to Father Maguire, who prior to the outbreak of the war, was on record as having advocated cooperation with Germany if this could secure Irish unity.[19] Healy's internment briefly became something of a cause célèbre in northern nationalist circles, but it did not have a comparable impact on the Dublin government. Kept abreast of the circumstances leading to Healy's arrest through British Home Office briefings of the

Irish High Commissioner in London, John Dulanty, Dublin's position was one of marked reluctance to take up Healy's case. Pressed in the Dáil, in late July, to make a statement as to whether his government would make representation to the British to secure Healy's immediate release, de Valera bluntly replied 'I do not think that official intervention on our part would help'.[20] De Valera's coolness was probably linked to his concerns that the British, fearful of their security being compromised by rogue Irish nationalist collaboration with Nazi Germany, would be prepared to take pre-emptory action which would imperil Irish neutrality: in 1940 it was believed that Britain would go so far as to invade the South.[21] De Valera also likely knew that contacts between representatives of northern nationalist groups and officials of the Axis Legations in Dublin were already established (the meetings that had taken place in August and November 1940); information to which the British government were not privy. As a consequence Dulanty duly informed Healy, in Brixton Prison, that Dublin could do little to assist him and advised that he cooperate fully with the British authorities if he wished to establish his innocence. Furthermore, the Irish government took steps to ensure that Healy's colleagues and supporters in Northern Ireland tone down their efforts to raise Healy's internment as a political campaign issue. This was clear when one of Healy's close political associates, Senator Thomas McLaughlin, called at the offices of the Irish Department of External Affairs (DEA) in Dublin in August 1941. McLaughlin's visit followed on from a series of meetings in support of Healy, held in Belfast in July and August, at which the Dublin government were called upon 'to take all necessary steps' to gain Healy's 'immediate release'.[22] McLaughlin's reception, however, was not as he would have anticipated or wished. In the course of his discussions with senior DEA officials McLaughlin was apprised of the Department's view that Healy's imminent release was 'somewhat remote in view of the extreme imprudence of Mr Healy's letter to Father Maguire'. He was also advised 'very strongly' not to embark on a proposed public campaign of protest against Healy's internment, the outcome of which, it was pointed out to him, might provoke the British government to publish the June 1941 letter with 'very serious consequences' for 'the other Nationalist M.P.s in the Six County area'.[23] From the documents relating to this meeting it is evident that the tenor of the encounter was one of delicacy and candour. McLaughlin's own contact with the German Legation in Dublin the previous year was not alluded to outright, but there was a perceptible bluntness both in the DEA officials' assumption that McLaughlin knew of the contents of Healy's letter and in their advice to him that he share this knowledge with his political colleagues 'so that their agitation might take a form consistent with the perils in which disclosure would involve them'.[24] By the end of the meeting McLaughlin's acquiescence with the directives of the DEA was complete and unconditional, thereafter the question of Healy's internment effectively disappeared from Nationalist statements protesting against the internment of republicans in the North.

Clandestine contacts and meetings between northern nationalist representatives and the Axis Legations in Dublin were understandably seen as a dangerous and risky business that could potentially cause serious embarrassment to de Valera and result in grave political repercussions. For this reason it was imperative that the British authorities did not get wind of them. Healy's indiscretion sailed far too close to that wind and as a corollary Dublin was determined to keep him at arm's length.

The consequences of the continued political stasis of the nationalist political organisations, borne out by the constant repetition of anti-partitionist statements shorn of practical recommendations, were not lost on all nationalist representatives – particularly those in urban working-class areas of Belfast. In January 1942 two Nationalist councillors representing the Falls ward in Belfast, Frank Hanna and James Collins, defected to the Northern Ireland Labour Party (NILP). In their resignation statements both men emphasised the gulf that had opened up between the leadership of orthodox Nationalism (as represented by the NCU and the array of elected representatives who were former members of the National League) and the Catholic electorate in their constituencies; Hanna felt that 'effective and proper representation' for his constituents could now 'only be secured under the aegis of a strong Labour Party' while Collins more forcefully castigated those who had allowed the Catholic minority 'to sink deeply into the slough of despair'.[25] The defection of Hanna and Collins did not mean any lessening of their nationalism. They were both staunchly anti-partitionist but they were also politically astute enough to realise that they could not afford to ignore either the immediate economic and social concerns of their constituents or the unpopularity of the innately conservative and dilatory response to those concerns from the orthodox Nationalist leadership. The movement to more labourist and left-wing positions in Catholic urban constituencies was not lost on nationalist political representatives. Their response to counter their declining influence – attacking the NILP as pro-partition and attempting to reposition themselves as champions of social and economic radicalism – was, however, enfeebled by their political inactivity regarding social and economic issues at the expense of an almost exclusive concentration on the 'Border' issue.[26]

There were still opportunities in Belfast for a more militant anti-partitionism. Following the death in August 1942 of Richard Byrne, the non-abstentionist Nationalist MP for the Stormont constituency of Falls, abstentionist Nationalist MPs and Nationalist Senators (but significantly not Byrne's sole parliamentary colleague still attending at Stormont, T.J. Campbell) unanimously supported Eamon Donnelly's candidacy for the seat on an abstentionist ticket. In the ensuing November by-election Donnelly, who had retired from his Leix-Offaly Dail seat in 1937, had several advantages over his anti-abstentionist nationalist competitor.[27] Donnelly was the secretary of a committee formed to campaign for the reprieve of Tom Williams, a young but experienced local IRA man who had been sentenced to death for his part in the killing of an RUC officer in April 1941,[28] and he was also secretary of the Green Cross Fund which was financially supporting the dependents of interned IRA men[29] from the Falls area. Williams's execution in September, and the ensuing Catholic anger it generated, probably guaranteed Donnelly's electoral success.[30] His victory was immediately followed by an attempt to extend the influence of the NCU throughout Northern Ireland. Donnelly announced a grand plan to unite northern nationalists with political parties in Southern Ireland[31] and made known his intention to form a new political organisation the object of which was to 'keep Partition a paramount issue in the minds of the Irish people'.[32] This proposal invariably emphasised abstentionism as its core principle; all nationalist MPs and Senators were welcome to join, but only if they turned their back on the Stormont parliament.

However, Donnelly's assumption that his election 'had had repercussions all over Ireland' and that his influence on the Southern political establishment was such that 'with the proper approaches made and contact effected [sic] on right lines, a solution is not only possible, but probable'[33] had no basis in objective reality. In fact Donnelly, who had for some considerable time played the role of republican gadfly within de Valera's Fianna Fail, had long expended what remaining political cachet he had in southern politics. In the North a Westminster by-election in the constituency of West Belfast in February 1943 revealed just how tenuous the appeal of Donnelly's traditional anti-partitionism was amongst Belfast's Catholic electorate in the changing material circumstances brought about by the war. Unemployment rates in Northern Ireland had steadily declined since 1941 (full employment was achieved by 1944) as the demand for military-related products – from servicemen's uniforms to warships – increased. With increased security of employment came a determination to protect favourable wages and work conditions through industrial militancy, optimum conditions in fact for parties of the Left.[34] The contrast with the situation in the south of Ireland could hardly have been greater. There unemployment was growing (reaching 70,000 by 1943),[35] basic foodstuffs were in short supply and the cost of living was spiralling upwards (an increase of around 40 per cent between 1939 and 1944).[36] A strategy of territorial unity as a cure-all panacea, which paid precious little attention to questions of material welfare, now looked decidedly less attractive to West Belfast's nationalist electorate who demanded something more substantial than Donnelly's abstentionism.[37] This they found in Jack Beattie, the socialist anti-partitionist NILP candidate, who impressively took the seat (which had returned a Unionist representative since 1920) while Hugh Corvin, who stood for the Donnelly NCU group, lost his deposit.[38] As Henry Patterson has observed, the Catholic working class in Belfast at this time 'was inclined to express its nationalism in a pragmatic and left of centre way'.[39]

There were other nationalist voices proffering strategic alternatives at this time. Ultach in his polemical article *Orange Terror*, published in 1943, railed against anti-Catholic discrimination, which he saw as endemic in Northern Ireland, but, in a departure from traditional nationalism, he called for British government intercession as a necessary step to ensure Catholic integration into a normalised and democratic political system which, in turn, would allow for constitutional change to evolve as the result of persuasion and freely given consent.' This proposal was met with disdain from Donnelly (because of its intrinsic moderation) and dismissal from the Bishop of Down and Connor, Daniel Mageean, partly on the more reasonable grounds that British intercession had been called for in the past but had never materialised.[40] Mageean's position was however informed by a deeply entrenched ideological anti-partitionism which imposed severe constraints on his support for political action that sought to accommodate unionist (even liberal unionist) opinion. For Mageean the rights of the nation were sacrosanct above all else:

> Even were its regime [Northern Ireland] one of justice and equality, of liberty and fair play ... we should still oppose the dismemberment of our fatherland. For we are Irish and until we are united with our brethren of the rest of Ireland, not only are we deprived of our rights as Irishmen but the historic Irish nation, unnaturally divisioned, is robbed of its glory and greatness. Partition is an evil which only its removal can remedy.[41]

The sincerity and conviction of Bishop Mageean's opinion, however, offered little in the way of a discernible strategy that could deliver the desired goal of Irish unity.

The question of how to bring an end to partition with the consent of Northern Ireland's Protestant population was, however, considered by the Protestant nationalist writer and journalist Capt. Dennis Ireland[42] and the small group of Protestant anti-partitionists who made up the Ulster Union Club (UUC). Established by Capt. Ireland in February 1941, his intention was to recapture the liberal and democratic spirit of the radical Ulster Protestant tradition ('Once outstandingly liberal in politics, once so intellectually fearless') which, he claimed, had 'grown obscurantist and reactionary' as a consequence of intransigent Ulster Unionist Party dominance.[43] Ireland was

particularly forthright in his condemnation of the practice of the gerrymandering of electoral constituencies and of anti-Catholic sectarian employment
practices. He was also an enthusiastic supporter of de Valera's right to pursue
a neutrality policy in the war. The Belfast-based UUC found favour among
nationalist commentators who warmly welcomed the public profile of these
'right-thinking non-Catholics' and spoke approvingly of their mission to 'ed-
ucate non-Catholic opinion on the question of Irish nationality'.[44] However,
whatever prospect Capt. Ireland held out of influencing Protestant opinion was
indubitably, and irreparably, damaged by the revelation, in 1942, that some
members of his group were also active members of the IRA. RUC raids on the
Club's premises in Belfast and on homes of UUC members, in March 1942,
uncovered arms and a substantial amount of 'seditious literature' linked to the
IRA.[45] If Ireland's role as proselytiser of 'non-Catholic opinion' was now no
longer possible he still, nonetheless, continued to enjoy a receptive, if mixed,
audience among constitutional nationalists. Capt. Ireland's distinctiveness as
an Ulster Protestant nationalist ensured that his views and opinions received a
level of attention that far outweighed his actual influence; and Ireland had definite thoughts on what was necessary for Nationalism to become a serious and
leading political force in Northern Ireland. Speaking at an event in the Gresham
Hotel, Dublin, in March 1943, Ireland gave an address ('An Ulster Protestant
Looks at Partition') in which he urged the formation of a united non-sectarian
Nationalist Party in Northern Ireland which could attract Protestants into its
ranks, called for the adoption of a modern economic programme with broad
appeal, and recommended federalism as a preliminary stage to Irish unity.[46]
In making this contribution Ireland enjoyed the advantage of being unbur-
dened by the weight of intra-nationalist competition and rivalry so prevalent in
the North and for that reason his ideas at least broached the thorny problem,
usually left unspoken, of how divisions between Catholics and Protestants in
the North were to be addressed and resolved in an envisaged future unitary
state. Writing in his *Frontier Sentinel* editorial Joseph Connellan readily admitted that nationalist schism had left 'the people … bewildered and helpless,
seeking … the guidance they ought to have and which is denied them', and
acknowledged the attractiveness of Ireland's proposals.[47] However, Connellan
also pointed out that the success of Ireland's proposed non-sectarian party and
federalist solution depended on the potential for Protestant unionists to be
won across to the nationalist side by force of reasoned argument and appeals to
mutual self-interest, and this he thought unlikely. Connellan's pessimism was
partly premised on his reading of the course of Irish history since 1798, and
in particular he emphasised the corrupting effects of material privilege on the
ancestors of 'the Dissenters of '98' whose once 'noble spirit' had been replaced

by the self-seeking allure of 'a place in the British sun' which, Connellan maintained, Ulster protestants had 'proved in our own time [that] they will go to any lengths to retain'.[48] But Connellan's questioning of Ireland's innovative thinking was not solely the result of a deterministic understanding of Irish history, for there was something much more pressing that impacted on the subject of winning the hearts and minds of Protestant Unionists – the outcome of the war. This Connellan posed in the following frank way:

> Whether the Ulster Scot will ever prove amenable to reason and acknowledge the necessity for national unity *before the direful march of events compels a recognition of a quite different kind* is a poser, the *answer to which must await developments.*[49] [Emphasis added.]

Clearly any strategy to win the consent of Ulster Protestants to an eventual change in Northern Ireland's constitutional status would be rendered unnecessary in the circumstances of Britain's defeat in the war: Irish unity would then become a *fait accompli* which unionists would be compelled to accept. The upshot of this 'wait and see' policy – which echoed that of Cardinal MacRory[50] – was to reinforce a policy of inaction and to prevent any serious reflection on the obstacles preventing Protestants from embracing the cause of Irish unity. On the latter Father Thomas Maguire, in reply to Capt. Ireland, offered a robust judgement. Protestants, he declared, were unreliable allies, unlikely to 'stay the course', and prone to fall away when 'flesh-pots were offered'.[51] In an forthright attack on Ireland (and Ernest Blythe who shared the platform with Capt. Ireland in the Gresham Hotel) Maguire made clear that these unattractive failings also applied to Protestant nationalists: 'The National mentality of the Protestants who joined the Nationalist ranks was a quite different brand from the national mentality of the Gaels. Therein lies the snag to national coalescence, not alone in the North but in the South as well.'[52]

Ulster Protestants, to whom Maguire gave 'the highest praise as good church-goers, and really loyal to their religion', were, he asserted, inveterate realists who would only be swayed by the removal of English 'swag' and not the pleadings of '"turncoats" … of their own sort'. Talk of federalism and a non-sectarian Nationalist Party was, he believed, an unhelpful distraction from the only inevitable outcome, 'an all-Ireland Parliament, where Catholics must dominate'.[53]

There was now little other than the Green Cross Fund campaign to galvanise nationalist political action, a campaign circumscribed by the duration of the Unionist government's internment policy and one that tended to add to the bitter political animosities between Unionists and Nationalists. However, the difficulties encountered by de Valera in the southern Irish general election of

1943, faced as he was with a deteriorating economic situation and increased support for opposition parties,[54] ensured that his frequent pronouncements on partition (alongside the alleged threat posed by communism) received regular coverage in nationalist newspapers in the North. There was of course a glaring disparity between the unwavering consistency of de Valera's inaction in relation to the northern Catholic minority and statements which appeared to prioritise partition; such as that delivered at an election rally in Dunmancray, Co. Cork, in May 1943: 'There were now left only two of the big national objectives remaining to be accomplished – the unification of the country into a single state and the restoration of the language'.[55] That these statements were not met with incredulity by northern nationalists but were taken at face value merely served to preserve an unhelpful illusion of immediacy and purposefulness on behalf of de Valera and the Irish political establishment.

The concerns of the Catholic Church, which now began to increasingly focus on the likely consequences of anticipated developments in the post-war period, further consolidated the conservative outlook of the main nationalist political groupings and, in doing so, further reduced whatever limited capacity they had to challenge the rising tide of labourist politics in Catholic urban areas. The Church was especially apprehensive of the blueprint for future social reconstruction outlined in the Beveridge Plan, the implications of which were seen as fundamentally malign.[56] In January 1944 the leading clerical intellectual Revd Dr Peter McKevitt, Professor of Sociology at St. Patrick's College Maynooth (the hub of Catholic intellectual thinking in Ireland) delivered a lecture on 'Post-War Problems' in which he gave warning of the latent dangers that underlay any expansion of the State's social role, 'the more we load the State with duties, the greater the powers we must give it over the arranging of our lives'. The inevitable result, McKevitt argued, was a 'transference of responsibility to the State', which would mean not only an extension of State power in the realm of industrial relations but also, and more disturbingly, a loss of 'personal control over our activities'.[57]

Throughout 1944 and 1945 the Lenten Pastorals of the Irish Catholic Bishops, taking their lead from McKevitt's analysis, warned of the incipient but mounting dangers that expanded State power posed to Catholic religious and social values. As the war came to a conclusion the Revd Dr Neil Farren, Bishop of Derry, cautioned that the growth of State control was 'the result of a pagan concept of society', while his colleague, Bishop Daniel Mageean, spoke of 'Christian culture and civilisation' being 'threatened in Europe by certain campaigns and movements having for their objects the destruction of religion and the imposition of atheism'.[58]

The fear that Catholic social mores were being undermined and threatened became a constant refrain from both the clergy and nationalist spokesmen who warned of the dangers posed to Catholic values by attacks on Christian morality (measured by the increase in divorce rates in England) and the rise in irreligion.[59] In part this defensive response was a consequence of the disturbance to Northern Ireland's parochial and conventional way of life brought about by the stationing of large numbers of Allied troops during the war. Of American troops alone some 300,000 passed through Northern Ireland between 1942 and 1945.[60] The billeting of American troops was an issue of perceptible consternation for nationalists; the USA had been long regarded as a major power sympathetic to the objectives of Irish nationalists, but the physical presence of their troops now demonstrated not only the USA's support for their British allies but also the importance of Northern Ireland's contribution to the war effort. The advantages of this were not lost on the Unionist government. However, even the presence of so many 'guests' could not stymie the expression of crass and petty sectarian attitudes that were so commonplace in local political exchanges and which drew attention to the less agreeable side of Northern Ireland. During the course of a parliamentary debate at Stormont, in February 1944, attention was drawn to the fact that an Orange Hall at Portrush, a predominantly protestant town, had been used to celebrate Mass for Catholic American soldiers on Christmas Day. In a preposterously callous interjection William Lowry, the Minister of Home Affairs, made the comment – 'Preparations are being made for its fumigation.'[61] Called upon by T.J. Campbell and Jack Beattie to withdraw the remark, which they insisted was a slur on the American troops who had attended the service, Lowry declined, claiming, somewhat disingenuously, that he had understood that it was the Hibernian Order who had used the Hall and that he had not made (nor meant) any derogatory reference to matters of religious observation. Coming just a day after Basil Brooke had effusively extended the welcome and hospitality of the House to the American troops ('with a heart and a half')[62] Lowry's comment was a potential cause of considerable embarrassment. In a quick about turn Lowry acknowledged that he was at fault and, in a letter to the Bishop of Derry, the Revd Dr Farren,[63] apologised in unreservedly contrite terms,

> Speaking with all the reverence for a faith I do not hold and with respect for what I believe to be the Central Mystery of the Faith I assure your Lordship that no insult was intended by me to the American Roman Catholic Chaplains in the exercise of their sacred functions or to those who were present … in the most unreserved and unqualified manner I withdraw my facetious interjection and express my deep regret for permitting myself to make it.[64]

For nationalists the import of this incident, which had the potential to paint Brooke's administration as irredeemably sectarian, was lessened by the fact that both de Valera and Cardinal MacRory had condemned the introduction of American troops into Northern Ireland in 1942[65] and this had set the tone for repeated attacks on their presence from pulpit and political platform in the North. In Derry Paddy Maxwell MP responded to the arrival of the first US troop units in the city with characteristic bellicosity: 'there is nothing we can do to physically throw the American troops out of Northern Ireland, or we would do so'.[66] Maxwell's bluster was however soon followed by more ominous developments when in April 1943 Hugh McAteer, the IRA's commander-in-chief, read a statement at a Republican Easter commemoration in Belfast in which he denounced the presence of American troops and warned that they would be targeted by the IRA.[67] This characteristically brutal response from the IRA found little support, but continued American criticism of Irish neutrality, and their demands on de Valera to expel Axis diplomats from Ireland in February 1944, guaranteed an automatic and impulsive defence of de Valera and a further wave of political condemnation, both clerical and lay, of the USA.[68]

What is particularly striking about the world of rural nationalism in Northern Ireland at this time is the obstinacy of its refusal to countenance any change to its traditional values and customs, and the depth of the indignation that greeted even signs of moderate change. This resistance to change and adaptation in Northern Ireland was not confined to nationalists, as British and American service personnel discovered when they encountered the rigidity of the stultifying and pleasure-free Presbyterian Sunday.[69] However, the nationalist sense of being a 'people apart', persecuted by unionists in the North and abandoned by their fellow nationalists in the South, elevated and exaggerated their suspicions of contact with so-called 'alien' influences which were seen as a form of cultural contamination, the consequences of which could only prove deleterious to the native 'Gaels'. This was symbolised by the rather arcane call for the Down Board of the Gaelic Athletic Association (GAA) to extend the policing activities of its Vigilance Committee (which had been set up in 1944 to ensure 'foreign' games were not played at sporting events) to social gatherings in order to ensure, in the words of one supportive correspondent to the *Frontier Sentinel*, that 'Shoneenism and West Britonism, with all their works and pomps' could be 'utterly destroyed'.[70] What was at issue here was the appearance of 'modern', and thus inappropriate, dances at GAA fund-raising functions.[71] This was no isolated flippancy but rather a viewpoint with strong clerical support. It coincided with a strong denunciation from the Bishop of Clogher, the Revd Dr Eugene O'Callaghan, of the moral evils arising from the dance halls which he regarded as 'dens of vice' leading the young to 'courses of unchecked pleasure',[72] a sentiment echoed by Bishop Mageean in a wider lament on the iniquities of change and its damaging effect on Catholic morality:

> we have skipped our moral moorings. Juvenile delinquency, indulgence in drink by young girls, the dance craze, dangerous friendships between boys and girls in their teens, the lack of parental control, dishonesty, the rush to get rich quickly, and the desire to have what is generally called a 'good time' are on the increase, and are weakening the moral fibre of the community.[73]

However, if the circumstances wrought by wartime exigencies placed strain on the Church's efforts to contain the recreational activities and sexual proclivities of Catholic youth then further strains of a political nature were to add to northern nationalist disquiet, particularly as they emanated from a wholly unwelcome source. In April 1944 Sean MacEntee, Minister for Local Government and Public Health in de Valera's government, delivered a speech ('Ireland After the War') at the Mansion House, Dublin, in the course of which he discounted any possibility of allowing northern representatives access to the Dáil. He was also sharply critical of the disunity among northern nationalists and disparaging of their confrontational tactics with unionists. MacEntee stated plainly his view that any solution to partition which did not consider the views of unionists was unworkable. In contrast to the northern nationalists' vitriolic condemnation of the Unionist administration MacEntee advocated instead 'friendship and good neighbourliness' on both sides of the border. This, he suggested, could be better achieved by leaving constitutional and political questions to one side and concentrating instead on the mutual benefits to be derived from joint co-operation in the less contentious areas of sport, agriculture, the development of natural resources and tourism.[74]

Predictably both Healy and Donnelly reacted to his speech with outrage and promptly issued a public retort in which they accused MacEntee of a shabby betrayal of the North. His reply to them, in what was a damaging public exchange widely covered in the nationalist press, clearly revealed how out of touch the northern nationalist leadership was with significant elements of the Fianna Fail government:

> Under diversified leadership the Nationalists of the Six Counties for twenty-two years have been condemned to political futility. For their own salvation they must become politically effective. To do this they must get together on a line of policy which will be coldly realistic, based on a recognition of the fundamental fact that conditions, as they exist today, are not what they might have been if the Treaty had been rejected in 1922. They must remember also that this is 1944, and that Time Marches On![75]

Revealingly, south of the border expressions of support for the tactics of the northern nationalists, and criticism of MacEntee, appear to have been confined to the more unrepresentative and marginalised quarters of southern Irish politics: the Irish Republican Army Old Comrades Association and the leadership of Córas na Poblachta,[76] a republican organisation now in the final throes of its political disintegration.[77]

MacEntee's intervention did not prevent northern nationalist political representatives issuing public expressions of support for de Valera when the latter called a snap general election in May 1944 – an election which restored Fianna Fail's parliamentary majority. Indeed, de Valera's neutrality policy continued to be widely admired as a snub to the British and support for him, from both the NCU and Healy, remained undiminished.[78] However, MacEntee's criticisms did rekindle some discussion of the desirability of a unified and coordinated Nationalist political machine in the North; it also provided the opportunity for those representatives who had long opposed the practice of abstentionism to voice their concerns that the tactic was eroding Nationalist support in Belfast at the expense of other anti-partitionist groups. One such occasion was a large gathering of national and local Nationalist representatives held in St Mary's Hall, Belfast, in June 1944. Among those present was T.J. Campbell MP – since the death of his colleague Richard Byrne the only Nationalist MP regularly attending Stormont – and two of the five Nationalist Senators who regularly attended the Northern Ireland Senate.[79] The major theme of the meeting was an appeal for unity amongst the nationalist community, but this was combined with criticism of the abstentionist tactics of the NCU. Senator T.S. McAllister[80] spoke of his regret that the nationalist electorate, who, he claimed, had 'laboured and sacrificed for the rights to the franchise', were now being denied the opportunity to exercise that franchise. What this denial resulted in, he declared, was a surrender of seats to the Unionist Party and to the NILP; a party which, he pointed out, was 'amalgamated with and controlled by the English labour organisations'[81] and thus by inference was a unionist party in all but name. His colleague, the recently elected Senator J.G. Lennon,[82] also warned of the danger of allowing 'the representation which really belonged to the Catholic people of the Six Counties to pass into hands which had no right to hold it'. These 'hands' to which Lennon referred were those of the West Belfast anti-partitionist MP Jack Beattie, who had in fact recently been expelled from the NILP.[83] For Lennon it was clearly the case that the Protestantism of men like Jack Beattie rendered them unrepresentative of the Catholic electorate: 'The name "Catholic" in the North was synonymous with "Nationalist". It typified to their opponents a man opposed to Partition and one who owed allegiance to the Holy Father.'[84] Such attacks on Beattie were unlikely to stem the tide of support for him; his creditable record as a hard-working representative on behalf of his constituents matched his anti-partitionism. However, the speakers at this event were concerned not just with current electoral loss but also with the present strategy and future direction of constitutional nationalism. And here there were certain areas of contradiction within the abstentionist nationalist camp – usually left neglected and unremarked upon – which now received attention. A Mr John Hopkins now bluntly identified them – the abstentionist MPs had, since the last general election in 1938, continued to draw their Parliamentary salaries despite their refusal to take their seats at Stormont;[85] they had also nominated nationalist members to serve in the Northern Ireland Senate in the full knowledge that such nominees had, since 1929, not only drawn their salaries but had also fulfilled their duties as Senators.[86] The discrepancy was obvious – the militancy of the abstentionist MPs incurred no hardship or financial penalty to themselves whatsoever, indeed quite the reverse. Their staunchly avowed political principles thus appeared to be unattractively elastic. Speaker after speaker urged unity, an all too familiar refrain from Nationalist platforms, but there was a nucleus of realism in the contributions from the platform that recognised the changing circumstances created by the new context of a forthcoming Allied victory in the war. This was summed up by T.J. Campbell who urged that nationalists 'must not lose the benefits they could obtain by concerted action when big opportunities arose, and they might come soon'. For Campbell the goal of any future campaign should be 'to capture and hold for Ireland every Parliamentary seat the Nationalists could win'. Furthermore, electoral competition was to be at the heart of a strategy of political involvement and activism which would broadcast Catholic grievances and aspirations in all elected assemblies including the Westminster parliament, which, it was suggested by one speaker, was 'the greatest public platform in the world'.[87]

Attendance at Westminster may not have been at the forefront of Eamon Donnelly's priorities, however, the growing frequency of the Catholic hierarchy's publicly expressed anxieties over the 'growth of state control', the implementation of Beveridge, and the dangers these developments allegedly posed to the institution of the family, did not allow for a policy of inaction. Nationalist politicians had to confront the fact that post-war reforms were to be introduced in Northern Ireland as a result of legislation passed through Westminster. Donnelly's preferred response was for a more familiar 'all-Ireland' strategy that was resolute in tone but amorphous in content. This he outlined to the Fianna Fail Ard Fheis, in Dublin, in October 1944:

> I have come with this message … The North East elected representatives … intend to get together and clear the ground for what it is worth.

And we are going to ask the principal organisations here, Fianna Fail, Fine Gael, Labour and so on, to give us two or three representatives each who, with the North East Nationalist representatives, will form a body to hammer out proposals to be submitted at the psychological moment, when the war is over, to make partition the burning question it used to be years ago before it became submerged in matters not so important.[88]

Donnelly was at this time mortally ill and in the weeks following his health deteriorated rapidly. He died aged seventy-seven in a Dublin nursing home on 29 December. His death heralded the decline of orthodox constitutional nationalism in Belfast; it also removed one of the most ardent supporters of parliamentary abstentionism from the political scene.

Donnelly's absence did not result in an abrupt nationalist Pauline conversion to parliamentary attendance, however, and in the run-up to the post-war Stormont general election of June 1945 there were early indications that nationalist representatives were caught off guard and unprepared. Certainly unionists anticipated that they would face the fractured nationalist opposition of old. In May 1945 the former Prime Minister, J.M. Andrews, with some satisfaction, summed up the situation as he saw it:

They are hopelessly divided between those who are willing to take part in the deliberations of our Ulster Parliament and those who disfranchise the constituencies which elect them by refusing to do so.[89]

Given the history of rancorous division within nationalism Andrews' assessment was entirely understandable. It was a view shared by independent commentators who also cast doubt on the abilities of T.J. Campbell to win over 'die-hard' abstentionists.[90] However, as the election campaign got under way there were signs that a combination of electoral competition for the Catholic vote, clerical pressure, and a growing awareness of general Catholic dissatisfaction with abstentionism, were together impacting on Nationalist political calculations. At a meeting of the Fermanagh Nationalist Convention in May, Cahir Healy's indubitable influence was evident in the convention's decision to abandon abstentionism; meanwhile in Derry, where Patrick Maxwell was again selected to contest the Foyle constituency, it was decided that he would not run on an explicitly abstentionist ticket; this matter being left to be resolved only after the election.[91] By early June the Nationalist election campaign was showing signs of a purposefulness that was decidedly absent in the previous general election of 1938. In that year the decision by the NCU not to contest South Down, Mourne and South Armagh had surrendered what were safe nationalist seats to their political opponents; now all three Nationalist constituency associations announced that the seats would be contested.[92] However, although unnamed but reputedly senior Nationalist political figures were quoted in the press as stating that the abstention policy was soon to 'be thrown overboard',[93] this did not represent a settling of deep-seated discontents and divisions within that diverse political entity which was subsumed, in press reports, under the title the Nationalist Party. The question of leadership and policy direction remained unresolved. An *Irish Times* correspondent covering the election revealed to his readers some of the peculiarities of the party system north of the border; in regards to leadership he pointed out appearances were deceptive and even though T.J. Campbell had been frequently quoted in the press as party leader, and indeed had figured large as a speaker on the platforms of other Nationalist candidates in the current election, 'he is not the leader' and that in fact the correspondent had discovered 'after careful enquiry that the Nationalists have no official leader of their party'.[94] He also perceptively captured the essence of disunity that underlay constitutional nationalism in Northern Ireland; 'There is something wrong with the Nationalist Party in the North,' he observed, '[o]n the surface they seem united but there is good deal of opposition in the ranks to the conduct of party policy'. Chief among the policy disagreements was the issue of abstentionism but it was believed that 'after the election the party will meet, and it is fairly certain that they will, at least, agree to a modified, if not a regular attendance at Stormont'.[95] However, party policy was not something that was determined centrally by a party executive, indeed the deconstructed nature of nationalist politics in the North meant that party policy and electoral strategy was to a large extent contingent on whom one asked to articulate it. Out in the constituencies there was a tendency for candidates to express their politics in more idiosyncratic ways that reflected localised concerns.

A case in point is Malachi Conlon who was selected as the candidate for the constituency of South Armagh. A newcomer to politics, Conlon's relative youthfulness, at the age of 33, made him something of a rarity in nationalist politics. Described in his election material as a local farmer, Conlon in fact shared the journalistic background common to many of his political colleagues having spent a number of years working on the editorial staff of the *Dundalk Examiner*. At a series of meetings throughout the constituency in early June, in the days before and after his selection for the candidacy, Conlon's election platforms hosted a variety of local speakers who defined the issues that were to dominate his campaign. Members of the clergy spoke of their concerns that the Unionist government would attempt to 'filch' the Church's rights over Catholic schools and the education of Catholic children, well-known local farmers professed confidence in Conlon as a man who had 'the interests of the farmers at heart' while other prominent local figures looked forward to ending the incongruity of South Armagh being represented by a member of the NILP (the hardworking sitting MP Paddy Agnew),[96] a party that was considered to be communistic and therefore incompatible with Catholic values.[97] Conlon himself appears to have married localised concerns with an internationalist perspective on politics that combined a potent mix of Catholic devotionalism, anti-partitionism, anti-communism, Anglophobia and anti-Semitism. This he elucidated upon at an election meeting in Crossmaglen in June when he warned his audience of the dangers they faced in the post-war world:

> Since the war a new evil, or rather an old evil in a new guise, had risen up among the nations. Europe was shattered with years of war and the Communist Jew was seeking his chance to prey on the broken nations. England itself was ready for the sowing of Communism, because she had thrown to the winds all her regard for religion and clean standards of religion. If we remained shackled to England we would not be in a position to defend ourselves against the squalid vermin of Communism, with which England was now infested. That was one of the many reasons why they should fight against Partition.[98]

Conlon's campaign against Agnew involved the political subterfuge of acknowledging his opponent's hard-earned and well-deserved reputation ('Mr Agnew is a Catholic, and I believe a decent man') while at the same time suggesting that he was a stooge being manipulated by alien and malign forces: 'Can Mr Agnew deny the affection of his Party for Moscow?'[99] While Conlon's supporters echoed such expressions of anti-communist sentiment on election platforms, Conlon's vigorous anti-Semitism, which revealed the Communist and Jewish threat to be synonymous and which received prominence in his election manifesto,[100] appears to have been, on this occasion at least, publicly stated only by the candidate himself.[101]

The zealous tone of Conlon's rhetoric added a new dimension to the election campaign in South Armagh; however, his candidature also highlighted some of the deficiencies of Nationalist organisation in the constituency: Conlon as an energetic and ambitious young man was decidedly atypical of the stalwarts of constitutional nationalist politics in Armagh. As a frustrated and irate supporter of Conlon was to point out at the time, most of the speakers who shared his campaign platforms during the election campaign were elderly men in their sixties, many of whom had been prominent in local politics for thirty years.[102] There was little sign of any organic renewal here.

Despite the decision to run candidates in all potentially winnable seats the Nationalist campaign was overall defined by an odd mixture of enthusiasm and complacency. To an extent this was determined by the absence of electoral competition in many of the constituencies that hosted Nationalist candidates. When the results were announced on 10 July, of the ten seats won by nationalist candidates (standing as Anti-Partitionists), six were returned unopposed and without electoral contest: T.J. Campbell (Belfast Central); Joseph Francis Stewart (East Tyrone); Michael McGurk (Mid Tyrone); Alex Donnelly (West Tyrone); Cahir Healy (South Fermanagh); Eddie McAteer (Mid Derry). Of the four contests that did take place, resulting in nationalist success, all were in relatively safe seats: Malachi Conlon (South Armagh); James McSparran (Mourne); Peter Murney (South Down) and Patrick Maxwell (Foyle).[103] However, there was also disappointment. In Eamon Donnelly's former seat in the Belfast Falls constituency, a seat which had lain vacant since his death, the Ant-Partitionist candidate, local publican J.M. McGlade, came in a poor third in a three-way contest with two left-nationalist candidates – John Collins representing Jack Beattie's Federation of Labour[104] and the winning candidate Harry Diamond standing as a Socialist Republican.[105] It was not the case that the Anti-Partitionist Nationalists had conducted their election campaign in the city oblivious to the social and economic concerns that were foremost in the minds of the electorate in working-class districts of Belfast. T.J. Campbell, in particular, gave prominence to the issues of poverty, health, housing and social welfare.[106] Nonetheless, Diamond's victory revealed the vulnerability of conservative nationalism in Belfast. His campaign left the working-class electorate in Falls in little doubt as to the vigour of his anti-partitionism or his objection to the continued detention of republican internees. Furthermore, his depiction of the Nationalists as a 'middle class party' was entirely accurate and his damaging accusation that they held 'no regard for the full rights of workers'[107] clearly struck home with an electorate whose material concerns were paramount[108] and who were broadly sympathetic to Diamond's enthusiasm for the incoming Labour government in Britain: a development he heartily applauded.[109]

When the election dust had settled the outcome might have appeared to belie pre-election predictions by political observers that the 'Nationalists Party' would receive a 'heavy, if not a fatal knock'.[110] In retrospect this may have seemed an unnecessarily pessimistic forecast. And yet the ability of orthodox nationalism to return more MPs in 1945 than in 1938 (ten as opposed to six)[111] must be seen in context. In one respect the 1945 general election represented a major advance; however, in effect that advance amounted to successfully retaining safe seats and recapturing 'lost' seats. The real highlight of the election, however, was the surge in support for various left-of-centre parties (especially in Belfast);[112] and, even though nationalists could delight over Unionist losses,[113] McGlade's poor showing in the Falls was telling, signalling as it did, what was to shortly become the rapid and final demise of orthodox nationalism in the city.

The writing on the wall for constitutional nationalists was mixed; they had emerged from the war period having made little political headway on their major demands and although, in the 1945 election, they had achieved electoral stability the future was one of an all too familiar uncertainty. But it was not one without a glimmer of possibility.

Notes

1 C. Norton, 'An Earnest Endeavour for Peace? Unionist Opinion and the Craig/Collins Peace Pact of 30 March 1922', *Etudes Irlandaises* 32: 1 (Spring 2007), pp. 91–108.
2 P. Buckland, *James Craig* (Dublin, Gill & Macmillan, 1980), p. 109.
3 G. Walker, *A History of the Ulster Unionist Party: Protest, Pragmatism and Pessimism* (Manchester, Manchester University Press), p. 96.
4 *Ibid.*, p. 89; see also H. Patterson and E. Kaufman, *Unionism and Orangeism in Northern Ireland since 1945: The Decline of the Loyal Family* (Manchester, Manchester University Press, 2007) p. 10.
5 On the background to this discontent see Colin Read, 'Protestant Challenges to the "Protestant State": Ulster Unionism and Independent Unionism in Northern Ireland, 1921–39', *Twentieth Century British History* 19: 4 (2008), pp. 419–445.
6 *Frontier Sentinel*, 5 April 1941.
7 B. Barton, *Northern Ireland in the Second World War* (Belfast Ulster Historical Foundation, 1995), pp. 52–53. The astute Wickham also informed London that conscription was decidedly unpopular amongst the Protestant community who were unprepared to shoulder the burden of responsibility in the face of Catholic refusal to do so. See Russell Rees, *Labour and the Northern Ireland Problem 1945–1951: The Missed Opportunity* (Dublin, Irish Academic Press, 2009), p. 26.
8 *Frontier Sentinel*, 24 May 1941.
9 *Ibid.*
10 Barton, *Northern Ireland*, p. 53; *Frontier Sentinel*, 31 May 1941.
11 Russell Rees, *Labour and the Northern Ireland Problem*, p. 25.
12 *Frontier Sentinel*, 21 June 1941.
13 Walker, *A History of the Unionist Party*, p. 91.
14 *Frontier Sentinel*, 13 December 1941.
15 *Frontier Sentinel*, 20 September 1941.
16 For a detailed account see C. Norton, 'The Internment of Cahir Healy M.P., Brixton Prison July 1941–December 1942', *Twentieth Century British History* 18: 2 (2007), pp. 170–193.
17 *Ibid.*
18 See A.W. Brian Simpson, *In the Highest Degree Odious: Detention Without Trial in Wartime Britain* (Clarendon, Oxford, 1992).
19 Maguire made these comments in March 1939. PRO, HO114/22162 249815, RUC report on Revd Fr. T. Maguire.
20 Norton, 'Cahir Healy', p. 177.
21 B. Girvin, *The Emergency: Neutral Ireland 1939–45* (London, Pan Books, 2007), p. 168; see also R. Fisk, *In Time of War: Ireland, Ulster and the Price of Neutrality 1939–45* (Dublin, Gill & Macmillan, 1983), pp. 233, 241.

22 *Irish News*, 8 August 1941, also *Irish Times*, 11 August 1941.

23 Norton, 'Cahir Healy', p. 179.

24 *Ibid.*

25 *Frontier Sentinel*, 10 January 1942.

26 *Frontier Sentinel*, 21 March 1942.

27 The non-abstentionist George McGouran, a local doctor, who had been nominated by T.J. Campbell. See M. Farrell, *Northern Ireland: The Orange State* (London, Pluto Press, 1978), p. 170.

28 R. English, *Armed Struggle: A History of the IRA* (London, Macmillan, 2003), p. 68.

29 The number of IRA internees in Northern Ireland reached 500 by October 1942. *Irish Times*, 5 December 1942.

30 Previous elections in the Stormont Falls constituency had seen close contests between Richard Byrne and NILP candidates, on this occasion the NILP candidate was relegated to third place. See S. Elliott, *Northern Ireland Parliamentary Election Results 1921–72* (Chichester, Political Reference Publications, 1978), p. 42.

31 *Irish News*, 7 November 1942.

32 *Frontier Sentinel*, 12 December 1942.

33 *Ibid.*

34 Senia Paseta, 'Northern Ireland and the Second World War', in *Northern Ireland: A Divided Community, 1921–1972* (Gale Digital Collection), www.gale.com/DigitalCollections.

35 R. Dunphy, *The Making of Fianna Fail Power in Ireland 1923–1948*, p. 223.

36 Girvin, *The Emergency*, p. 228.

37 There was a strong tradition of support for left-wing, anti-partition candidates in West Belfast. Ironically, one such former incumbent – William McMullan, a Protestant anti-partitionist member of the NILP who held the seat between 1925–29 – speaking at an Irish Labour Party event in Dublin in 1938, and addressing the issue of material welfare, was highly critical of those Catholics in the North 'who were opposed to coming in with the South, because they benefited from the better social services available under the "step by step" policy in the Six Counties', *Irish Times*, 5 December 1938.

38 E. Staunton, *The Nationalists of Northern Ireland 1918–1973* (Dublin, Columba Press, 2001), p. 153.

39 H. Patterson, *Ireland Since 1939: The Persistence of Conflict* (Dublin, Penguin Ireland, 2006), p. 35.

40 Ultach, 'The Persecution of Catholics in Northern Ireland', *Capuchin Annual* (1943); M. Elliott, *The Catholics of Ulster: A History* (London, Allen Lane, 2000), p. 394; P. Bew, *Ireland: The Politics of Emnity 1789–2006* (Oxford, Oxford University Press, 2007), p. 462.

41 Ultach, 'The Persecution of Catholics in Northern Ireland', p. 37.

42 Dennis Ireland (1894–1974) was a Northern Ireland-born freelance writer, journalist and broadcaster. He saw military service with the British army in World War I, being invalided out of the forces with the rank of Captain. Thereafter he worked for his family's linen firm until the 1930s at which time he devoted himself to a career as a writer. He was a member of the Irish Senate 1949–51.

43 *Frontier Sentinel*, 22 February 1941.

44 *Frontier Sentinel*, 8 March 1941.

45 *Belfast Newsletter*, 19 March 1942; *Frontier Sentinel*, 21 March 1942; see also John Gray (ed.), *Thomas Carnduff: Life and Writings* (Belfast, 1994), p. 46. At this time UUC member John Graham was the IRA's Northern intelligence officer, director of publicity and editor of the *Republican News*, see Farrell, *Orange State*, p. 164.

46 *Irish Times*, 20 March 1943 On this occasion Ireland shared the platform with the Northern-born Protestant nationalist politician Ernest Blythe.

47 *Frontier Sentinel*, 3 April 1943.

48 *Ibid.*

49 *Ibid.*

50 MacRory at this time professed his hope that the provisions of the Atlantic Charter, the set of principles intended to create the foundations for a lasting peace which were drawn up by Churchill and Roosevelt in August 1941, would 'be certain to bring partition in Ireland to a speedy end'. However, he simultaneously held out the hope that in the event of the victory of the Axis powers 'they would see the folly and absurdity of dividing or partitioning a small island like ours, made one by God'. *Frontier Sentinel*, 10 April 1943.

51 *Frontier Sentinel*, 3 April 1943.

52 *Ibid.*

53 *Ibid.*

54 The election saw a drop in support for Fianna Fail of 10 per cent, a loss of ten seats and the loss of its majority in the Dail. Patterson, *Ireland*, pp. 68–70.

55 *Frontier Sentinel*, 22 May 1943.

56 On the theological reasoning behind the Church's concerns see Daithí Ó Corráin, *Rendering to God and Caesar: The Irish Churches and the Two States in Ireland, 1949–73* (Manchester University Press, Manchester, 2006), p. 118.

57 *Frontier Sentinel*, 29 January 1944.

58 *Frontier Sentinel*, 15 February 1945.

59 See for example Joseph Connellan's leaders 'The Servile State', *Frontier Sentinel*, 7 October 1944 and 'Immorality Rampant', *Frontier Sentinel*, 25 November 1944.

60 T. Bartlett and K. Jeffrey, *A Military History of Ireland* (Cambridge, Cambridge University Press, 1996), p. 440.

61 House of Commons (Northern Ireland) Debates, Volume 27 (1944, 45), pp. 89–90.

62 House of Commons (Northern Ireland) Debates, Volume 27 (1944, 45), pp. 27–28.

63 Oliver Rafferty has pointed out that Bishop Farren, who played a key role in attending to the spiritual welfare of American service personnel stationed in Northern Ireland, had close links with the American government. In 1947 he was awarded the US Medal of Freedom in recognition of his pastoral duties to American troops. Oliver P. Rafferty, *Catholicism in Ulster 1603–1983* (Dublin, Gill & Macmillan, 1994), p. 243.

64 *Frontier Sentinel*, 12 February 1944.

65 Bartlett and Jeffrey, *A Military History of Ireland*, p. 441.

66 *Irish News*, 28 January 1942.

67 *Irish News*, 24 April 1943.

68 In response to the demands from David Gray, the United States Minister to Ireland, Cardinal MacRory retorted 'The fact is, Eire deserves credit in the circumstances for not having allied herself with the Axis nations and offered them hospitality and assistance.' *Frontier Sentinel*, 26 February 1944.

69 When Belfast City Council refused to allow cinemas to open on a Sunday the army took the step of commandeering a cinema and running it themselves. See Bartlett and Jeffrey, *A Military History of Ireland*, p. 441.

70 *Frontier Sentinel*, 12 February 1944.

71 A response to this implacable conservatism came from an anonymous correspondent (Modern and Liking it) who, complaining of the 'out of date' céilidh formats of the dances in Newry Town Hall, wrote 'We the youth of today cannot possibly be expected to always live in the past.' *Frontier Sentinel*, 19 August 1944.

72 *Frontier Sentinel*, 26 February 1944.

73 *Frontier Sentinel*, 17 February 1945.

74 *Frontier Sentinel*, 22 April 1944.

75 *Ibid.*

76 See PRONI, D2991/B/23/5, Letter To Cahir Healy from Owen McCarthy, Hon Secretary, Irish Republican Army, Old Comrades Association, 25 April 1944; PRONI, D2991/B/23/2, Letter to Cahir Healy from the Central Committee of Córas na Poblachta, 29 April 1944.

77 The decline of Córas na Poblachta followed its unsuccessful attempt to contest the Irish general election in 1943. Its election programme on this occasion strongly emphasised its plan to end partition, the chief points of this plan were expounded upon at its final election rally in Dublin in June 1943: '1) That Northern representatives be admitted to the Dáil; 2) that steps be taken to make all government departments partition-conscious; 3) that Radio Eireann be used daily in an anti-partition campaign, and thus break the stations silence on the matter; 4) that the young people in our schools be made partition conscious and, in particular, be made aware that our people in the North were committed to England's war because we had deserted them; 5) that money be set aside to support a virile campaign in the six counties to deal with the question of partition; 6) that our Army and Civil Service should be open to our people in the North', *Irish Times*, 21 June 1943. On the demise of Córas na Poblachta see also R.M. Douglas, 'The Pro-Axis Underground in Ireland, 1939–1943', *The Historical Journal* 49: 4 (2006), p. 175.

78 Staunton, *Nationalists*, pp. 55–56.

79 Senators McAllister (Ballymena) and Lennon (Armagh) were in attendance at the meeting. Of the other Nationalist Senators, Senator John McHugh, was a long-time opponent of abstention and his absence may be accounted for by ill health, he died the following year. The other two Nationalist Senators at this time were the Belfast-based Thaddeus Lynch and Joseph Maguire. The latter was Deputy Speaker in the Senate 1939–42.

80 Thomas Stanislaus McAllister was at this time Deputy Speaker in the Senate, a post he had previously held 1930–32. McAllister had formerly been MP for Antrim in the Northern Ireland parliament (1925–29).

81 *Frontier Sentinel*, 24 June 1944.

82 A solicitor by occupation, Lennon was elected to the Senate in 1944 possibly as a replacement for Senator Thomas McLaughlin who died in April 1944.
83 Ironically his expulsion resulted from his refusal to move the writ for a Senate by-election on the death of McLaughlin, an action apparently accounted for by his concern not to antagonise the Nationalist members. See Farrell, *Orange State*, p. 172.
84 *Frontier Sentinel*, 24 June 1944.
85 *Ibid.*
86 *Ibid.*
87 *Ibid.* This contribution came from Alderman T. Agnew.
88 *Frontier Sentinel*, 14 October 1944.
89 *Irish Times*, 30 May 1945.
90 *Irish Times*, 31 May 1945.
91 *Ibid.*
92 *Frontier Sentinel*, 9 June 1945.
93 *Irish Times*, 11 June 1945.
94 *Irish Times*, 12 June 1945.
95 *Ibid.*
96 On Paddy Agnew see A. Edwards, *A History of the Northern Ireland Labour Party: Democratic Socialism and Sectarianism* (Manchester, Manchester University Press, 2009), p. 20.
97 *Frontier Sentinel*, 9 June 1945. 'No matter what a man's private opinion might be, he was discredited by the people of South Armagh if he had any connection with the Labour Party.'
98 *Ibid.*
99 See Conlon's election manifesto, *Frontier Sentinel*, 9 June 1945.
100 'There are two flags in the sand – the Hammer and Sickle of the Communist Jew – and the flag of our own land. Which flag do you support?' *Ibid.*
101 However Enda Staunton points out that others in the Conlon camp did vilify Agnew as a 'communist atheistic Jew'. See Staunton, *The Nationalists*, p. 160. Anti-Semitic currents persisted in Ireland in the post-war period despite knowledge of the Holocaust. In 1953 a series of lectures in Newry Cathedral, delivered by members of the Redemptorist Order on the theme 'Enemies of the Church', included a lecture by Revd H. Kerr on 'The Jews'. Father Kerr regarded all Jews as being part of a diabolical international conspiracy and had little time for recent reports of Jewish persecution in the Soviet Union and Eastern Europe, 'Do not be misled by such reports. Whatever may be the cause of all this, you can rest assured that Judaism is still deeply rooted in Communism.' But, Father Kerr's anti-Semitism went beyond 'Jewish and Atheistic Communism': 'Wall Street was controlled by the Jews, as was the BBC and several other British institutions and even in Ireland – even in the City of Dublin – their power was growing and growing in many directions, especially in property market, where they were even buying up the ground-rents of Convents.' See *Frontier Sentinel*, 31 January 1953. On anti-Semitism in Ireland at this time see also E. Delaney, 'Political Catholicism in Post-War Ireland: The Revd Denis Fahey and Maria Duce, 1945–54', *Journal of Ecclesiastical History* 52: 3 (July 2001), pp. 487–511.
102 *Frontier Sentinel*, 23 June 1945.

103 Maxwell had been returned to this seat unopposed in 1938.
104 The Federation set up by Beattie following his resignation from the NILP. He had initially declared that he would not be 'the medium through which any new party would be formed' and later defended the establishment of the Federation on the grounds that a federation was not a party. The organisation was made up of ex-members of the West Belfast Labour Party who followed Beattie out of the NILP. Beattie described the social programme of the Federation as being '100 per cent the social policy of the Labour Party'. *Irish Times*, 2 February 1945. Somewhat ironically in the 1945 election Beattie held on to his Stormont seat in Pottinger standing as an 'Independent Labour' candidate. See G. Walker, *The Politics of Frustration: Harry Midgley and the Failure of Labour in Northern Ireland* (Manchester, Manchester University Press), p. 168.
105 Diamond had previously unsuccessfully contested the seat as an abstentionist Republican in the 1930's. Abstentionism he now considered to be a policy 'rejected by the people'. See PRONI, D2991//3/6, *Northern Star* 1: 4 (August 1945).
106 Brendan Lynn, *Holding the Ground: The Nationalist Party in Northern Ireland, 1945–72* (Aldershot, Ashgate, 1997), p. 16.
107 *Irish News*, 9 June 1945 cited in Lynn, *Holding the Ground*, p. 17.
108 A fact noted with some perspicacity by a Belfast based Catholic priest 'of some standing' who had earlier, in an *Irish Times* article, emphasised the importance of material issues over national aspirations: ' … at present there are many Catholics in the North who are by no means anxious to be included in Eire in its present economic condition', *Irish Times*, 12 June 1945.
109 See 'Churchill Out!', *Northern Star* 1: 4 (August 1945).
110 *Irish Times*, 2 February 1945.
111 There was in fact an additional nationalist candidate returned to Stormont. Dr Frederick McSorely, standing as an Independent, took one of the Queen's University seats.
112 Parties of the left won 32 per cent of the total vote. In Belfast the combined vote of the NILP, Harry Midgley's Commonwealth Labour Party and the Communist Party came to an impressive 40 per cent as compared to 50 per cent for the Unionist Party. See Patterson, *Ireland*, p. 49; Walker, *Harry Midgley*, p. 168.
113 'Shocks for Tories', *Frontier Sentinel*, 21 July 1945.

4

The Irish Anti-Partition League: possibilities and pitfalls, 1945–49

The question in 1945 was to what degree could the elected nationalist representatives take advantage of the altered political landscape resulting from the return of a Labour government at Westminster to raise, what one observer of the election had termed, the 'burning sense of grievance' their constituents felt in regard to the issues of discrimination in employment and housing, franchise gerrymandering and internment?[1] As Russell Rees has argued, there were distinct prospects here. The Labour Party was traditionally regarded as sympathetic to the united Ireland aspiration of Irish nationalism, and the return of Attlee's administration with a landslide majority – a cause of consternation among members of the Unionist cabinet – proved to be a major impetus in the decision of the elected Nationalist MPs to take their seats at Stormont.[2] Furthermore, a number of Labour Party backbenchers (some thirty in all), who shared a common concern over Catholic disadvantage in Northern Ireland, banded together to form a ginger group, the Friends of Ireland (FOI), to ensure 'that the province's affairs were kept before the House of Commons'.[3] In the run-up to the Westminster election (in July) the decision by the Tyrone and Fermanagh Nationalist Convention – which reselected the sitting abstentionist MPs Anthony Mulvey and Patrick Cunningham as candidates – to postpone any decision on abstention until after the election appeared to signal recognition of the potential of a new political dawn.[4]

Within weeks of Mulvey and Cunningham's successful re-election a reconvened convention voted overwhelmingly (by 113 votes to 23) to abandon abstentionism[5] and shortly afterwards both men travelled to London to take their seats at Westminster. In a joint press statement they explained that their decision was taken 'at the request of the people of our constituency' and in anticipation of the 'more enlightened and progressive methods' of the Labour government.[6] However, they also made it abundantly clear that their primary demand, in fact the only demand mentioned in the statement, was 'the abolition of Partition and the right of our nation to be controlled by a democratically-elected government for the entire thirty-two counties'.[7] This was a statement that was suggestive more of self-imposed constraints rather than the enlightenment and progressivism of the Labour government, which was so welcomed. Nonetheless, there was undoubtedly a frisson of expectation that the new post-war political order heralded a significant opportunity for change. But how was constitutional nationalism to transform itself into a united political force that could win the confidence of Ulster Protestants and demonstrate a mature and realisable strategy to both Dublin and London? It is clear that some did devote attention to these issues.

In an open public letter the ubiquitous Father Maguire, anticipating a forthcoming convention to establish a new anti-partition organisation in the North, spoke of the need to develop not only what he referred to as an 'external policy' (i.e. 'ending the evils of Partition') but also an 'internal policy' which would address important economic and social issues that were of concern to both communities within the 'Six Counties'. The scope of his suggested internal policy was broad:

> Our internal policy must determine our attitude to many questions – (1) Nationalisation of rail and road transport, shipbuilding, monopolies and key industries; (2) education – the language; (3) division of landed estates so that the standard of agricultural output may be stabilised and greater extension of peasant proprietorship; (4) long-term loans for farmers; (5) housing, not alone for industrial workers, but for farmers and farm labourers, with a purchase scheme for the latter; (6) drainage; (7) sanitation, sewerage and water schemes for all towns and villages; (8) workers' security insurance; (9) land reclamation – forestry; (10) development of our bogs and roads thereto; (11) departmental amalgamation and all-round reduction of ministerial salaries; (12) segregation of real revenue from the British financial doles, so that we may test whether these Six Counties to be an economic unit or not.[8]

Maguire felt that pursuance of the internal policy should take precedence over the external policy: 'We must work our internal policy as if we had no external policy to bother us, and in the hope that our constructive talents may one day early our [sic] being handed the reins of authority by the electorate of these Six Counties.' Only once this goal had been reached would the partition issue be settled (and here he had no hard and fast prescription, holding out the possibility of either a federal arrangement or a unitary state) with any settlement being predicated on 'ample safeguards for the Protestant minority'.[9] There was undoubtedly an element of wishful thinking creeping in here, but there were also echoes of a Devlinite social reformism which offered more than one-dimensional anti-partitionism. However, some short time later Maguire's views appear to have been modified by his reading of a recently published pamphlet by Cahir Healy (*The Mutilation of a Nation*)[10] which detailed a litany of wrongs perpetrated against Catholics by the Unionist government. Maguire's now frequent references to Healy's cataloguing of numerous examples of discrimination and injustices visited upon northern Catholics since 1920 seems to have rekindled in him a compassionate identification with the Catholic community's collective sense of historical injustice, political and economic subservience and social humiliation (what Marianne Elliott has called its 'highly sensitised victim psychology')[11] and to have awakened a strong sense of moral indignation. As a result Maguire returned to a more familiar Manichaean outlook. His earlier suggestion that nationalists should concentrate their attentions on internal policies and upon winning support across the sectarian divide was now discarded in favour of a simple demand for the British government to disengage: 'Can anyone be so mentally befogged as to think that the Orangemen – or their kith and kin – could ever be converted to cooperate with the pro-Irish and to drive the English out? There is only one way to solve the problem – insist on England clearing out.' Reconciliation between unionists and nationalists was now less compelling and consigned to some undetermined future: 'Let time and circumstances assuage our differences when England goes.'[12]

The Anti-Partition Convention, alluded to by Father Maguire in his open letter, met in Dungannon on 14 November to launch the Irish Anti-Partition League (IAPL). Reportage of the convention – presided over by James McSparran MP and attended by all the recently elected Northern Ireland Nationalist MPs, Senators, Westminster MPs and upwards of 480 delegates – was constrained by the organisers' attempted imposition of a strict censorship on journalists, which resulted in a press walk-out.[13] However, while the deliberations of the convention remained unavailable the official communiqué, detailing the resolutions passed, suggested little evidence of any consideration of Maguire's earlier innovative ideas relating to a broad range of 'internal policies'. The main resolution was a demand for 'the re-unification and freedom of our country' while supplementary resolutions dealing with 'internal' issues were limited to a protest against gerrymandering in local government electoral districts and a demand for 'the unconditional release of ... political prisoners and internees in the gaols of the Six Counties'.[14] As to its composition this new organisation fell short of its proclaimed intention to 'consolidate all anti-partition forces in the Six Counties';[15] it was effectively representative of conservative, middle-class rural nationalism. Harry Diamond, the Socialist Republican MP for Belfast Falls, refused to attend the convention on the grounds that the new organisation 'was being founded on a sectarian basis'. The left-nationalist Westminster MP for West Belfast, Jack Beattie, also failed to attend the convention claiming that he was detained in London on parliamentary business, while it was reported that Capt. Denis Ireland had sent apologies for his non-attendance.[16] Even within the conservative nationalist bloc there were signs of unease as to the outcome of the new political formation and the nationalist post-election policy of parliamentary attendance. In November the *Derry Journal* singled out Cahir Healy for attack when it misrepresented a speech he delivered in Stormont in which he offered to back the Unionist government 'all the way'[17] if they withheld Northern Ireland's Imperial Contribution (some £34 million) from Westminster. Healy's comments, taken out of context by the paper, appeared to suggest that he was prepared to offer general support to the government. His response – a vigorous defence of the attendance policy – was strongly supported by many of his parliamentary colleagues who regarded the episode as 'a deliberate effort … to wreck the Irish Anti-Partition League'.[18] There was also an early hiccup when T.J. Campbell, the IAPL's only remaining elected representative in Belfast, announced his acceptance of a county court judgeship in December; a decision which necessitated forfeiting his parliamentary seat and severing his links with the IAPL. This level of engagement with the institutions of the State went far beyond that considered desirable by his IAPL colleagues. However, although party collegiality was markedly absent on this occasion, criticism of Campbell was nonetheless muted; for, as a clerical correspondent with Cahir Healy observed, had Campbell refused to accept his elevation into the judiciary, when 'the denial of distributive justice is one of our grievances', the result would have been a propaganda coup for the Unionist government.[19] The need to prevent Campbell's example setting a precedent that others may follow was addressed by Eddie McAteer MP who spoke of 'purging our ranks of defections for high places', but the absence of an unqualified condemnation of Campbell led Peter Murney to publicly disassociate himself from the Parliamentary Party at Stormont (although he retained his membership of the IAPL).[20]

The lack of an established culture of nationalist party political structures, discipline and loyalties was evident in the complex interplay of relationships that now emerged in the IAPL. In the absence of a pre-existing programme of opposition newly attending IAPL MPs at Stormont adopted a strategy designed to unify members in a common purpose and appeal to a broad spectrum of nationalist opinion. And, it was the emotive issue of the release of internees and prosecuted IRA activists that provided the lowest common denominator for such a strategy and which figured prominently in early parliamentary exchanges, much to the ire of the Unionist benches.[21]

Meanwhile, Anthony Mulvey's attendance in the Westminster parliament,[22] where he was taking his seat for the first time since 1935, elevated his status significantly – he even became the recipient of offers from both Healy and Father Maguire to use their influence to secure a civil service position (as a superintendent for exams) for his daughter in the South.[23] But it was the relationship between the IAPL and the Friends of Ireland group, a relationship that held out the prospect of British Labour parliamentarians raising Catholic grievances in the British parliament, which was of consequence; and here there were fundamental strategic and ideological differences between the IAPL and the Friends. The driving force behind the Friends, Hugh Delargy, MP for Manchester Platting, had made known to Mulvey his disagreement with Healy's presentation of the problem in Northern Ireland (in his publication, *The Mutilation of a Nation*) as one of rampant anti-Catholic persecution ('I do not like his pamphlet'). Delargy thought the archaic confessional nature of Healy's 'Catholic persecution angle … peculiar to handle in England' and suggested instead that a more profitable approach would be to portray the political impasse in Northern Ireland as resulting from the Unionist government's 'persecution of a minority', which would also encompass 'Labour and progressive organisations'.[24] This attempt to present the political/religious divide as a conflict between a broadly left of centre opposition and a conservative reactionary government received a mixed reception from the North's anti-partitionists. The Friends were predominantly on the left of the Labour Party and thus held a political outlook that was an anathema to many socially and politically conservative nationalists, some of whom were unable to restrain themselves from publicly expressing their misgivings; Capt. Denis Ireland, for example, warned the readers of the nationalist daily paper the *Irish News* of his fears that the FOI 'are friends of Ireland only in order that the Irish may be turned into good little Socialists like themselves'.[25] Nor did the candidature of the British Labour Party member and close associate of the FOI, Desmond Donnelly, for the Westminster parliamentary by-election in South Down in June 1946 do much to enhance relations between the IAPL and the Friends. Donnelly, standing under the banner of the Northern Ireland Labour Party (NILP), was contesting a constituency whose previous incumbent had been the Independent Unionist, Revd James Little,[26] a clergyman of outspoken populist views. The IAPL had not contested the constituency in the July 1945 election[27] and, no doubt presuming that the result of the by-election would be a foregone conclusion, again chose not to put forward a candidate. In fact, although an Ulster Unionist was returned, Donnelly came in a credible second place capturing just over 29 per cent of the vote and beating two Independent Unionist candidates.[28] That the FOI had supported Donnelly [29] and endorsed the NILP was reason enough, in the parochial and bitterly divided politics of Northern Ireland, to reinforce IAPL suspicion and distrust. In correspondence to Cahir Healy in October Father Maguire warned: 'these "Friends" have no plan or policy [and] … they are only playing their own game. We should upset that.'[30]

But, while suspicious and distrustful of outside (i.e. British) influences, Father Maguire was acutely aware that the absence of unity and cooperation amongst anti-partitionists in Ireland could result in the IAPL slipping back into the ineffectual posturing of its political predecessors. In calling for the establishment of a Joint Advisory Council representative of all anti-partition positions, he appeared to take seriously the need for a coordinated campaign incorporating those outside the ranks of the IAPL. However, Father Maguire was somewhat of a mercurial figure and his suggestion that Capt. Dennis Ireland should be nominated for T.J. Campbell's vacant seat in Belfast and that he should be declared parliamentary leader of all anti-partition parties[31] may be considered typical of his idiosyncratic interventions. But, nonetheless, his concerns about the IAPL's lack of leadership and organisation were prescient, and in a letter to Mulvey, in September 1946, these were expressed dramatically but with some accuracy,

> Oh for a Parnell or a Davitt!!! … 'Cunningham & Mulvey' must be a voice crying in the wilderness unless you and the fellows who have assumed leadership get down to political brass tacks. It is not being done. You are nothing at Westminster without a vigorous party at home. You have not this – N or S. I think you have got to get a grip of the wide scale our appeal should take.[32]

Others chose not to address these misgivings, preferring instead to adopt a more familiar stance that promised much but offered little beyond sloganeering. Speaking in Manchester in April 1946, Capt. Ireland announced that the 'fight against Partition' was entering 'its last phase' (though he did offer the caveat 'How long that last phase will last is not for me to say')[33] while at an IAPL meeting in Newry, in the same month, Eddie McAteer MP told his audience that they 'must now prepare themselves to take over power in the Six Counties'.[34]

At a more mundane level there were signs that the IAPL's involvement in the prisoner amnesty campaign, the confrontational political agenda of which was effectively being set by republicans, was replicating inconsistencies evident in the earlier Green Cross campaign. This was revealed in the case of David Fleming, a 32-year-old IRA man from Kerry imprisoned in Crumlin Road gaol in Belfast,[35] who embarked on a hunger strike in March 1946 and who rapidly became the focus of the amnesty campaign in the North. In his support rallies were held, petitions to the British and Northern Ireland governments demanding his release were delivered, and condemnations of the Unionist government (as 'fascist') were made – as were accusations that the conditions in Crumlin Road were 'no better than Belsen',[36] the Nazi concentration camp. However, at the exact same time that Fleming was on hunger strike in Crumlin Road, an IRA member from Belfast, Sam McCaughey, was also on a hunger and thirst strike in Portlaoise Prison, Dublin. In Dublin a public protest meeting in support of McCaughey, held in College Green in May, was roughly dispersed by a police baton charge, while a petition calling for his release was bluntly refused by de Valera who declared his decision in the matter to be 'irrevocable'. Fleming's plight received much sympathetic comment from IAPL and other anti-partitionist politicians – including dire warnings from Eddie McAteer that 'Belsen was followed by Nuremberg ... there would be no exception in the case of Stormont.'[37] In contrast McCaughey's hunger strike was reported in the nationalist press with the minimum of detail and a marked absence of statements condemning de Valera's inflexibility. When, during a Stormont parliamentary debate on 21 May, Edmund Warnock, the Minister of Home Affairs, pointed to this discrepancy[38] Cahir Healy replied that the two cases were entirely different. McCaughey, he pointed out, was hunger striking for unconditional release whereas Fleming's protest was for 'better conditions'.[39] This was somewhat disingenuous on Healy's behalf as IAPL representatives, along with other anti-partitionists, were indeed calling for Fleming's 'immediate release' as part of 'an amnesty for all political prisoners' and had forcibly made this point at a mass demonstration in Belfast on 27 April.[40] The outcome of the two cases could not have been more different; McCaughey was to die in Portlaoise Prison on 11 May[41] while Fleming was later released from prison on humanitarian grounds.[42]

The prioritising of the amnesty campaign and the stridency of statements in relation to IRA convicted prisoners (the last of the internees having been released in December 1945)[43] left little space for the IAPL to develop an oppositional programme at Stormont that could constructively work in tandem with Mulvey's more visible Westminster profile and his efforts to galvanise the support of Labour backbenchers eager to address issues of Catholic disadvantage in Northern Ireland. This was a serious failing for in fact this juncture held out at least the prospect of some quite interesting developments. As Henry Patterson has pointed out, the Unionist government at this time was increasingly dependent on British financial support to fund post-1945 welfarism; a dependency which convinced the Unionist Prime Minister, Basil Brooke, of the necessity of presenting to the British government 'a more emollient public face from Ulster Unionism'.[44] This public face entailed a more accommodating approach to Catholics, an approach for which Brooke had the support of liberals within his party. If this was a moment upon which the IAPL could capitalise to improve the situation of Catholics in Northern Ireland there is little evidence that its stridently confrontational tactics at Stormont did anything to bring that closer. It is of little surprise that IAPL tactics in the Stormont parliament found favour amongst republicans; however, even they could point to the essential incoherence of a strategy that appeared to reject Stormont but accept Westminster; an incongruity stressed by a young Derry solicitor's assistant and republican sympathiser, Ciaran McAnally, in correspondence with Cahir Healy,

> you yourself speak with one voice at Westminster and with another to the Anti-Partition League audiences. I saw a Derry Journal report recently where you stated that efficient or inefficient, you wanted *no* Stormont Administration. But why was that attitude not adopted towards a Westminster audience? I can only conclude that an artificial enthusiasm is being fomented in the Six Counties which will pass off as did other Anti-Partition Leagues in the past.[45]

The absence of a more nuanced and pragmatic IAPL approach to parliamentary politics also meant adopting a uniformly negative stance on all policies enacted by the Unionist government. This meant that post-war social, educational and welfare provision introduced by Stormont, for example, was invariably traduced as worthless to the Catholic population even when there was evidence to the contrary. This could have unforeseen and embarrassing consequences, as in January 1948 when the southern-based President of the Irish National Teachers Organisation, Sean Brosnan, while addressing a teachers' conference in Belfast, lavished praise on the Stormont government for the benefits (citing higher teachers' salaries and lower class sizes) that had followed from the introduction of the 1947 Education Act. Brosnan congratulated the Unionist administration for leading the country 'in the whole field of education' and suggested that the '6-County people should count their blessings under the Act'. He also made the point that teachers in the South had little prospect of achieving the benefits enjoyed by their northern colleagues. In response the *Ulster Herald* (edited by Anthony Mulvey), lamenting the 'running down and belittling' of the southern State, described Brosnan's comments as 'most unfortunate and unseemly'.[46]

The introduction at Westminster of the Northern Ireland Bill in March 1947 marked what Bob Purdie has called the 'high point' of the relationship between the IAPL and the FOI. The Bill extended the legislative power of the Northern Ireland parliament (restricted by the Ireland Act, 1920) enabling it to enact welfare provisions that were being introduced in the rest of Britain. It also contained clauses pertaining to law and order issues and thus its introduction in the House of Commons became the occasion for the Friends (and in particular one of its leading members Geoffrey Bing) to raise the peculiarities and iniquities that existed in Northern Ireland.[47] However, while the relationship between Mulvey and the Friends may have developed at this time, in contrast the relationship between the IAPL and the Attlee administration deteriorated. There were clear signs of this when in March, addressing the Cardiff branch of the IAPL, Mulvey intimated his growing distrust of the Labour government, which he accused of attempting 'to extend the power of the "Tory Junta" at Belfast'.[48]

As expectations of the Attlee government faded, developments in southern politics were to become more central to IAPL calculations. A general election in February 1948, fought against a backdrop of economic stagnancy, high emigration, and a general weariness with de Valera's government,[49] saw Fianna Fáil ejected from office and replaced by a coalition government that included Fine Gael and Clann na Poblachta. The latter, a left-of-centre party set up by Sean MacBride (a former IRA Chief of Staff in the 1930s) in 1946 and bringing together liberals and republican discontents, had, during the election campaign, emphasised partition and attacked Fianna Fáil over its failure to resolve it. MacBride's own answer to the problem was revealed on the election canvass to be a twin policy of improving welfare provision in the South to match that in the North (which, considering the disparity in welfare provision on both sides of the border, was a proposal nebulous in the extreme),[50] and the proposed granting of a 'right of audience' in the Dáil to anti-partitionist representatives elected in Northern Ireland.[51] However, such was the degree of scepticism held about southern politicians by the more experienced nationalist representatives in the North that MacBride's policies elicited little initial enthusiasm. In an exchange of letters between MacBride and Healy before the election, the tone of which was decidedly formal and cool, Healy was cautious and non-committal when pressed by MacBride for a response to his 'right of audience' proposal: 'Your proposal … is, I think, an idea that the late Eamon Donnelly MP pushed for a time without success with F.F.. We have not discussed the matter of late, but will give it consideration as soon as we are invited.'[52] With Mulvey still active in Westminster the *Ulster Herald* was downright dismissive of the proposal, criticising it as 'altogether unworkable and unacceptable'.[53]

Scepticism, however, was soon to be abandoned in the heady atmosphere that accompanied political change in the South. With de Valera out of office, rhetorical anti-partitionism was reignited as a staple ingredient of inter-party competition. De Valera now spoke in terms of the people of the North being 'coerced' and of the urgency for partition to be addressed: 'The cry that should go out on every lip was: "Partition must go".'[54] More dramatically, on a tour of Canada in September 1948, the coalition Prime Minister, John A. Costello, announced that Ireland would sever its links with the Commonwealth and declare a Republic. The effects of this on nationalist opinion in the North were soon in evidence. The *Derry Journal*, while expressing surprise that a Fine Gael Taoiseach had snapped 'the last thread of connection in any shape or form with the British Crown', felt that the way was now clear for all political parties in the South to concentrate on 'the one remaining question of Partition'.[55] This heightening of expectations, and inevitably of political passions, was to have a profound impact on one area of Northern Ireland's politics that had long struggled to remain above sectarian and ethnic division: labour and socialist politics.

In September 1948 the NILP split and its anti-partitionist element, under the leadership of a senior party figure Jack Macgougan, combined with Harry Diamond's small Socialist Republican Party in declaring their joint aim of integrating with the southern-based IrLP. The NILP, a cross-confessional party which had been in existence since the inception of the Northern Ireland state, had traditionally adopted a pluralist position on the constitutional question: party members united in pursuit of social justice but were free to argue the merits/demerits of the Union or Irish Unity.[56] By 1945, however, support for the Allied war effort, coupled with the desire that Northern Ireland should share in the benefits anticipated from the British Labour Party's post-war social and economic reforms, brought about a redefinition of the NILP's stance on the constitutional question. The NILP's manifesto for the Stormont general election of 1945 now stated that as a democratic party it would not seek a change in the constitutional status of Northern Ireland 'except by the expressed will of the majority of the people';[57] a commitment which undoubtedly made a significant contribution to the substantial increase in electoral support for the non-nationalist Left in that election.[58] There were those within the NILP who felt its 'broad church' approach had tilted too far towards a pro-Union position, but in fact the most pro-Union elements had left the party in 1942 (to form the Commonwealth Labour Party)[59] and in 1945 Jack Macgougan, the most articulate and dynamic anti-partitionist in the NILP,[60] was elected Party Chairman. From 1946 Macgougan was to enjoy close contacts with leading members of the FOI, his introduction to the FOI coming via his friendship with Desmond Donnelly, a friendship which dated from the time of the South Down by-election in 1946 when Macgougan acted as Donnelly's director of elections. This connection to the FOI promised much. In May 1947 Donnelly had written to Macgougan with an offer – from himself and Geoffrey Bing MP – to prepare a draft manifesto for a united Labour movement in Ireland. Donnelly and Bing suggested that such a manifesto should contain 'immediate objectives' for both the NILP and the IrLP 'in their separate spheres' and a 'collective policy' between the two parties 'aimed at ultimately abolishing partition'. These strategic objectives were to be based on a detailed investigation into Northern Ireland's economic relationship with Britain (to ascertain whether this was a relationship of dependency) and a review of the economic resources available in both Northern and Southern Ireland.[61] Macgougan, however, rejected the offer. He felt that as there was little prospect of Labour government's being elected on either side of the border anytime in the immediate future the Donnelly-Bing proposal was but a distraction from the fundamental goal of ending partition.[62] Macgougan was convinced that the only way to advance towards the secular socialist politics he espoused was through an imposed solution on Northern Ireland, i.e. unilateral action by the British parliament to bring an end to partition. This prescription was essentially based on an idealised notion of the progressive potential that inclusion in southern politics would bring – as compared to what he felt was the backward sectarian politics inherent in the North.[63] However, his visceral belief that territorial unification would create the conditions allowing for more benign political, economic and ideological developments in Ireland lacked substance. Macgougan candidly admitted to his FOI associates that he had 'never found out the exact extent to which the Northern standard of life and social services are subsidized by Britain'; a major omission on his behalf. Perhaps unsurprisingly both Donnelly and Bing did not share his optimism and indeed viewed the prospect of a divided Labour movement in Northern Ireland with alarm. Bing cautioned Macgougan that the break-up of the NILP would be counter-productive and advised against this course of action.[64] However, by 1948 Macgougan was steadfast in his chosen path; his decision to leave the NILP no doubt influenced by what appeared to be, on the surface at least, a genuine determination on behalf of the major parties in the South to settle the border question.

This view could only have been bolstered by a series of linked events in late 1948 and early 1949: the passing of the Republic of Ireland Act in December 1948, the Coalition government's calling of an All-Party Anti-Partitionist Conference – which met for the first time at the Mansion House, Dublin, on 27 January 1949 – and the ensuing establishment of an all-party anti-partition committee (the Mansion House Committee) made up of the Taoiseach John A. Costello; William Norton, Tánaiste and leader of the Labour Party; Seán MacBride, Minister for External Affairs and leader of Clann na Poblachta; Eamon de Valera, leader of Fianna Fáil; and Frank Aiken, a former Fianna Fáil minister. There was a concomitant Unionist response to all this. In February 1949 Brooke called a snap Northern Ireland general election, enabling him to take advantage of a situation in which the constitutional question would be the dominant, and divisive, issue. It was indeed to prove to be an election that reinstated, what Graham Walker has called 'ethnic political priorities and imperatives' after the exceptional left-right politics of the 1945 general election.[65] The decision by the Mansion House Committee to raise and make available funds to anti-partition candidates in the North, funds which were collected after Mass at Catholic churches throughout the South on a chosen Sunday in January, enabled the IAPL to contest a record number of seats, return nine

MPs[66] and increase their share of the vote to its highest level since 1921.[67] However, it also ensured a sectarian hue to the election that only served to deliver a substantial boost to the Unionist Party, enabling it to consolidate its support at the expense of Independent Unionists and the NILP.[68] A pre-election statement from the Belfast representatives of the all-party committee of the Anti-Partition Fund claiming that Brooke's 'puppet throne is being shaken' and that the upcoming 'fake election will do nothing to strengthen his position'[69] could not have been further from the truth.

There does appear to have been some scepticism on the nationalist side as to the wisdom of the 'chapel gates' collection[70] but the IAPL as a body welcomed it, informing the Mansion House Committee that in 'occupied Ireland' they took 'new courage from this decision'.[71] The upbeat tone of IAPL statements issued immediately following the 1949 election appeared to signal a renewed confidence in the ability of the organisation to influence politics on an all-Ireland level. Addressing a large anti-partition demonstration in Dungannon, in March, Cahir Healy claimed that the IAPL had 'worked a miracle' by bringing together all nationalist political parties in the Mansion House Committee 'to hammer out a unified policy'; his fellow speaker and colleague Joseph Stewart considered the support for the anti-partition campaign now so substantial at a national level that 'No power on earth could prevent the re-union of the country.'[72] And yet the question as to the nature of this 'unified policy', and how it would succeed in overcoming unionist resistance to their inclusion in a unitary settlement, remained extant.[73]

Eddie McAteer, in a letter to Sean MacBride (Minister of External Affairs in the coalition government) sent in early March, now pressed the latter on his earlier proposal to grant northern anti-partitionists the 'right of audience' in the Dail. McAteer declared he was 'convinced it would do an immense amount of good', even though he clearly had not given a great deal of thought to its operation or practical effectiveness: 'All … I want is a token gesture … I am only concerned with the symbolism of the thing.'[74] MacBride, in response, put the matter in the hands of Cecil Lavery, the Attorney General, who swiftly reported that although the Irish Constitution prevented granting 'membership' of the Dail to northern representatives it was nonetheless possible to nominate northern nationalists to sit in the Irish Senate. Furthermore, a 'right of audience' in either House could be granted 'possibly under rules of procedure and certainly by legislation'.[75] The IAPL at its annual convention at the end of March took up the 'right of audience' issue with some gusto, recommending that Dublin be requested to give the matter their attention 'as soon as possible'; at the same time the members of the convention intimated that parliamentary abstentionism was back on the agenda: IAPL attendance at Stormont since the election had been irregular and now it was proposed that any decision regarding attendance be left 'to the discretion' of individual elected representatives.[76]

IAPL enthusiasms of early 1949 were dampened by the introduction, in May, of the Ireland Bill at Westminster. Designed as a response to the Republic of Ireland Act (which became effective on Easter Monday 1949)[77] the Ireland Bill clarified the British government's relationship with the new Irish Republic while at the same time offering a guarantee that there would be no change in the constitutional status of Northern Ireland 'without the consent of the Parliament of Northern Ireland'.[78] Costello denounced the Bill in the Dáil[79] and at a mass demonstration (of over 100,000 people) in Dublin on 20 May condemned the 'affront to … national dignity' resulting from the 'insolent British claim to legislate for part of Ireland'.[80] Introducing IAPL representatives Senator Lennon, Malachi Conlon and Eddie McAteer to the platform – to be greeted with 'thunderous cheers' – Costello assured them that they could 'bring back to the North a special message that the Twenty-six Counties were behind their efforts' and that 'they were not isolated and alone'.[81] Whatever solace this brought to northern nationalists at the time, the enactment by the British government of the Ireland Act (1949) in June brought the first flurry of criticism directed towards the Costello government. Joseph Connellan (now a Stormont MP) writing in the *Frontier Sentinel* acknowledged Costello's continued rhetorical commitment to the 'Partition issue', but he also pointedly noted Dublin's lack of concrete action on the matter.[82] Considering the vehemence of Costello's statement in the Dáil on 10 May when protesting the Ireland Bill – 'We can hit the British Government in their prestige and in their pride and in their pocket'[83] – mounting criticism of Dublin was understandable as the northern nationalist sense of isolation grew.[84] By August the *Derry Journal* splenetically observed that the existing relationship between Britain and Ireland (one, it pointed out, in which Ireland provided Britain with foodstuffs 'essential for her very existence', allowed the recruitment of Irish workers into British labour unions and even provided soldiers for the British army) meant that the 'hitting has been all on the other side'. The All-Party Committee was accused of having 'gone into a state of hibernation' and the demand was made that it should now 'act or else make way for those who will'.[85] Such views were now being monitored, recorded and assessed[86] by the Information Section of the Republic's Department of External Affairs, operating under the direction of Conor Cruise O'Brien.[87] Set up by Sean MacBride, the Minister of External Affairs, the role of the Information Section was to coordinate an international anti-partition propaganda campaign and to liaise between MacBride and northern nationalist leaders.[88] Although some later accounts of O'Brien's career suggested his 'enthusiastic' support for the anti-partition policies of his minister at this time[89]

(O'Brien himself gave a more nuanced picture of his attitudes in this period)[90] the Information Section reports in the DEA files reveal O'Brien and his staff to have quickly come to regard traditionalist Nationalist positions in Northern Ireland as sclerotic and as part of the problem. Hand-written comments on an *Irish News* report detailing a large Ancient Order of Hibernians rally in Dungiven, Co. Derry, in August, which was addressed by Joseph Stewart MP and an array of Hibernian speakers and at which nationalist grievances and traditional solutions to partition were aired, disclose not only the early divergence in views that was opening up between O'Brien and northern nationalist leaders but also the discernment of his critical eye:

1 The problem of N I is seen by every speaker in this report as one of British *occupation* of the North not one of divided communities. The discrimination, it is assumed, would cease if the British Army pulled out. No doubt if one dug deep enough in the consciousness of these speakers they would concede that the discrimination, gerrymandering etc arose *locally* not from Britain and that even were the British Army to pull out the problem would have to be tackled locally with a protestant community weakened by the loss of support from Britain. The references to Sir Basil Brooke & his like seem to tilt at the Unionist *Ascendancy*. No reference is made to the aspirations of the Protestant working class.
2 It is possible, from speeches such as these, to appreciate something of Protestant distrust of Catholicism.[91]

O'Brien's cautious, and critical, view of events in the North was informed by the reports of Captain Seamus McCall who, acting on behalf of the DEA, regularly visited Northern Ireland to furnish the Information Section with relevant materials for its propaganda activities. McCall also acted as a liaison officer between the DEA and the North's anti-partitionists. His reports, covering the period 1949 to the mid-1950s, provide a fascinating snapshot of political, social and economic developments in Northern Ireland in this period. Much of the substance of these reports is based on information gleaned from contacts that McCall encountered, or cultivated, on his visits. They are detailed, often containing firsthand accounts as well as information from both named and anonymous sources. Inevitably, the very nature of McCall's method of data collection, i.e. private personal conversations, meant some of the information supplied to him was uncorroborated. In his first report of October 1949 McCall provided Dublin with a pessimistic assessment of what he regarded to be the parlous state of IAPL organisation and morale. Hints of an IRA reorganisation in the North, he suggested, had revealed the fragility of IAPL unity and purpose. Rumours were circulating that, in anticipation of an outbreak of republican violence and the possible collapse of the IAPL, its Chairman, James McSparran – allegedly 'in the running' for a judgeship – was preparing to abandon the organisation; furthermore, other senior members of the IAPL (named as Conlon and McAteer) were said to be contemplating 'going over' to the republicans. While the latter supposition was based on 'not very reliable evidence' McCall did nonetheless recount a recent conversation he had had with Malachi Conlon in which Conlon had vented his frustration over the 'bickering and jealousy' within the IAPL, a body Conlon considered to be at 'sixes and sevens'.[92] This engagement, with what was the largely alien world of northern politics, heralded what was to be an uneasy, and often acrimonious, relationship between the DEA and northern anti-partitionists. The very nature of this relationship was a complex one fraught with difficulties; constitutional nationalists in the North had consistently appealed to the South for assistance, support and direction and yet at the same time they were fiercely independent of Dublin, towards which they harboured a barely disguised scepticism founded on what they regarded to be the cavalier and self-serving conduct of Irish governments in the past.[93]

For its part the Irish government, through the Information Section, arranged for propaganda and publicity events on behalf of the IAPL; but they quickly came to realise that they were not in a position to compel the IAPL to conform to Dublin's strategies or directives. Both sides weighed each other up with the watchfulness of allies who had combined to secure an end but who had slightly different ends in mind. An account of an anti-partition speaking tour in the USA in November 1949,[94] a tour probably organised by Conor Cruise O'Brien, reveals a sense of trepidation that such events could easily rebound to the embarrassment of the Irish government. The tour combined IAPL members Malachi Conlon and Senator J.G. Lennon with the legendary militant IRA figure Tom Barry.[95] The latter's inclusion on the tour may possibly have been calculated to draw large Irish American audiences unfamiliar with the relatively unknown Conlon and Lennon. However, Barry was a man of radical and extreme views, which he invariably delivered in an incendiary style. His 'call to arms' at a large public gathering in New York on 17 November and his claim that 'the Irish Government has set aside $100,000 to buy guns'[96] could not have been the kind of publicity Costello's government relished. O'Brien was 'relieved' to learn of the 'relatively unenthusiastic reception' given to Barry on this occasion.[97] In comparison Conlon's tour speech, delivered at numerous venues, repeated familiar themes in a highly emotive and exaggerated manner – Northern Ireland was a fascist state, Unionism was akin to Nazism, the treatment of Catholics in Northern Ireland was the same as that meted out to the Jews in Nazi Germany.[98] Amidst this picture of Catholic degradation and despair Conlon pointedly emphasised that the route to deliverance was at hand, made possible by the 'magnificent Unity' that existed in Ireland as a result of the formation of the IAPL in the North and the All-Party Mansion House Committee in the South.[99] However, as we shall see, this suggestion of fraternal accord and partnership was far from the reality.

Notes

1 *Irish Times*, 12 June 1945.

2 Russell Rees, *Labour and the Northern Ireland Problem 1945–51: The Missed Opportunity* (Dublin, Irish Academic Pres, 2009), pp. 1, 105.

3 *Ibid.*, pp. 64–65. On the Friends of Ireland see Bob Purdie, 'The Friends of Ireland: British Labour and Irish Nationalism, 1945–49', in Tom Gallagher and James O'Connell (eds), *Contemporary Irish Studies* (Manchester, Manchester University Press, 1983).

4 *Irish Times*, 9 June 1945. At the Convention Cahir Healy was proposed as an alternative candidate to the wholly ineffective Cunningham but lost the nomination on the toss of a coin.

5 *Irish Times*, 11 August 1945.

6 *Frontier Sentinel*, 25 August 1945.

7 *Ibid.* This emphasis on the maximalist demand to end Partition formed the core of Mulvey's maiden speech in the House of Commons on 30 August 1945. See *Frontier Sentinel*, 1 September 1945.

8 *Frontier Sentinel*, 15 September 1945.

9 *Ibid.*

10 Cahir Healy, *The Mutilation of a Nation: The Story of the Partition of Ireland* (Derry, The Derry Journal Ltd, 1945).

11 M. Elliott, *The Catholics of Ulster: A History* (London, Allen Lane, 2000), p. 384.

12 *Frontier Sentinel*, 3 November 1945.

13 The press were told they could attend the convention only if they gave a prior undertaking to publish only statements supplied by the convention organisers. *Irish Times*, 15 November 1945.

14 *Frontier Sentinel*, 17 November 1945.

15 See B. Lynn, 'The Irish Anti-Partition League and the Political Realities of Partition, 1945–9', *Irish Historical Studies* xxxiv: 135 (May 2000), p. 321.

16 *Frontier Sentinel*, 17 November 1945. There is some doubt regarding Ireland's invitation and his apology for non-attendance. At the AGM of the Ulster Union Club, held less than two weeks after the Dungannon convention, the Secretary (Ford Graham) when called upon to explain why the Club had not been represented at Dungannon replied that no invitation to attend had been received. It is possible that Ireland may have been invited in a personal capacity and not as President of the Ulster Union Club. See *Frontier Sentinel*, 26 November 1945.

17 House of Commons (Northern Ireland) Debates, Volume 29 (1945, 46), p. 1398.

18 *Frontier Sentinel*, 8 December 1945.

19 Lynn, 'The Irish Anti-Partition League', p. 325.

20 *Ibid.*, see also *Frontier Sentinel*, 22 December 1945.

21 See for example the Stormont debate on Conlon's motion the 'Release of Political Prisoners and Internees' that took place on 30 October 1945. House of Commons (Northern Ireland) Debates, Volume 29 (1945, 46), pp. 911–945.

22 His colleague, Patrick Cunningham, appears to have been an infrequent attendee at Westminster. There is no record that he ever spoke in the House of Commons.

23 See PRONI, D1862/F/7, Cahir Healy Papers, Maguire to Mulvey, 'For the Clones job I believe Miss Mulvey will get 100% support if the qualifications of the other two candidates are not before the Board and Mr F O'Duffy says it is not likely – if they are he will have to support the locals though he would prefer to support Miss Mulvey … '; also PRONI, D1862/F/4 Healy to Mulvey 11 October 1945, ' … I was told by Father McC that your daughter would get the post. Johnston has the last word there in such matters … and when he was agreeable I knew she was right. I think these people owe something to the Six County folks, whom they have left, like Cinderella, up here.'

24 PRONI, D1862/B/5, A.J. Mulvey papers, Hugh Delargy MP to Mulvey, 6 November 1945.

25 Cited in Purdie, 'The Friends of Ireland', p. 82.

26 Little contested the seat in July 1945 following his failure to be nominated by the Unionist Party. In Stormont Little adopted the title of the Democratic Unionist Party and criticised Unionist misgivings of Attlee's government. Little's death was the reason for the by-election.

27 In the run-up to the July election the *Frontier Sentinel* ran with the editorial 'Don't Vote', calling on nationalists and anti-partitionists to boycott the constituency. See *Frontier Sentinel*, 30 June 1945.

28 See John Harbinson, 'A History of the Northern Ireland Labour Party' (unpublished M.Sc. thesis, Queen's University Belfast, 1966), pp. 196–200.

29 The FOI contributed £400 towards Donnelly's election expenses, see Purdie, 'The Friends of Ireland', p. 83; also T. Cradden, *Trade Unionism, Socialism and Partition, The Labour Movement in Northern Ireland 1939–1953* (Belfast, December Publications, 1993), p. 150.

30 PRONI, D2991/B/144/21, Cahir Healy papers, Maguire to Healy, 30 October 1946. The hostility shown by elements of Nationalist opinion towards the FOI was not lost on the Friends themselves. Harry McGhee (MP for Penistone, Yorkshire) brought Mulvey's attention to the edition of the *Derry Journal* (18 October 1946) which published 'a beastly sectarian attack on the "Friends"'. PRONI, D1862/F/1, M.J. Mulvey papers, McGhee to Mulvey, 2 November 1946.

31 *Frontier Sentinel*, 30 March 1946.

32 PRONI, D1862/F/7, M.J. Mulvey papers, Maguire to Mulvey, 24 September 1946.

33 *Frontier Sentinel*, 6 April 1946.

34 *Frontier Sentinel*, 20 April 1946.

35 Fleming had been arrested in Belfast in September 1942 following a police raid on the publicity headquarters of the IRA Northern Command. He was later charged with a number of offences including the attempted murder of a police officer. See T.P. Coogan, *The IRA* (New York, Palgrave, 2002), p. 183, also House of Commons (Northern Ireland) Debates, Volume 30 (1946/47), p. 738.

36 *Frontier Sentinel*, 11 May 1946.

37 *Frontier Sentinel*, 4 May 1946.

38 House of Commons (Northern Ireland) Debates, Volume 30 (1946/47), p. 744.

39 *Ibid.*, p. 726.

40 *Frontier Sentinel*, 4 May 1946.

41 It appears that McCaughey's refusal to wear prison clothes had resulted in him being kept naked in his cell since 1941. See M. Farrell, *Northern Ireland: The Orange State* (London, Pluto Press, 1978), p. 182.

42 Although J. Bowyer Bell claims that Fleming was released in the same month that McCaughey died, the Fleming case was still being debated in Stormont in November 1946. By this time IAPL members were pressing the government to release Fleming into the care of a mental institution, on the grounds that he was suffering from 'religious mania'. Warnock now made it known that he was prepared to consider Fleming's release (as a depoliticised issue) on humanitarian grounds. See J. Bowyer Bell, *The Secret Army: The IRA 1916–1979* (Dublin, The Academy Press, 1983), p. 243; House of Commons (Northern Ireland) Debates, Volume 30 (1946/47), pp. 2791–2794.

43 *Frontier Sentinel*, 29 December 1945.

44 Henry Patterson, *Ireland Since 1939: The Persistence of Conflict* (Dublin, Penguin Ireland, 2006), p. 119.

45 PRONI, D1862/F/6, M.J. Mulvey papers, McAnally to Healy, Good Friday 1947. At this time McAnally believed that 'The lesson of the Anglo-Irish conflict is that England bows to force and the threat of force'. By the mid-1960s McAnally (or Ciaran Mac an Aili as he was now better known) had moved from this position, he was by that time president of the Irish Pacifist Association and a force for moderation actively encouraging the Republican Movement to abandon militarism and embark on a campaign of civil rights in the North. See Bob Purdie, *Politics in the Streets: The Origins of the Civil Rights Movement in Northern Ireland* (Belfast, Blackstaff Press, 1990), p. 132; Sean Swan, *Official Irish Republicanism, 1962 to 1972* (Lulu.com, 2008), p.105. However, Mac an Aili still did not think that constitutional methods of bringing reform to the North were apposite, instead he advocated 'a new departure' of civil disobedience. This he envisaged as a mass non-violent campaign, but he appeared nonetheless to see state judicial, or violent, suppression of such a campaign as an inevitable response leading to change. See Ciaran Mac an Aili, 'Uniting Ireland: Violence or Non Violence', *Hibernia* (January 1962), p. 15.

46 *Ulster Herald*, 10 January 1948.

47 Purdie, 'The Friends of Ireland', pp. 87, 90.

48 *Irish Times*, 17 March 1947.

49 D. Keogh, *Twentieth-Century Ireland: Nation and State* (Dublin, Gill & Macmillan, 1994), p.182.

50 On this disparity see Patterson, *Ireland Since 1939*, p. 120.

51 See E. Keane, *An Irish Statesman and Revolutionary: The Nationalist and Internationalist Politics of Sean MacBride* (London, I.B. Tauris, 2006), p. 81. Keane, generously, judges that both proposals were 'far sighted' and suggests that they anticipated developments in the late 1990s; namely the Good Friday Agreement. For an incisive and more critical account of MacBride in this period see Eithne MacDermott, *Clann na Poblachta* (Cork, Cork University Press, 1998) p. 136.

52 PRONI, D2991/B/60/1, MacBride to Healy, 13 January 1948 D2991/B/60/2, Healy to MacBride 20 January 1948.

53 *Ulster Herald*, 24 January 1948.

54 *Irish Times*, 9 August 1948. De Valera was speaking at Clonmellon, Co. Westmeath.

55 *Derry Journal*, 6 September 1948.

56 On the background to labour politics in the North see C. Norton, 'The Left in Northern Ireland 1921–1932', *Labour History Review* 60: 1 (Spring 1995), pp. 3–20.

57 NILP Manifesto 1945, cited in C. Norton, 'The Irish Labour Party in Northern Ireland, 1949–1958', *Saothar* 21 (1996), p. 47.

58 The non-nationalist Left comprising the NILP, the Commonwealth Labour Party and the Communist Party. See Cradden, *Trade Unionism, Socialism and Partition*, pp. 41–50.

59 See Graham Walker, *The Politics of Frustration: Harry Midgley and the Failure of Labour in Northern Ireland* (Manchester, Manchester University Press, 1985), Chapter 7.

60 See C. Norton, 'Jack Macgougan (1913–1998)', in K. Gildart and D. Howell (eds), *Dictionary of Labour Biography Volume XIII* (London, Palgrave Macmillan, 2010). pp. 232–237.

61 Donnelly to Macgougan, 14 May 1947 cited in C. Norton, 'The Irish Labour Party in Northern Ireland, 1949–1958', *Saothar* 21 (1996), p. 49. The proposal advanced a number of areas in which socialist planning could best be implemented: collective farming, cooperative buying and selling for small farmers, machinery pools, the application of scientific methods to agriculture, and the abandonment of de Valera's policy of economic protectionism in the South.

62 *Ibid.*

63 Macgougan held a deeply pessimistic view of both northern Protestants and Catholics; the former described as occupying a position 'akin to [that] held by the Cossacks in Russia' while the latter were 'equally as narrow minded, undemocratic and terribly scared of socialism'. In marked contrast he considered the southern Irish to be 'democratically minded and traditionally so'. Macgougan to Donnelly 23 May 1947, *Ibid.*

64 Geoffrey Bing MP to Macgougan, 15 November 1948, cited in *Ibid.*, p. 50.

65 G. Walker, *A History of the Ulster Unionist Party: Protest, Pragmatism and Pessimism* (Manchester, Manchester University Press, 2004), p. 111.

66 Malachi Conlon, South Armagh; Joseph Connellan, South Down; Cahir Healy, South Fermanagh; Patrick Maxwell, Foyle; Eddie McAteer, Mid Londonderry; Edward McCullagh, Mid Tyrone; James McSparran, Mourne; Roderick O'Connor, West Tyrone; Joseph Francis Stewart, East Tyrone. Dr Eileen Hickey, nominated by Catholic Queen's University graduates, was elected for one of the Queen's University seats as an Independent. Two left-wing anti-partitionists were elected in Belfast; Harry Diamond, Belfast Falls; and Francis Hanna, Belfast Central. Although both men were at this time associated with Macgougan's nascent Irish Labour Party they stood under the titles Socialist Republican and Independent Labour respectively.

67 Rees, *Labour and the Northern Ireland Problem*, p. 138.

68 Prior to the election the NILP reiterated its commitment to the 'no change without the will of the majority' policy and attempted to counter Brooke's assertion that the election was a plebiscite on the border, but with little success. The electorate rejected

all nine of its candidates. See *Irish Times*, 1 February 1949; D. Harkness, *Northern Ireland Since 1920* (Dublin, Criterion Press, 1983), p. 120.

69 *Irish Times*, 1 February 1949.

70 E. Staunton, *The Nationalists of Northern Ireland 1918–1973* (Dublin, Columba Press, 2001), p. 362 fn. 21.

71 Telegram sent by the Secretaries of the IAPL (Malachi Conlon and Senator JG Lennon) to the Mansion House Committee, *Frontier Sentinel*, 5 February 1949.

72 *Irish Times*, 18 March 1949.

73 In fact Unionist opposition was treated as something to be challenged and subdued rather than conciliated. For example Father L. Gilmartin, delivering an address to mark the opening of an IAPL branch in Kinawaley, Co. Fermanagh (of which he was appointed chairman) in March spoke optimistically of the border 'going in your day and my day' but offered little evidence of any serious consideration of the place for Unionists in the new Ireland. On the contrary Father Gilmartin considered Unionists to be 'traitors to their own country'. Such comments can only have reinforced Protestant prejudices as to the controlling and manipulative tendencies of the Catholic Church. Cahir Healy, speaking at the same event, proposed repatriation of Unionists to the British mainland. *The Irish Weekly*, 12 March 1949.

74 NAI, DFA 305/14/29, McAteer to MacBride, 5 March 1949.

75 *Ibid*. Report of Cecil Lavery, Attorney General, 10 March 1949.

76 *Irish Times*, 31 March 1949; *Irish Times*, 11 April 1949.

77 Republican response to this was negative in the extreme. In May the publication of the republican movement, the *United Irishman*, bearing the headline 'Action – Not Words!', published the IRA Army Council's Easter Statement which announced that recent developments 'in no way altered the fundamental position' and that the 26-County Republic 'cannot be accepted as a genuine advance towards the goal of free united Ireland unless followed by certain definitive steps which would translate the empty formulae and pious hopes into reality.' See *United Irishman*, May 1949.

78 M.J. Cunningham, *British Government Policy in Northern Ireland 1969–2000*. (Manchester, Manchester University Press, 2001), p. 3.

79 Parliamentary Debates Dáil Éireann, Volume 115, 10 May 1949, pp. 785–818.

80 *Frontier Sentinel*, 21 May 1949.

81 *Ibid*.

82 *Frontier Sentinel*, 9 July 1949.

83 Parliamentary Debates Dáil Éireann, Volume 115, 10 May 1949, p. 807.

84 Hopes that President Truman would intervene to persuade Britain to relent on partition was now abandoned on the grounds that Truman was a Freemason, therefore anti-Catholic, and in complete accord with 'his fellow-Freemasons in London'. *Frontier Sentinel*, 30 July 1949.

85 *Derry Journal*, 12 August 1949.

86 NAI, DFA 305/14/12, 19 August 1949 A hand-written comment on the report of the *Derry Journal* article read 'Rather disturbing'.

87 Conor Cruise O'Brien, *States of Ireland* (London, Panther Books, 1974), p. 134.

88 *Ibid*., p. 137.

89 See O'Brien's obituary in *The Times*, 20 December 2008.

90 'I came to look back on this phase of my career with growing distaste. I realised fairly early that the anti-partition campaign was doing no good, but it took me longer to realise it was doing serious harm.' Conor Cruise O'Brien, *Ancestral Voices: Religion and Nationalism in Ireland* (Dublin, Poolbeg Press, 1994), p. 137.

91 NAI, DFA 305/14/12, hand-written comments on *Irish News* article, 16 August 1949.

92 NAI, DFA 305/14/65, Report of Capt. Seamus McCall, October 1949.

93 This attitude was not just confined to the Irish government. The criticism, made by the left-republican radical, Peadar O'Donnell, of northern Nationalism's failure to fully comprehend what he perceived to be the true rebellious character of Orangeism, and his suggestion of a policy of reconciliation with Orangemen produced, in response, a lengthy article in the *Derry Journal* in which O'Donnell was summarily dismissed as a 'political simple Simon'. *Derry Journal*, 18 January 1950

94 The tour prefigured by a few months Basil Brooke's successful tour of the USA. See S Smyth, 'In Defence of Ulster: The Visit of Sir Basil Brooke to North America, Spring 1950', *The Canadian Journal of Irish Studies* 33: 2 (2007).

95 In the early 1920s Barry had commanded the flying column of the IRA's West Cork Brigade, a unit that acquired a reputation for its bold and particularly brutal military engagements. For a detailed account of Barry's role at this time see P. Hart, *The IRA and Its Enemies: Violence and Community in Cork 1916–1923* (Oxford, Oxford University Press, 2009), Chapter 2. A British intelligence report alleges that in 1939 Barry travelled to Nazi Germany in the company of Jupp Hoven, an Abwehr intelligence officer, for the purposes of discussing 'the future action of the IRA in the event of a European war'. UK National Archives, KV/3/120, Report by C. Liddell, 11 April 1943.

96 NAI, DFA 305/14/111, Pete Barnicle (Boston) to Conor Cruise O'Brien, 28 November 1949.

97 NAI, DFA 305/14/111, Conor Cruise O'Brien to Pete Barnicle (Boston), 5 December 1949.

98 As well as drawing on the example of European Jews persecuted by the Nazis to emphasise Catholic persecution Conlon also spoke admiringly of the communal solidarity of American Jews and of their success in the USA. It would seem that his earlier robust views had either moderated or else were reserved for Jews who were also communist.

99 NAI, DFA 305/14/111, copy of Malachi Conlon's American speech.

5

Deteriorating relations with Dublin, 1950–55

The Westminster general election of February 1950 was to reveal both an in-capacitating divisiveness among northern constitutional anti-partitionists, which placed very real constraints on their strategic options, and a deepening strain in relations with Dublin. In the months leading up to the election the Information Section of the Irish Government's Department of External Affairs (DEA) had become exasperated by the verbal attacks directed against the British Labour government (in the aftermath of the Ireland Act, 1949) by leading members of the IAPL. The decision taken by the British section of the IAPL, in October 1949, to stand candidates in opposition to British Labour Party candidates at the election had already resulted in the resignation of leading FOI member, Hugh Delargy, from the chairmanship of the League.[1] In November James McSparran's vituperative assault on Attlee's Labour Party, delivered in Glasgow to the Gorbals Branch of the IAPL, in which he claimed that the Labour Party was atheistic, anti-Catholic and pro-communist, stretched Conor Cruise O'Brien's patience with the IAPL Chairman. O'Brien's hand-written comment on the DEA report of McSparran's speech – 'Completely in char-acter. The man is an appalling liability'[2] – reveals his irritation. Shortly before the election Captain Seamus McCall had visited Belfast and found the IAPL Executive divided in their attitudes towards Dublin. Some, he reported, were demanding that Dublin play a greater role in providing 'active leadership' while others considered 'the people in Dublin' to be too 'concerned with their own selfish party interests than with the removal of the Border'. The latter favoured a policy of IAPL 'independent actions' designed to expose an Irish government which, they felt, 'was doing nothing for the people in the North'.[3] McCall was also frustrated in his attempts to convince the IAPL Executive to give their support to other anti-partition candidates in the election; namely the two can-didates from the IrLP (Jack Macgougan and Jack Beattie) who were standing in seats (South Down and West Belfast respectively) not being contested by the IAPL. His suggestion of cooperation, in order to maximise the chances of anti-partitionist electoral success, was 'scornfully rejected' by members of the Executive in what he saw as a pique of 'imbecile jealousy and selfish concern'.[4] And yet McCall himself displayed a characteristically cool attitude towards the IrLP. He called into question the integrity of their West Belfast candidate, Jack Beattie, accusing him of being unwilling to cooperate with party colleagues and suggesting that he may have appropriated political funds for his own use.[5] It was certainly true that Beattie had a reputation as a political maverick and that he was not a 'party man' by instinct, but McCall was aware that the IrLP leadership in Dublin had called for the release from prison of Beattie's Sinn Féin opponent in the election (the IRA man Jimmy Steele)[6] and that Beattie suspected that some of his Dublin comrades favoured his rival over his own candidature. This knowledge did not, however, lessen the severity of McCall's conclusion that Beattie was 'so little trusted that we should be better off with-out him'.[7]

The result of the election saw the return of Healy and Mulvey[8] – who were prevented from taking their seats at Westminster by their abstentionist-dom-inated local constituency organisations[9] – and the defeat of Macgougan and Beattie. In a post-election report sent to Frank Aiken, Macgougan placed the blame for their failure on a partial nationalist press which supported the IAPL candidates while at the same time calling on Catholics to abstain from voting in all other constituencies not being contested by the IAPL. Macgougan es-timated that the nationalist vote in the election was reduced by up to 50 per cent.[10] He was appreciative of McCall's efforts to undo this damage by 'visiting many of the clergy and pointing out the true facts',[11] but this obviously had made little impact. However, in the aftermath of the election an accommoda-tion between the IrLP and IAPL appeared to be at hand. In March Malachi Conlon (Secretary of the IAPL) contacted Macgougan with a proposal to form an All-Party Committee in the North on the same lines as that already in exist-ence in the Republic.[12] Tragically, before any further involvement Conlon died suddenly in the Mater Hospital, Belfast, succumbing to a heart attack on the morning of 27 March. He was thirty-eight years old.[13] Despite his loss repre-sentatives of the two parties met in Belfast in early June 1950 and a decision was tentatively arrived at to organise a Unity Conference in October to which all shades of nationalist opinion in the North would be invited to attend.[14] The prospects for united action were not, however, as they seemed. McCall had the opportunity of interviewing IAPL members shortly after the June meeting and his impression was that senior figures had little confidence in the success of the venture. McCall believed that McSparran was merely going through the mo-tions in order to demonstrate to Dublin that an attempt to unify anti-partition forces was being made. Indeed McSparran confided that he thought many anti-partition groups would decline an invitation to participate, and that even if a 'Unity Meeting' did get off the ground he was sure that any arrangement arrived at between the participants would break down at election times. McAteer had 'no hope for the success of the effort, but was willing to give it a fair trial'.[15] In his report to Dublin McCall also provided details of his now expanded role in the North which involved offering active assistance to IAPL representatives at Stormont: he furnished MPs with questions to raise in parliament, provided 'propaganda points' and suggested 'useful lines of argument'. He was convinced of the efficacy of his labours stressing the 'great importance of using Stormont for the purposes of putting over our point of view'. However, the shortcomings of the recipients of his efforts were, he felt, a serious obstacle to their success: 'owing to the general confusion of thought, the lack of any co-ordinated policy among themselves, the all too common tendency to regard politics not as a means to an end but an end in itself, and – sometimes – the pertinacity of spoiled children, it has been slow going.'[16]

What improvements he had been able to make in IAPL parliamentary performance, he believed, were constrained by the infrequent attendance of their MPs and, tellingly, the lack of interest shown by Irish national newspapers in Northern Ireland issues. However, it was the problem of what McCall termed a 'new distraction' that he was 'up against' that was to provide the basis for increased tensions between Dublin and the IAPL: this was the demand that IAPL parliamentary representatives in the North be given the right to take seats in either the Dáil or the Seanad.[17]

Sean McBride had returned to the theme of his earlier proposal of northern representatives taking seats in the Republic's parliamentary institutions when campaigning for Cahir Healy and Anthony Mulvey in the February Westminster general election. Speaking in St Patrick's Hall in Dungannon, MacBride concluded his speech with the following: 'Indeed, I hope that when Mr Cahir Healy and Mr Mulvey are elected by the people of Tyrone and Fermanagh, they will make a beginning in this direction by taking their seats in one or other of the Houses of Parliament in the Republic.'[18] But MacBride was not in fact holding out any prospect of such an eventuality in the near future. MacBride's speech revealed that he had modified his original proposal by changing the context in which it could take effect. He now suggested a 'federal solution' for Ireland, which would allow for a local parliament of 'limited jurisdiction' in the North and an all-Ireland parliament 'in which all parts of the country would be represented'.[19] It was thus only in the imagined future of an agreed federal settlement that northern nationalist representatives could claim their seats in an all-Ireland parliament. However, while McBride's proposal became increasingly speculative the whole issue of taking seats in Dublin was one that was becoming progressively more significant to the IAPL. At its annual convention in May 1950, a resolution recommending abstention from both Stormont and Westminster was defeated by 89 votes to 32; the majority still favoured attendance, but the continued absence of Healey and Mulvey from Westminster testified to the strength and influence of abstentionists within the constituencies. It was in this context that the question of taking seats in the Dáil or Seanad now took on something of a totemic quality; it was an issue around which the IAPL could unite and galvanise party opinion. A resolution proposing that a deputation of IAPL MPs and Senators should meet the Irish government and call upon them to allow 'Northern elected representatives seats in the Dáil and Senate' was passed by the convention.[20] However, when a deputation met with Costello and the Tánaiste, IrLP leader William Norton, in July, it was only to be rebuffed yet again on the grounds that 'in the absence of general agreement among members of the Dáil, the government was not prepared to promote the necessary legislation to permit members of the Six County Parliament to sit in either House of the Oireachtas'.[21]

Despite this, and in the absence of an agreed alternative policy, for the IAPL the symbolism of nationalist representatives entering the Irish parliament remained potent, even if its practicalities, and benefits to constituents, were not publicly considered. Privately Cahir Healy remained dismissive of the whole idea, confiding to Father Maguire that although 'a large section of our people think that something wonderful would develop if we were there' he was firmly of the opinion that '[n]umbers will believe anything a clever crank suggests – until they try it out and see the folly'.[22] In fact Healy had earlier acknowledged (at a public meeting in Fermanagh in August 1950) that conditions for Catholics in Northern Ireland could be improved substantially if they were prepared to compromise on their policy of non-compliance with the northern state. He was 'sure' that more active involvement in political matters would result in Catholics securing 'some public positions here and there' and filling 'a due proportion' of places in the RUC and the Civil Service. He also felt that in following such a course of action they would not be resigning themselves to the permanency of their position within Northern Ireland – the goal of Irish unity would be suspended not abandoned. This was what not, however, something that Healy was prepared to contemplate at this time; nationalists, he affirmed, 'wanted first and last the unity of the country and they would not exchange that demand for anything else'.[23]

As regards northerners taking seats in the Oireachtas it was of course already possible for Northern Ireland citizens to be nominated for, and elected to, the Seanad; and Capt. Dennis Ireland did just that, holding a seat in the Seanad from 1948 until 1951. Capt. Ireland's time in the Seanad seems to have been remarkably uneventful, he is on record of having risen to speak on only one occasion;[24] but Senator Ireland did nonetheless immerse himself in southern politics, even becoming a member of Clann Na Poblachta. However, Ireland was to find southern political idiosyncrasies, and the lack of sensitivity shown towards opinion north of the Border, at times unsettling. In February 1950 he felt compelled to resign his membership of the Clann because of 'alternative policies on Partition' that were being advanced by some within the party. These 'alternative policies' – the advocacy of physical force methods – while undoubtedly appealing to the more unrestrained republican wing of Clann Na Poblachta, held out little prospect of winning the hearts and minds of Ulster Protestants. In his letter of resignation Ireland set out his position:

> Seen from the angle of one whose fixed purpose it is not to get so far away from his fellow Protestants in the Six Counties as to become merely another Twenty-six County politician, the mere possibility, even the mere mention, of such alternative policies is another matter entirely; and I can only regretfully report that their effect is either likely to postpone the possibility of Irish reunion or to bring it about in a form that would be worse than useless.[25]

Ireland was later to withdraw his resignation following entreaties from MacBride, but he did so with the proviso that his continued support for the party could not be taken for granted,

> I withdraw my letter of [resignation] on the understanding that I feel very strongly in this matter of even indirect reference to force on the part of anybody in the Twenty-six Counties, and that I reserve my liberty of action should there at any time be a tendency towards such a policy – that is, on the part of any one, and excluding all considerations of party opinion in the matter.[26]

This tendency for the aspirations of Protestant or secular nationalists to become overwhelmed when confronted with the established verities of Irish nationalism was a problem that also confronted the northern section of the IrLP. From the outset Macgougan had been at pains to develop the IrLP as a secular alternative to traditional constitutional nationalism in Northern Ireland. By way of emphasising this he had stressed, during his election campaign in South Down in February, that his anti-partitionism was 'more than a sentimental desire … to rejoin the motherland', it was based instead on his belief that economic unity held out the potential for a substantial improvement in the economic and social life of the working class.[27] However, in an astute commentary on the IrLP Annual Conference, held in August 1950, the editor of the *Irish Times*, Robert Maire Smyllie, writing under the sobriquet 'Aknefton', observed that the new northern section of the IrLP now appeared to be comprised of two distinct groups. One group, he wrote, denounced the evils of partition while the second spoke of the advantages of unity. He cited Harry Diamond as being representative of the first group while as an example of the second group he quoted a Belfast delegate (John Kennedy) who spoke of the party's need to consider the rights of Protestants in a future united country: 'Unless you guarantee the recognition of their right to conduct their lives and to order their lives in accordance with their own beliefs, methods and ideas, you are infringing on their civil liberty as much as if you restricted their right to worship.'[28]

This issue of Protestant rights within the context of a united Ireland had proven to be a contentious one among the northern section prior to the conference. At a party gathering in Belfast, in June, held to discuss the forthcoming conference, a proposed resolution affirming the IrLPs adherence to the 'principles of Civil and Religious Liberty' and its commitment to 'guarantee to the protestant minority that they would not be forced to accept ethical standards different from those of their own faith', was opposed by Harry Diamond who regarded the resolution, plus another barring religious ceremony under the auspices of the party, as 'an implied insult to the majority of the people'.[29]

Notwithstanding the formation of a tentative IAPL/IrLP dominated Unity Council in October 1950[30] the internal tensions within both the IAPL and the IrLP were augmented by continuing rivalries between them. The extent of these rivalries were revealed in the course of two by-elections which took place in the final months of 1950 and which demonstrated to McCall just how difficult was his task of establishing unanimity amongst a broad section of nationalist opinion.[31] In the first, a Westminster by-election in West Belfast held in November, Jack Beattie narrowly failed (by 913 seats) to regain the seat he lost to a Unionist candidate in the February general election. In the election Beattie was the sole anti-partitionist candidate, his only opponent being a Unionist Party candidate; the young Queen's University law lecturer and Orange protagonist Thomas Teevan. However, McCall detected a distinct absence of IAPL support for Beattie's campaign. He felt that the decision by the main nationalist daily, the *Irish News*, to publish a Sinn Féin appeal for voters in the constituency to abstain from voting, was particularly harmful to Beattie's chances; more damagingly he alleged that several 'so-called' nationalists, including a 'prominent' IAPL member, had actively assisted in Teevan's successful campaign.[32]

The second election, which took place in December, was the Stormont by-election in South Armagh, called to replace the deceased Malachi Conlon. In this election the candidate supported by the IAPL was Charles McGleenan, who in 1935 had contested the Westminster seat of Armagh as an abstentionist Republican.[33] McGleenan's campaign was based on a pledge that if elected he would not attend Stormont but would instead seek to take his seat in the

Dáil. His only opponent in the election was Seamus McKearney of the IrLP. In his report on this election McCall revealed a caustic view of the 'South Armagh people' finding them 'for the most part, uneducated politically'. He was strongly critical of every aspect of McGleenan's campaign which he considered to be based on 'false reasoning, stunting and blatant dishonesty', and he made no secret of his wish to see McGleenan fail. [34] McCall's frustrations with the main body of constitutional nationalism in the North now poured forth; he thought while the original idea behind the IAPL had been 'a good one' it had now regrettably 'degenerated into a party machine for securing the return to Parliament of a few, largely useless, mainly selfish, out-of date politicians'. He complained bitterly of the scant regard he received for his efforts; he was tired of the demands made upon him by the IAPL, irritated by their lack of cooperation and angered by their hectoring tone and the misuse of funds provided by the Mansion House Committee.[35] McGleenan's subsequent election success brought yet a further anguished report from McCall. The IAPL in the aftermath of their victory were 'impossible'; they regarded the defeat of McKearney as a blow against 'the people in Dublin' who they suspected had engineered the contest in order to defeat McGleenan and they considered the result 'a clear decision by the electors of South Armagh in favour of seeking admission to the Oireachtas', even though McGleenan's vote was only half that achieved by Conlon in the 1949 Stormont election (5,581 as compared to 10,868).[36] McCall again despaired at the backwardness of South Armagh. It was, he wrote, 'like going back a whole generation in Irish history'; the IAPL consorted with 'gombeenmen' and smugglers and together they all shared 'a lively hatred of anyone who tries to "muscle-in" on their territory'.[37] The tone of disdain in his report, and his absence of empathy with the IAPL, is striking. McCall appears to have regarded those nationalists who prioritised anti-partitionism above all else, and who had remained remarkably loyal to Dublin, as errant and ungrateful children. They were to be cajoled and mollified but not necessarily treated with any fraternal regard. There is no evidence that his superiors in the DEA shared in McCall's acrimonious opinions to the same degree, but there was a perceptible air of detachment in Conor Cruise O'Brien's apologetic letter to Denis Devlin, a staff member in the Irish Legation in Rome, when requesting that 'a little official attention' be given to a 'bunch of northern Nationalists' who were there for an audience with the Pope in November. O'Brien thought the attention 'may do a lot to mollify them' following Dublin's latest refusal to admit them to the Dáil.[38] This attitude towards the IAPL – a mixture of paternalism and disapproval – which pervaded political opinion in the South, tended to account for the IAPL's lack of progress by reference to the inadequacies of its leading figures. There was little reflection on the strategy that the Mansion House Committee had itself advanced for some years. All the major party leaders in the Republic had engaged in bouts of, what was at times, bellicose anti-partition propaganda. The IAPL had dutifully emulated this in its attempts to expose the failings of the Unionist regime and of the Partition settlement of 1921; however, this had achieved little or no appreciable results. Their performance at Stormont served to increase unionist enmity towards them at a time when a revived Independent Unionism, critical of Brooke's alleged 'appeasement' of disloyal Catholics,[39] heralded the re-emergence of a revived and toxic sectarianism. Their activities at Westminster were equally unfruitful, though here they were faced with the insuperable obstacle of an establishment wary of becoming involved in the quagmire of the 'Irish question'. All in all the outcome of this was to place the IAPL in a weakened position. McCall could see the symptoms of this (though not its cause); he observed that McGleenan's candidature had attracted little enthusiasm among the IAPL leadership (even if some senior figures had canvassed for him), that his campaign failed to generate popular local support and that his public meetings were poorly attended. He also noted that while the IAPL presented Beattie's defeat in West Belfast and McGleenan's victory in South Armagh as evidence that the League had been 'rehabilitated', it was in fact, he thought, suffering from a 'very serious split'.[40]

This split was between its abstentionist and anti-abstentionist wings and it was exacerbated by the failure of the IAPL's current strategy; a failure that had opened up a space for more militant alternatives to develop. In South Armagh there were clear signs of this militancy in the increasing activities of Sinn Féin. At a ceilidh in Newry Town Hall organised by the South Armagh Sinn Féin Committee in August 1950, which attracted a sizeable audience of 500 people, an address by the Dublin Sinn Féiner (and IRA member) Sean Kearney left no doubt as to his party's limited appetite for constitutional methods: 'Sinn Féin did not intend to stand by constitutional means to achieve the freedom of Ireland, if such means proved of no avail, as they had done to date.'[41] It was in the face of this challenge that those senior IAPL members sceptical of pursuing entry to the Oireachtas found themselves in a position of having no option other than to give their support to abstentionists like McGleenan.

There were those in the Republic, deeply critical of the confrontational policies of the Mansion House Committee, who advanced a more liberal and gradual approach to ending partition; though they were in a minority. Ernest Blythe was one such member of this minority. A Lisburn-born Protestant na-tionalist, Gaelic enthusiast, 1916 participant and former Minister for Finance in the Cosgrave government, Blythe had censured Dublin's attempts to coerce Unionists into an all-Ireland settlement at the time of the formation of the Mansion House Committee in 1949. Instead he urged neighbourly cooperation and the 'peaceful persuasion' of unionists – a process which he thought could take between 20 to 50 years. He also recommended that northern Catholics should participate in 'public and social activities' in Northern Ireland.[42] Blythe returned to this theme in an article written in October 1950 for the golden jubilee edition of the Nationalist weekly review, *The Leader*. His acknowledge-ment of the democratic legitimacy of the northern state and his dismissal as 'utterly childish' any notion that the British government would 'ever be willing to use British bayonets to drive out from under the Union Jack a large group of people who would be bitterly resistant' won support in certain quarters – the *Irish Times*[43] and the Unionist daily *The Northern Whig*[44] – but was met with a (surprisingly) subdued response from the IAPL. Louis Lynch, an Omagh-based IAPL Senator in the Northern Ireland Senate, wrote a brief letter to the *Irish Times* taking issue with Blythe's description of Stormont as being a 'decent democratically-chosen Irish assembly … despite a slight lack of balance due to some gerrymandering', a description which, Lynch felt, took scant regard of the extent of anti-Catholic discrimination in certain Unionist-controlled local gov-ernment authorities. However, Lynch did not engage with Blythe's substantive criticisms of the fundamental flaws, and failures, of the anti-partition cam-paign.[45] The same was true of the *Frontier Sentinel* which, while reproducing Blythe's article in full, devoted more time to a character assassination of Blythe (including drawing attention to his allegedly Orange origins) than to a serious consideration of his argument.[46] Blythe's voice was to remain a persistent but largely ignored one.

In complete contrast to Blythe, however, McCall was fulsome in his praise of what he regarded to be the great successes of the initiatives taken by pol-iticians in the Republic. He pointed in particular to three 'events' which, he believed, had led to an 'improved situation in the North': these were de Valera's international tour, undertaken in the aftermath of his electoral defeat in 1948, which, McCall claimed, had raised anti-partition agitation above the confines of the 'local-goings on of the Six-County nationalists';[47] the declaration of the Republic in 1949; and, the 'church-gate' collection of that same year. There was little consideration here of the possible malign effects on unionist opinion of the exaggeratedly vigorous and martial language that de Valera had employed on his tour when addressing the issue of partition,[48] or of relationship between his three events and Brooke's success in the 1949 snap election. And, even though McCall acknowledged that some northern nationalists felt the church-gate collection had been 'a mistake', he remained convinced that the publicity resulting from 'the very fury which it aroused among our enemies' had in fact prevented an outbreak of sectarian violence 'which … would have ended in tragic disaster and would have made the "submerged third" the victims of a new and bigger "Orange Terror"'.[49] As a result of this rather strained logic McCall confidently concluded that the anti-partition campaign had played a fundamental role in forcing unionists to abandon their 'arrogant intolerance' and to become 'more circumspect'.[50] However, the political ramifications of this circumspection were nowhere spelt out. Inevitably the leadership of the IAPL were not credited as having made any contribution to this 'improved situation'; all that could be said, he wrote, was that the Unionist government's 'contemptuous' attitude towards them had become 'more good-humoured'.[51]

This last observation captures the essence of McCall's reports, for what they chronicle are the ineffectiveness, fragmentation and demise of the IAPL. The deterioration in its relations with the FOI, its reluctance to cooperate in joint projects with other anti-partitionists, and its internal jealousies and rivalries are all recorded in some detail.[52] Leading figures within the IAPL were now pursuing a number of very different political paths, which were neither complementary nor coordinated, and none of which showed any prospect of success. McGleenan epitomised the trend towards a growing, though highly negative, abstentionism. In January 1951 he announced that he would travel to Dublin to demand his seat in the Dáil, and 'squat on the lawn of Leinster House' if it was refused.[53] On past history his hopes of success may have seemed forlorn, and his request was indeed to be rebuffed in March,[54] but nonetheless the continued espousal of the Mansion House Committee's strident anti-partitionism and the attendant tendency of southern politicians to resort to highly emotive language and gestures in their dealings with Northern Ireland[55] may well have given some sustenance to the belief that a resolute and steadfast refusal to attend Stormont would ultimately find favour in Dublin. In contrast Anthony Mulvey, in March 1951, announced his decision, with Geoffrey Bing's active encouragement,[56] to take up his seat at Westminster. Mulvey, clearly with a wary eye on his abstentionist critics, emphasised the reluctance of his decision, which, he claimed, had been taken in response to 'the persuasion of his supporters' thus leaving him 'obliged to yield to the pressure of the Nationalist electorate'.[57] His brief time spent at Westminster was, however, depressingly unproductive. Despite the continued support of what remained of the FOI, neither of the main political parties showed much inclination to engage in any meaningful way with the issue of nationalist grievances. In the final parliamentary session in the House of Commons attended by Mulvey a motion calling for an amendment of the Government of Ireland Act (1920), to ensure a greater equality of rights for Catholics, was withdrawn by its proposer (in a poorly attended debate) without a vote being taken.[58] Even the minor success of having the motion discussed at all was deemed 'a failure' in Irish diplomatic circles in London on the grounds that the debate was premised on an assumption that a reformed Northern Ireland could address nationalist grievances and not on an acknowledgement that partition was in itself the problem.[59] Meanwhile, the most experienced and effective parliamentarian on the nationalist side, Cahir Healy, remained absent from Westminster, unable to overcome abstentionist resistance within his constituency organisation. He had anyway fallen from favour with the FOI. His continued friendship with Sir Oswald Mosley, which dated from their internment together in Brixton Prison during the war, and his association with the post-war Mosleyite far-right organisation, the Union Movement,[60] undoubtedly soured relations with the left-wing Friends and made future cooperation between them unlikely. Bing confided in McCall that he thought Healy 'not worth bothering about – likely to do more harm than good'.[61]

There was yet a further development within the IAPL, one that advanced a modified constitutional political strategy that incorporated a campaign of obstruction and civil disobedience. Eddie McAteer had initially broached this idea in 1948 with the publication of his pamphlet, *Irish Action*. In this he proposed a somewhat frivolous range of activities (including 'acting stupid') which were designed to hinder the operation of officialdom.[62] He was careful, at this time, to stress that such actions represented 'a bloodless way' to protest Catholic grievances and was specific in his instruction that he wanted 'no un-necessary risks'.[63] Early the following year, expressing fears that the 'climax of constitutional activity had been reached' and that the anti-partition movement could be put back 'for many years', he again suggested a civil disobedience campaign. Ominously, however, he now acknowledged the possibility of serious consequences that could result from such a campaign; he talked of 'counter-measures' that could be taken against northern nationalists and he made it abundantly clear that he envisaged that these might take the form of 'burnings and pogroms'.[64] The question of 'risks' had taken on a new dimension and new significance but nonetheless a strategy of civil disobedience remained, for McAteer, a possible avenue to explore and Dublin noted that he was still 'toying with the idea' in 1951.[65]

The collapse of the Coalition government in the Republic and resultant general election of May 1951, which saw the return of de Valera at the head of a Fianna Fáil government, brought little amelioration to the problems faced by constitutional nationalists in the North. What was to be in effect his policy of inaction on the North was dispassionately defended by de Valera during a Dáil debate on 19 July. It was, he held, 'the people in the North' themselves who constituted the main impediment to a successful national anti-partition policy; they were at 'sixes and sevens themselves regarding what policy they should pursue', allowing them entry to the Dáil would merely reproduce these antagonisms and disagreements in a different arena. He thought that northern nationalists should strive to overcome their differences, they should put together a 'body representative of the attitude of those who are against the partition' and from that appoint a 'small executive group' with whom his government could meet and consult. But even here de Valera added the deflating comment that he did not hold out 'any great hopes of what would be secured by it'.[66] This pronouncement was, the leader of the *Frontier Sentinel* declared, a 'bitter disclosure'.[67] In an angry and intemperate response the editorial chose to focus on one particular item of de Valera's Dáil speech; his declaration that 'force' as a means to resolve partition should not be contemplated. It questioned whether on this matter de Valera was 'correct in his assumption that he speaks for the nation' and pointed out that as northern nationalists had not been consulted 'it cannot be regarded as settled national policy'. It also reminded de Valera that he had himself 'once used force against the British with far less prospect of success than now appears in relation to Partition'. A solution brought about by force was, it recognised, 'inexpedient or even impossible at present', but nevertheless the categorical rejection of force under any circumstances was 'not to be thought of'.[68] Coming from a source that had been resolute in its loyal support of de Valera and Fianna Fáil since the 1920s this was a disquieting development to arise out of nearly four years of the Mansion House Committee's anti-partition propaganda efforts. It was also an indication of changes taking place within Northern Ireland itself where militant forces were preparing to challenge a fragmented and directionless constitutional movement. In anticipation of just such a development Father Maguire had counselled de Valera that if he failed to take up the reins of a nationally coordinated and purposive anti-partition campaign then, 'there will be reasons advanced for re-organisation of the IRA'. He too was critical of de Valera's renunciation of force, fearing that the withdrawal of its threat removed a possible bargaining counter against the 'Orangemen'. Maguire was not an advocate of force, 'None of us want another bloody Easter Day', he wrote, but he believed that the onus lay with de Valera to prevent violence re-emerging in the North and impressed upon him the full import of his responsibilities: 'remember, it depends on *you*.'[69] However, as John Bowman has suggested, de Valera drew the opposite conclusion to that hoped for by Maguire. De Valera believed, probably quite correctly, that his greater involvement in anti-partitionism would actually encourage extremism in the North rather than prevent it.[70]

Against this background the retiring IAPL Chairman, James McSparran, at the party's Annual Convention held in Armagh on 29 March 1953, delivered a positive and assured report on a year 'in which definite strides forward had been taken towards the achievement of Irish unity'.[71] He was, he declared, 'confident' that a solution to partition 'would be brought about in the course of a few years'.[72] However, McSparran's confidence masked a much grimmer reality. In actuality the IAPL was approaching a state of organisational morbidity. This was revealed in an exchange of letters between Cahir Healy and Patrick McGill, the IAPL General Secretary, in February 1953. Responding to suggestions made by McGill to keep members 'active and interested' Healy had replied that many League branches existed only 'upon paper', that they met infrequently and that communication between the leadership and the branches was virtually non-existent.[73] Another part of McSparran's address to the convention, however, came much closer to the truth. Turning his attention to 'twenty-six county politicians' he ventured that 'many politicians' in all of the political parties operating in the Republic, 'wanted to keep the question of Partition ... on the long finger'.[74] This was undoubtedly an accurate assessment. Since his return to power de Valera had shown little enthusiasm for continuing the activities of the Mansion House Committee; indeed Sean MacBride had in February communicated to Healy his belief that de Valera would 'wind it up soon'.[75] Cross-border relations with Dublin were at best tenuous.

The difficulties in maintaining a meaningful working relationship were evident in March 1953 when Conor Cruise O'Brien, who retained his position as Head of Information under the new Fianna Fáil administration,[76] visited the North to review the distribution of a pamphlet produced by his Information Section (*Ireland's Right to Unity*, specifically designed to be read by 'Unionist families') and to explore the possibility of producing a film documentary on anti-Catholic discrimination practices in the allocation of housing by certain Unionist-controlled local authorities.[77] O'Brien's report of the visit reveals the IAPL as an organisation lacking cohesion or an agreed sense of purpose and direction. At a meeting with the Executive of the IAPL O'Brien found that no progress had been made on the pamphlet's distribution. The task had been left to 'individual members' who had been given 'responsibility for distribution in their areas', but they had not made any attempt to fulfil the task. It was not just operational inefficiency that accounted for this failure; there was also a strong scepticism as to the worth of the Mansion House Committee's propaganda efforts. One member of the Executive from Fermanagh opined that 'no pamphlet would ever convince an Ulster Unionist' and 'questioned the wisdom of the whole project'. O'Brien believed that this was a view shared by other Executive members.[78] Through his discussions with Michael O'Neill MP (who had replaced Anthony Mulvey as the representative for Mid Ulster at the 1951 Westminster general election)[79]. O'Brien was also made aware of the general level of dissatisfaction with McSparran's chairmanship of the League.

While it was widely believed that McSparran held the position reluctantly, and retained it only because of the lack of agreement as to his successor, his continued absence from Executive meetings had led to a growing resentment over what O'Neill referred to as McSparran's 'absentee leadership'.[80] But it was not just disquiet over IAPL leadership issues that concerned its Executive members for O'Neill also revealed to O'Brien details of the continuing tussle within the IAPL over the future direction of its political strategy. By this time both O'Neill and Healy were attending Westminster[81] having arrived at a compromise with their constituency conventions that they would take their seats in Westminster only if they were refused seats in the Dáil.[82] At Westminster O'Neill's stance was remorselessly anti-partitionist and negative in the extreme; he attacked all British economic subsidies to Northern Ireland on the grounds that they propped up Stormont, regardless of the economic and social consequences that their withdrawal would have on his constituents: nationalists, he thought, 'would bear the necessary sacrifices willingly'.[83] However, despite his unflinching fealty to nationalist orthodoxy, O'Neill confided to O'Brien that in IAPL circles it was 'widely held that he and Mr Healy were "doing no good"'.[84] A meeting between O'Brien and Eddie McAteer in Derry confirmed this judgement. McAteer thought O'Neill and Healy 'too respectable' and was disparaging of them for not using the Westminster stage to carry out 'stunts' highlighting the anti-partitionist case.[85] McAteer's growing preference for extra-parliamentary activities was not without its risks, as he had himself earlier recognised, and which an IAPL St Patrick's Day rally in the city the previous March had demonstrated. The rally had descended into a violent clash between demonstrators and the RUC resulting in the worst violence the city had experienced since the 1920s.[86] O'Brien described a tinderbox situation in Derry; he found that post-war welfarism had done little to improve the position of Catholics and considered the city to be 'more explosive than it had been for many years'.[87] Despite this McAteer favoured a further staging of the St Patrick's demonstration in March 1953, even though he admitted to O'Brien that it would 'almost certainly have led to bloodshed'.[88] It was, O'Brien reported, opposition from the Bishop of Derry, Dr Niall Farren, which had been decisive in the cancellation of the demonstration and which had prevented any further deterioration of an increasingly volatile atmosphere. Dr O'Brien noted Dr Farren's disapproval of McAteer's confrontational anti-partition 'stunts' and the Bishop's own preference for focusing on 'the economic advancement of the Catholic community'.[89]

The Stormont election of September 1953 further added to the difficulties faced by the IAPL. In Foyle and Mid Londonderry the IAPL candidate and an Independent Nationalist non-abstentionist (Eddie McAteer and Paddy

Gormley[90] respectively) held their seats in the face of challenges from anti-partitionist abstentionist candidates.[91] However, in Mid Tyrone Liam Kelly, standing as an Anti-Partitionist, defeated the sitting IAPL candidate Edward McCullagh.[92] Kelly, a staunch physical force republican, had parted company with the IRA in 1951 (a result of his impatience over their lack of military activity) to form his own Tyrone-based armed group Saor Uladh.[93] In the run-up to the election he made it abundantly clear that he had absolutely no faith in constitutional methods: 'I believe in the use of force; the more the better, the sooner the better.'[94] Kelly's readiness to publicly broadcast such inflammatory and provocative views inevitably, and no doubt deliberately, set him on a path of confrontation with the authorities in Northern Ireland. His subsequent prosecution in December, leading to a twelve-month term of imprisonment and instant notoriety, merely served to elevate Kelly to the role of republican martyr and allowed him the opportunity to seize the public eye from the IAPL by announcing the formation of a new republican political party: Fianna Uladh.[95] The setback of Kelly's election was to be further compounded by Sean MacBride's endorsement of Fianna Uladh and his nomination of Kelly (while he was still imprisoned) for a seat in the Irish Seanad, a seat to which Kelly was duly elected in 1954.[96] The enthusiasm with which MacBride and his Clann na Poblachta colleagues had embraced Kelly, and other abstentionist candidates, in the 1953 Stormont election stood in marked contrast with the reluctance of politicians from the main southern parties to demonstrate a similar solidarity with the IAPL; a fact not lost on an increasingly embittered Cahir Healy who gave vent to his frustrations in a letter to the Cavan-based Irish Senator, Patrick Baxter, who had declined an invitation to support the IAPL in Mid Derry. The tone of exasperation is unmistakeable in Healy's curt reference to the short-term and instrumentalist attitude of the southern political parties 'who use Partition as a sort of big stick to use upon each other'.[97] In yet a further blow to the IAPL its sister organisation in the South, the Anti-Partition Association (which attracted a more robustly republican element to its ranks),[98] took the opportunity presented by the emergence of Kelly's Fianna Uladh to distance itself from the IAPL.[99] In a prolonged correspondence with senior figures in the Association, Healy, who had attacked abstentionists as 'a disgruntled minority' who 'could criticise when they could not produce the remedy',[100] railed against the 'extremists' who were intent on 'pulling down' the IAPL[101] and categorically rejected an attempted rapprochement from Patrick O'Reilly, the Association's Chairman, with the wounded retort, 'Do you think we enjoy being spat upon?'[102]

In Belfast, where the IAPL were unable to field any candidates in the 1953 Stormont general election, the successful return of two labour nationalists (in Belfast Central and Falls) was achieved in the face of continued anti-partitionist political fracturing which resulted in four labour nationalist groups challenging each other in the constituencies: the Irish Labour Party (Beattie, Macgougan); Independent Labour (Frank Hanna), Republican Labour (Harry Diamond) and Independent Irish Labour (Tim O'Sullivan). Macgougan's IrLP now attempted to distinguish itself from its rivals by emphasising its non-sectarianism, but its performance was dismal. In Belfast Central, Hanna, whose election leaflet brazenly proclaimed 'Mr Frank Hanna … is a zealous Catholic, and champion of social justice along the lines adumbrated in Social Encyclicals',[103] topped the poll while Beattie came last of four candidates. In the Falls constituency the picture was repeated; Harry Diamond topped the poll and Macgougan came in third behind the Independent Irish Labour candidate O'Sullivan. Diamond had previously made known his view that 'In my opinion there [is] no room for any but Catholics in the National movement.'[104] Macgougan's heroic vision of an all-Ireland non-sectarian socialism had fallen prey to the endemic ethnic rivalries of Belfast politics. In a letter sent after the election a party colleague of Macgougan, Tom Kelly, the chairman of the IrLP's Newry Branch, succinctly, if acerbically, captured the truth of the situation: 'The position in Belfast' he wrote 'seems to be gone to Hell altogether'.[105]

While Belfast's nationalist politics settled into a sectarian equilibrium, the IAPL grew increasingly concerned by challenges within its own heartlands. It was in this context, and following the return in May 1954 of a new Coalition government in the Republic which was dependent upon (but did not include) Clann na Poblachta, that Cahir Healy, called upon the Taoiseach, J.A. Costello, to throw a lifeline to IAPL elected representatives by allowing them access to the Dáil or Seanad. Healy pointed out that the situation was now radically changed by Kelly's election to the Seanad (which Costello, anxious to retain the support of MacBride, had supported). If Costello failed to conciliate the reasonable requests of constitutional nationalists, Healy warned, then 'it may well be assumed in the North that the physical force policy is the only one which meets with approval down here'.[106] The issue of seats in Dublin for northern nationalist representatives was now presented not as an end in itself but as the only means to prevent the IAPL from being electorally damaged by an abstentionist republican challenge. This challenge, it was alleged, could only result in winnable Nationalist seats being lost to Unionists which could result in a fatally damaging increase in apathy among the nationalist electorate.[107] For his part Costello had already set out his position on the 'right of audience' during a Dáil debate in October; he was decidedly against it, believing that there was no guarantee that this concession would secure the position of constitutional nationalists in the North against the republicans. Costello's preference was for the establishment of a Unity Council, representative of nationalist opinion in the North, which would work in close liaison with the Dáil;[108] a policy which Seamus McCall had so little success in implementing in 1950. In the light of this judgement, and the subsequent rejection of Eddie McAteer's request for a 'courtesy audience' with the Taoiseach to petition for the repeal of his decision,[109] the IAPL hoped that Costello's criticisms of Sinn Féin, Fianna Uladh and other sundry abstentionists – voiced in his Dáil speech – would at least translate into a policy of preference for them when it came to the composition of the Unity Council. It was in with this hope that Patrick McGill, Secretary of the IAPL, wrote to Costello asking for clarification of the membership of the proposed Unity Council.[110] When consulted by the Department of the Taoiseach on this matter, Conor Cruise O'Brien suggested that the Taoiseach's reply should 'be such as to strengthen the hands of those who desire to exclude Sinn Féin and to weaken those – numerous enough within the League – who give covert encouragement to "the Armagh-Omagh policy"'.[111] The latter reference was to the IRA raids on Gough Military Barracks, Armagh in June and Omagh Barracks in October 1954 and indicated O'Brien's awareness of the corrosive effects of IRA violence on the constitutional nationalist body politic.[112] O'Brien's advice, contained in a memorandum to Maurice Moynihan, Secretary to the Department of the Taoiseach, was that Costello should give heart to the IAPL's constitutional non-abstentionists by stating that only elected parliamentary representatives to Stormont or Westminster would be eligible for membership of the Unity Council, thus ensuring that it would consist almost wholly of IAPL representatives. However, Costello chose not to take this advice and instead his reply to McGill referred to the desirability of contacts between the Irish government and 'nationalist opinion in the Six Counties', an altogether much more non-committal, and for the IAPL disheartening, choice of words.[113]

The announcement by Sinn Féin in January that they would contest all Northern Ireland seats in the next Westminster general election provided yet a further occasion for the IAPL to attempt to persuade the Irish government to firm up its support for them. A deputation made up of Eddie McAteer, Cahir Healy, Michael O'Neill, Joe Stewart and Patrick McGill met with Costello and the Minister of External Affairs, Liam Cosgrave, on 17 January 1955. On the following day they had a subsequent meeting with Conor Cruise O'Brien to discuss 'matters arising'.[114] Significantly this meeting revealed these senior IAPL figures to be overly concerned with matters peripheral to the much larger question of maintaining their dominant position in the face of an electoral challenge in the North; they were perturbed about the decrease in activity of the Anti-Partition League in Britain; they thought the Irish government should increase its anti-partition propaganda efforts abroad; and they were particularly concerned about the 'denationalising effects on … the younger generation of Nationalist families' of 'Ulster is British' propaganda which, they suspected, would pour forth from a newly opened television station in the North.[115] When eventually the conversation did turn to the forthcoming Westminster general election O'Brien was made acutely aware both of the deep pessimism within the IAPL and of a division of opinion over the most apposite electoral tactic to adopt. All members of the deputation were resigned to losing the IAPL held seats of Fermanagh and South Tyrone and Mid Ulster – but to Unionist candidates and not to Sinn Féin, for they were convinced that although Sinn Féin were in possession of considerable funds they were lacking in the necessary experience required for an electoral campaign and had little prospect of attracting the votes of moderate nationalists. The main concern of the deputation therefore centred on damage limitation to the IAPL. And here lay the division over electoral tactics which were outlined to O'Brien. Firstly, there were those who felt that the IAPL should not stand any candidates in the election at all. This position envisaged a scenario in which the Unionists would take both seats and Sinn Féin would be revealed as electorally and organisationally weak. By not standing, it was reasoned, the IAPL would avoid the accusation of splitting the nationalist vote and thus could not be held responsible for the loss of the seats. The outcome, it was assumed, would result in the Catholic electorate returning to its 'old allegiance' – i.e. the IAPL – at the next election. However, some of those who favoured this position also pointed to the potentially high political risks involved in allowing Sinn Féin to gain prestige from being the sole anti-partitionist party to fight the election, even if they did lose. Secondly, there were those who advocated putting candidates forward; but here there was a further consideration – if IAPL candidates did stand, should they run as abstentionists or non-abstentionists? Again, there was divided opinion on this issue. On the one hand it was thought an abstentionist candidate might attract some votes from Sinn Féin, however, on the other hand it was feared that an abstentionist candidate could act as a disincentive for some nationalists to come out to vote – thus votes would be lost on an abstentionist ticket. The delegation were at least united in making an appeal to the Irish government to publicly support IAPL candidates, in the event of them standing (and here Michael O'Neill pointedly mentioned the support Liam Kelly had received from some quarters in the Republic during the 1953 Stormont election); however, this was met with the usual rejoinder that the government was anxious not to be seen 'taking sides' in the 'internal divisions between Nationalists in the Six Counties'.[116] The Irish government's reticence and air of detachment, coupled with the deputation's tortuous logic, indecision and lack of unity did not augur well for IAPL prospects in the face of any future challenge from Sinn Féin.

Indeed, at the IAPL Annual Convention, held in Belfast on 30 March 1955, there was little sign of enthusiasm for the forthcoming Westminster contest. In his presidential address James McSparran rejected the tactic of physical force (whose advocates, he noted, were being encountered at 'every meeting and convention') on the grounds of practicability: 'I don't believe physical force is a policy that would produce results at the present time.'[117] Avoiding any direct reference to Sinn Féin, the general tenor of his speech communicated a palpable sense of inertia – 'people must be patient'; 'the organisation was doing nothing spectacular'[118] – an impression compounded by the annual report of the general al secretary, Patrick McGill, which made no reference to any single recent local or national political, economic or social initiative of significance. It was left to Eddie McAteer to broach the thorny issue of the election. In his speech to the Convention McAteer suggested that the nationalist electoral conventions for Fermanagh and South Tyrone and Mid Ulster should support contesting the seats currently held by the IAPL, 'even if it meant … the loss of the constituencies to Unionists'; but the apparent vigour of these comments was then moderated by his assertion that the IAPL (which he himself referred to as 'a loosely organised controlling organisation') would make no effort to persuade or influence the decisions of the local constituency bodies.[119] McAteer's caution was undoubtedly dictated by the necessity of avoiding further dissension and division within an increasingly fissiparous IAPL; but the passionate rhetoric so characteristic of the IAPL and its predecessors, with its promise of major initiatives and imminent Irish unity, was now markedly absent from the convention platform and McAteer said little that could inspire a concerted effort to fight the election with confidence. McAteer's own assessment of future political prospects was indeed remarkably sober, he announced that the IAPL 'had no master plan to solve partition' and that the 'problem of Irish independence which existed for centuries, was unlikely to be solved in a handful of years'.[120] This realistic perspective, very likely influenced by his recent contacts with the Irish government,[121] was refreshingly candid; however, in the absence of some strategic overview for the future direction of constitutional nationalist politics, it was also disarmingly negative.

Notes

1 *Irish Times*, 31 October 1949.
2 NAI, DFA 305/14/12, Report on McSparran's speech at Glasgow, 16 November 1949.
3 NAI, DFA 305/14/38, Interim report from the North, 15 February 1950.
4 *Ibid.*

5 *Ibid.*

6 Steele was Sinn Féin's only candidate in the 1950 election.

7 NAI, DFA 305/14/38, Interim report from the North, 15 February 1950.

8 Elected to the new constituencies of Fermanagh and South Tyrone and Mid Ulster respectively.

9 *Irish Times*, 24 March 1950. See also B. Lynn, *Holding the Ground: The Nationalist Party in Northern Ireland, 1945–72* (Aldershot, Ashgate, 1997), pp. 91–93.

10 PRONI, D1050/17/38 Macgougan to Frank Aiken, 6 March 1950.

11 *Ibid.*

12 PRONI, D1050/17/44, Jack Macgougan papers, Conlon to Macgougan, 7 March 1950.

13 *Frontier Sentinel*, 1 April 1950.

14 PRONI, D1050/17/44 , Jack Macgougan papers, Minutes of meeting between the IrLP and IAPL, Belfast, 5 June 1950.

15 NAI, DFA 305/14/65, Report from the North, 10 June 1950.

16 *Ibid.*

17 *Ibid.*

18 *Frontier Sentinel*, 8 February 1950.

19 *Ibid.*

20 *Irish Times*, 13 May 1950.

21 *Irish Times*, 1 August 1950; see also *Frontier Sentinel*, 5 August 1950.

22 PRONI, D2991/B/145, Cahir Healy papers, Healy to Maguire, 5 November 1950. See also Lynn, *Holding the Ground*, p. 96. Healy continued to point out the downside of Dáil representation for northern Nationalists. See reportage of his comments at the Fermanagh Nationalist Convention in 1952, *Irish Press*, 13 November 1952.

23 *Irish News*, 7 August 1950, cited in E. Staunton, *The Nationalists of Northern Ireland 1918–1973* (Dublin, Columba Press, 2001), p. 167.

24 On 22 June 1949.

25 PRONI, D3137/7, Denis Ireland papers, Ireland to the Secretary, Clann Na Poblachta, 21 February 1950.

26 PRONI, D3137/7, Denis Ireland papers, Ireland to Sean MacBride, 6 March 1950.

27 PRONI, D1050/17/42, Jack Macgougan papers, Macgougan election speech delivered during 1950 South Down election campaign.

28 *Irish Times*, 2 September 1950.

29 PRONI, D1050/17/126, Jack Macgougan papers, Minutes of meeting of IrLP Resident Committee, 16 June 1950.

30 The draft constitution of the Unity Council, which affirmed its 'devotion to the spiritual and moral values which constitute the virtues of religious and political liberty and the rule of law', made little concession to Macgougan's secular nationalism. PRONI, D1050/17/44 Unity Conference Report, 1 October 1950.

31 See NAI, DFA 305/14/65, Report from the North, 9 November 1950.

32 NAI, DFA 305/14/65, Report from the North, 4 December 1950.

33 See Chapter 1, n. 40.

34 NAI, DFA 305/14/65, Report from the North, 4 December 1950.

35 *Ibid.*

36 NAI, DFA 305/14/65, Report from the North, 10 December 1950.

37 *Ibid.*

38 The Nationalists in question were McAteer and McCarroll, both of whom, O'Brien wrote, 'are decent men and do not belong to the Molly Maquire section of the League. McAteer is, perhaps not very bright but is respected for his sincerity; McCarroll is quite a good journalist – very Fianna Fail in outlook but with an open mind in some things.' NAI, DFA 305/14/164, O'Brien to Devlin, 11 November 1950. The Embassy's account of the visit echoed similar sentiments to O'Brien's. McAteer and McCarroll, whose visit coincided with that of a party of forty Irish pilgrims, were said to have remained aloof and to have lacked 'the easy cheerfulness of the other pilgrims'. The latter group apparently thought 'the Derry fellows were a bit too full of themselves'. *Ibid.*, J.P. Walshe to O'Brien, 21 November 1950.

39 See the discussion of this in Henry Patterson, 'Party versus Order: Ulster Unionism and the Flags and Emblems Act', *Contemporary British History* 13: 4 (Winter 1999), pp. 105–129.

40 NAI, DFA 305/14/65 Report from the North, 10 December 1950.

41 *Frontier Sentinel*, 5 August 1950.

42 H. Patterson, *Ireland Since 1939: The Persistence of Conflict* (Dublin, Penguin Ireland, 2006), pp. 100–101.

43 See D. Ó Corráin, '"Ireland in his Heart North and South": The Contribution of Ernest Blythe to the Partition Question', *Irish Historical Studies* XXXV: 137 (May 2006), p. 66.

44 *Northern Whig*, 30 October 1950. O'Brien commented on the *Whig* article, 'I'm afraid Blythe's 'tributes' to the 6-Co Govt. will be used against us repeatedly'. See NAI, DFA 305/14/62.

45 *Ulster Herald*, 11 November 1950.

46 *Frontier Sentinel*, 4 November 1950. The editorial leader concluded 'Great will be the rejoicing in Lisburn at the return to the Orange orchard of the grower who once went a-foraging in the Republican desert.'

47 NAI, DFA 305/14/65, Report from the North, April 1951.

48 In Philadelphia, for example, de Valera decreed 'The struggle is not over … The British are still occupying Six of our Counties … we are asking the people of America … to help us in that fight', cited in T.P. Coogan, *De Valera: Long Fellow, Long Shadow* (London, Hutchinson, 1993), p. 639.

49 NAI, DFA 305/14/65 Report from the North, April 1951.

50 *Ibid.*

51 *Ibid.*

52 *Ibid.* also Report from the North, 24 January 1951; Report from the North, 21 March 1951.

53 *Sunday Express*, 21 January 1951.

54 Lynn, *Holding the Ground*, p. 100.

55 For example, the address delivered by Frank Aiken TD, at the unveiling of a memorial to members of the IRA's 4th northern Division, held at Mullaghbawn, South Armagh at Easter, in which he expounded on 'the mountains and fields of Ulster, reddened for seven centuries with the blood of an unconquerable people' could more easily be

taken as an encouragement for McGleenan's radical abstentionism than for a policy of cooperation and conciliation with the northern state. See the *Frontier Sentinel*, 31 March 1951. There was a certain irony in Aitken's remarks. The IRA's 4th Northern Division, of which he had been commanding officer in the early 1920s, had a particularly fearsome reputation, its members being responsible for the brutal massacre of six Protestant civilians at Altnaveigh near Newry in June 1922. See P. Bew, *Ireland: The Politics of Enmity 1789–2006* (Oxford, Oxford University Press), p. 436. However, at the time of his Mullaghbawn oration Conor Cruise O'Brien regarded Aiken to be far removed from his earlier republican radicalism. O'Brien describes Aiken in this period as 'a very serious and thoughtful man, profoundly ecumenical by disposition, bordering on pacifism, and always aware … of the explosive potential of sectarian political relations in northern Ireland'. This makes Aiken's Mullaghbawn speech doubly ironic. See Conor Cruise O'Brien, *Memoir*, pp. 163, 165.

56 NAI, DFA 305/14/65, Report from the North, 24 January 1951.
57 *Frontier Sentinel*, 3 March 1951.
58 *Frontier Sentinel*, 9 June 1951 see also Lynn, *Holding the Ground*, p. 102.
59 For details of the report on the debate sent by the Irish Ambassador in London see E. Staunton, *The Nationalists*, p. 177.
60 See C. Norton, 'The Internment of Cahir Healy M.P., Brixton Prison, July 1941– December 1942', *Twentieth Century British History* 18: 2 (2007), pp. 191–192.
61 NAI, DFA 305/14/65, Report from the North, 24 January 1951.
62 B. Purdie, *Politics in the Streets: The Origins of the Civil Rights Movement in Northern Ireland* (Belfast, Blackstaff Press, 1990), p. 41.
63 M. McAteer, *Irish Action: New Thoughts on an Old Subject* (Ballyshannon, Donegal Democrat, October 1948), reprint (Belfast, Athol Books, 1979), p. 52.
64 *Irish Times*, 10 January 1949.
65 NAI, DFA 305/14/65, Report from the North, 21 March 1951.
66 Dáil Éireann, Volume 126, 19 July 1951.
67 *Frontier Sentinel*, 28 July 1951. Made all the more bitter by defeat of a motion (by 82 votes to 42) calling for northern parliamentary representatives to be allowed entry to the Dáil, proposed by Sean MacBride.
68 *Frontier Sentinel*, 28 July 1951.
69 PRONI, D2991/B/144/50, Cahir Healy papers, Maguire to de Valera, 27 July 1951.
70 Bowman, *De Valera*, p. 282.
71 *Frontier Sentinel*, 9 May 1953.
72 *Ibid.*
73 PRONI, D2991/B/24, Cahir Healy papers, Healy to McGill, 9 February 1953, cited in Lynn, *Holding the Ground*, p. 108.
74 *Frontier Sentinel*, 9 May 1953.
75 See Lynn, *Holding the Ground*, also Bowman, *De Valera*, p. 282.
76 O'Brien, *Memoir*, p. 162.
77 The town of Fintona was raised as such an example. See NIA, DFA 305/14/2/3, Report by C.C. O'Brien on visit to North, 23–25 March 1953. For details of the idea to produce the film documentary see also O'Brien, *Memoir*, p. 162.

78 NAI, DFA 305/14/2/3, Report by C.C. O'Brien on visit to North, 23–25 March 1953.

79 Mulvey had stood down citing his poor health as the reason for ending his political career; he was sixty-seven years old in 1951 and died in 1957 at the age of seventy-four. Healy was returned as MP for Fermanagh and South Tyrone at the election.

80 At the IAPL convention in March 1953 McSparran was elected to the new and titular position of President. McAteer became the chairman while Cahir Healy, Joe Connellan, Charles McGlennan and Joe Stewart were elected as vice-chairmen. *Frontier Sentinel*, 9 May 1953.

81 O'Neill having made his maiden speech in February 1952.

82 See PRONI, D2991/B/51/1, Cahir Healy papers, Healy to J.A. Costello, July 1954 for details of this arrangement.

83 PRONI, D2991/B/30/4, Cahir Healy papers, M. O'Neill to C. Healy, 22 March 1953. O'Neill was also unwilling to work on behalf of significant farming interests such as the Ulster Farmers Union, which he saw as a Unionist front organisation.

84 NAI, DFA 305/14/2/3, Report by C.C. O'Brien on visit to North, 23–25 March 1953.

85 *Ibid.*

86 M. Farrell, *Northern Ireland: The Orange State* (London, Pluto Press, 1978), p. 203.

87 NAI, DFA 305/14/2/3 Report by C.C. O'Brien on visit to North, 23–25 March 1953.

88 *Ibid.*

89 *Ibid.*

90 Gormley later claimed that his candidacy resulted from local dissatisfaction with the 'worthless and discredited' IAPL organisation in the constituency. He was, however, supported in his election campaign by Healy, Lennon and other senior IAPL figures. See Lynn, *Holding the Ground*, pp. 110–111.

91 McAteer was challenged by Patrick Maxwell who had held the seat since 1937 but whose candidature was overturned by the local constituency association who opposed his abstentionism. Gormley had a narrow victory (584 votes) over his republican rival T.B. Agnew. The other successfully returned candidates were, James McSparran (Mourne), Joe Connellan (South Down), Charles McGleenan (South Armagh), Cahir Healy (Fermanagh South), Patrick Stewart (East Tyrone) and Roderick O'Connor (West Tyrone). The latter four were elected unopposed although Stewart only secured the nomination for his constituency, against an abstentionist, on the toss of a coin. Dr Eileen Hickey was again elected as an Independent candidate for Queen's University.

92 Kelly's victory with 4,178 votes (55.3 per cent) to McCullagh's 3,376 (44.7 per cent) was achieved in a campaign in which McCullagh refused to hold any public meetings, in the expressed hope of preventing 'discord'. In complete contrast Kelly campaigned vigorously. See Lynn, *Holding the Ground*, p. 111, 258.

93 R. English, *Armed Struggle: A History of the IRA* (London, Macmillan, 2003), p. 72.

94 Cited in Farrell, *The Orange State*, p. 205.

95 *Ibid.*, p. 206.

96 See J. Maguire, 'Internment, the IRA and the Lawless Case in Ireland: 1957–61', *Journal of the Oxford University History Society*, Michaelmas 2004, pp. 2–3. It has been

claimed that MacBride wrote the address that Kelly delivered from the dock during his trial. See *Saoirse-Irish Freedom*, December 2003, www.iol.ie/~saoirse/2003/dec03.pdf, p. 14.

97 PRONI, D2991/B/65/4, Cahir Healy papers, Healy to Baxter, 20 October 1953.

98 J. Bowyer Bell, *The Secret Army: The IRA 1916–1979* (Dublin, Academic Press, 1983), p. 249.

99 See PRONI, D2991/B/49/13, Cahir Healy papers, Chairman's Address, Anti-Partition Association Ard Fheis, 1953.

100 Healy had made these comments at the Ancient Order of Hibernians St Patrick's Day celebration at Donaghmore, Co. Tyrone on 17 March. See *Irish Times*, 18 March 1954.

101 PRONI, D2991/B/49/21, Cahir Healy papers, Healy to Maura Comerford, 25 March 1954.

102 PRONI, D2991/B/49/19, Cahir Healy papers, Healy to Patrick O'Reilly, 22 March 1954.

103 C. Norton, 'The Irish Labour Party in Northern Ireland, 1949–1958', *Saothar* 21 (1996), p. 53.

104 Quoted in G. Walker, *Intimate Strangers: Political and Cultural Interaction between Scotland and Ulster in Modern Times* (Edinburgh, John Donald Publishers, 1995), p. 141.

105 Norton 'The Irish Labour Party', p. 54.

106 PRONI, D2991/B/51/1, Cahir Healy papers, Healy to J. A. Costello, July 1954.

107 PRONI, D2991/B/51/3, Cahir Healy papers, Memo to J. A. Costello, 3 November 1954.

108 Dáil Éireann, Volume 147, 28 October 1954.

109 *Irish Times*, 15 October 1954.

110 NAI, DFA 305/14/29/2, P McGill to J. A. Costello, 18 November 1954.

111 NAI, DFA 305/14/29/2, C.C. O'Brien to Maurice Moynihan, 23 November 1954.

112 An immediate consequence of the Gough Barracks raid was the restoration by the Stormont government of special security powers to the RUC, a measure which those members of the IAPL wholly opposed to IRA violence, such as Joseph Stewart, were inevitably compelled to condemn. See *Irish Times*, 18 June 1954.

113 NAI, DFA 305/14/29/2, J.A. Costello to P. McGill, 23 November 1954. O'Brien was informed by Maurice Moynihan, Secretary to the Department of the Taoiseach, that Costello felt 'it would be better not to appear in any way to dictate the choice of representation on the Council'. This is contained in a hand-written comment on the following correspondence NAI, DFA 305/14/29/2, M. Moynihan to C. C. O'Brien, 23 November 1954.

114 McAteer did not attend this second meeting.

115 NAI, DFA 305/14/281, Memorandum of meeting between C.C. O'Brien and a deputation from the North, 18 January 1955. Among the suggestions made by the deputation was that the Irish government 'give consideration' to building a television station 'at a point which could reach at least the border areas in the Six Counties'. Ironically, Unionists detected an anti-government bias in the BBC's policy of

providing broadcasting opportunities to an array of viewpoints. See Patterson, *Ireland Since 1939*, p. 182.

116 NAI, DFA 305/14/281, Memorandum. O'Brien did intimate that if a northern-based 'Unity Council' could put forward agreed candidates then it 'might be possible' for the leaders of the parliamentary parties in the Republic to endorse these candidates. However, as O'Brien was careful to point out, this was a 'very ticklish matter' and he did not speak with the authority of the Taoiseach on this matter. In fact, as far as IAPL attempts to establish an anti-partitionist Unity Council were concerned, the whole notion remained as nebulous as ever. O'Brien favoured the idea of establishing a 'Unity Committee' or 'Partition Brains Trust' to advise the government on cross-border matters. He envisaged that such a body would draw its membership from intellectuals, businessmen, industrialists, lawyers, journalists, etc. throughout Ireland. He did not see any place on such a body for northern political representatives: ' … it would interfere with the coolness and detachment which are necessary to the effective working of an advisory body'. However, even this idea proved too proactive for the government and never saw the light of day. See NAI, DFA 305/14/280, hand-written note from C.C. O'Brien to Dr Kiernan, 24 March 1955 and C.C. O'Brien to Mr Horan, 31 December 1959.

117 *Frontier Sentinel*, 9 April 1955. There was a human cost to the physical force tactic that McGill did not touch upon in his address. Some two weeks earlier, on the evening of the 5 March, the B Specials had been mobilised alongside the RUC in response to intelligence received of a planned IRA raid on Omagh military barracks. The 50-strong IRA unit which was to carry out the raid withdrew in the face of the unexpectedly high security activity, but during the night the B Specials opened fire on a van killing 18-year-old Arthur Leonard and seriously wounding his companion 16-year-old Clare Mallon. Both young people were innocent victims of what appears to have been an edgy B Special unit anticipating an IRA attack. See Bowyer Bell, *The IRA*, pp. 267–268.

118 *Frontier Sentinel*, 9 April 1955.

119 *Irish Times*, 31 March 1955.

120 *Ibid*.

121 *Ibid*. McAteer spoke cautiously of 'happy improvements in the working relationship between the Irish Government and the League' with which they were 'reasonably satisfied' and 'moderately confident' of progress in an intensified 'anti-partition drive'. However, on these improvements he 'could not give details'.

6

The Sinn Féin challenge and the birth of the Nationalist Party, 1955–59

When it came to competition for the anti-partitionist vote the political initiative now passed to Sinn Féin which was considerably advantaged by the IAPL's disunity and organisational fragility.[1] Announcing its intention to contest all twelve Westminster constituencies in Northern Ireland at the forthcoming general election in May 1955,[2] Sinn Féin's boldness and militancy was publicly demonstrated by the nomination of eight IRA prisoners as candidates. All the nominees were serving custodial sentences in prisons either in Northern Ireland or England. The proposed candidates for the two nationalist-held seats of Mid Ulster and Fermanagh and South Tyrone (respectively Tom Mitchell and Phil Clarke) were both young Dublin men[3] serving lengthy sentences in Crumlin Road Prison, Belfast, arising from their involvement in the IRA raid on Omagh barracks in October 1954.[4] Sinn Féin now presented itself as the only party able to give northern Catholics the opportunity of unambiguously voicing their anti-partitionism and opposition to 'Britain's unjust claim to a right to rule over Irish territory', and on this rather flimsy basis it appealed directly to the constituency conventions ('With all the sincerity at its command') not to 'split the vote'.[5] The tactic was successful. In early May the Nationalist convention[6] in Fermanagh and South Tyrone, elected the Sinn Féin candidate, Phil Clarke, as its chosen candidate.[7] At the convention Cahir Healy, having decided at the age of seventy-eight to retire from political life and not contest the seat, spoke vigorously in opposition to Sinn Féin's abstentionism and mounted an energetic attempt to promote his preferred IAPL candidate (Francis Traynor), but to no avail.[8] The decision of Healy's old associate, Father Thomas Maguire, to nominate Clarke was symptomatic of the IAPL's current malaise; although the elderly priest's action was possibly more a result of his receptiveness to political seduction and flattery rather than a renunciation of constitutionalism.[9] One week later, on 13 May, the Nationalist convention for the Mid Ulster constituency decided unanimously not to select a candidate, and, in so doing, left the field open to Sinn Féin's Tom Mitchell.[10]

It was only in West Belfast that Sinn Féin faced an anti-partitionist challenge. Here Jack Beattie was nominated as a candidate for the Irish Labour Party (IrLP), though not, it should be noted, with the support of all the Administrative Council members of the party in Dublin, some of whom favoured giving Sinn Féin a clear run.[11] By this time the IrLP Belfast branches were so badly organised and short of funds that Beattie's campaign was run without election posters, transport or personation agents.[12] And yet, despite these very real constraints, Beattie's rejection of abstentionism, his emphasis on defending 'the old-age pensioners, the sick, the children and the unemployed', and his portrayal of Sinn Féin as a party peddling an empty politics of gesture and symbolism ('Sinn Féin … seemed content to go on waving flags, while every day people left the country')[13] struck a chord with the local electorate. Beyond a vague commitment to 'organise and develop the resources of the nation for the benefit of its citizens irrespective of class or creed' Sinn Féin's election manifesto, in comparison, was notably reticent on social and economic issues[14] and some commentators noted the disparity between Sinn Féin's heady idealism and the immediate and tangible concerns of the 40,000 unemployed in Northern Ireland as a major weakness of the republican campaign.[15]

That Sinn Féin's overall electoral success was not assured is evidenced by its own early warning that the election outcome was not 'an end in itself' and that a poor showing would not 'in any way affect the determination of Republicans to forge ahead towards their objective … the right of Ireland to full and complete freedom';[16] an objective which they held 'must never be put in issue through referendum of a section of the population, *nor of the people of the country at large.*'[17] (Emphasis added.) However, republicans did play down their militarism during the election campaign; Catholic voters were not being asked to endorse the activities of the IRA.[18] Even so, the more exuberant outpourings of a group of young IRA militants based around the left-wing IRA man Joseph Christle[19] proved difficult to repress. In April Christle, and his associate Seamus Sorahan, while touring Co. Galway in a surprisingly open recruitment drive for the IRA, announced that 'in the foreseeable future the military move would be made against the border' and that 'the republican movement were going to tackle the border with guns in their hands'.[20] Sorahan returned to this theme at Sinn Féin's first open-air election meeting in Belfast on 15 May when he warned that if the campaign to end the border by constitutional means failed then the next recourse would be violence: 'it will inevitably and inexorably come to the use of the gun. There will be nothing for it but the use of physical force – the gun, the rifle and the hand-grenade – in an effort to take by force what was taken from us by force.'[21] Such expressions of unbridled militarism (exceptional though they were) may well have alienated moderate Catholic opinion and rebounded on Sinn Féin's electoral potential; however, the day after Sorahan had delivered his incendiary speech, a boon was to land in the lap of Sinn Féin in the shape of a statement issued by the Ulster Unionist Chief Whip, Colonel W.B. Topping. In this Topping announced that all convicted felons serving a prison term in excess of twelve months would be disqualified from taking their seats if elected, that all votes 'knowingly given to such a person' would be 'lost or thrown away', and that in such circumstances the seat would be awarded to the candidate with the next highest number of votes (which would result in Unionists taking the two Westminster seats normally held by Nationalists). Topping's statement was immediately seized upon by Sinn Féin as a deliberate attempt to 'frighten', 'bully' and ultimately disenfranchise nationalist voters.[22] The likely effect of Topping's intervention was to bring out the vote for Sinn Féin, especially in the closely fought constituencies of Mid Ulster and Fermanagh and South Tyrone; although it should be noted that in the days before the election there was evidence that nationalists in these constituencies saw their vote as being anti-Unionist rather than pro-Sinn Féin.[23]

The outcome of the election saw Unionists winning ten of the twelve Westminster seats, including Jack Beattie's seat in West Belfast (where Beattie came in second place comfortably outpolling Sinn Féin)[24], while Sinn Féin captured both Mid Ulster and Fermanagh and South Tyrone – though with much less support than their outgoing IAPL predecessors.[25] Overall Sinn Féin received a total of 152,310 votes. Michael Farrell, in his classic left-republican history of Northern Ireland, points out that this represented the biggest anti-partition vote since 1921 and an increase of almost 50,000 on the anti-partition vote recorded at the Stormont general election of 1949.[26] However, if compared to the previous Westminster election in 1951 the anti-partitionist vote in the three above constituencies actually fell from 98,988 to 84,763, a drop of 14,225 votes. In South Down the anti-partitionist vote fell from 26,976 in 1951[27] to 19,624, a drop of 7,352 votes. This pattern, a decline in nationalist voter turnout, was repeated in other constituencies previously contested by constitutional anti-partition candidates.[28] Cahir Healy was quick to point to these negatives of Sinn Féin's performance,[29] but there was little escaping the damage that had been done; the election was now over and Sinn Féin's success in taking Mid Ulster and Fermanagh and South Tyrone had both confounded IAPL predictions and revealed the folly of those who had favoured not contesting the seats. For their part, and despite their gains, Sinn Féin quickly reiterated its earlier position, i.e. that the outcome of the election would not deflect the party from pursuing 'the course it had set itself'.[30] At an election victory parade for Phil Clarke held in Dungannon on the evening of 4 June, the principal Sinn Féin speaker emphasised that republicans had not been won over wholesale to electoral politics; 'if war were necessary to free Ireland', he declared, 'they would not avoid it'.[31]

Sinn Féin's highly qualified success in the election had little impact on Dublin. Interestingly, the anti-partition policies of successive Irish governments had come in for some acerbic criticism from the Irish-American intellectual and Harvard University academic, John V. Kelleher, in an article ('Can Ireland Unite?') published in the *Atlantic Monthly* in April 1954. In this Kelleher admonished Irish governments for failing to acknowledge both the starkly contrasting material basis of the two states in Ireland, and, what he regarded as the obviously umbilical economic relationship between Northern Ireland and Britain. He was also dismissive of the notion that de Valera's 1937 Constitution, with its Catholic ethos and territorial claims, could provide the foundation for unification. Kelleher believed that failure to recognise these truths would condemn nationalist Ireland to a futile and destructive political cul-de-sac: 'The question is what time of day is it in the world? One sometimes gets the impression that de Valera and his fellow statesmen, pro and con, really accept time as another dimension and are studying how to move sideways in it, or on a slight backward bias, forever.'[32]

In fact, there was some rethinking on the question of North–South relations amongst the major parties in the Republic at this time and, since 1954, Fine Gael and Fianna Fáil had pursued a bipartisan policy towards the North that stressed 'cooperation' with the Stormont administration.[33] Reports sent back to Dublin from visits to the North by officials of the Department of External Affairs before the Westminster general election reconfirmed the Irish government's view that there was no alternative to its more conciliatory approach,[34] and the outcome of the election seemed only to reinforce cross-party bipartisanship. In a Dáil debate in July 1955 the Taoiseach John A. Costello and Eamon de Valera took the opportunity to roundly condemn violent attempts at resolving partition and they were at one in declaiming that future progress could only be advanced by greater economic and social cooperation between North and South.[35] The IAPL's position on this was mixed; they did not condone political violence but nor did they want to see Dublin abandon its former more aggressively critical stance towards the Stormont government. There were, however, definite limits to conciliation as Costello made clear in a Dáil statement in November in which he condemned republican violence while at the same time reaffirming his government's refusal to extradite to Northern Ireland any persons who had been engaged in 'armed political activities' in the 'Six Counties'.[36] Revisionist thinking was clearly not so advanced as to avoid Kelleher's warning of the pitfalls of a sideways move. Nor did it translate into a greater engagement with northern constitutionalists; indeed, the fact that the

Department of External Affairs was to conduct no further fact-finding visits to the North for the next five years[37] was very likely indicative of the Irish government's belief that as far as Northern policy was concerned the IAPL was best kept at arm's length.

In the North the travails of the IAPL were set to continue in the see-sawing of parliamentary by-elections which followed on from Unionist challenges to take Tom Mitchell's seat in Mid Ulster, on the grounds that his imprisonment as a convicted felon disqualified him from elective office (Phil Clarke having been unseated in June).[38] In the first of these by-elections, in August 1955, Mitchell re-contested the seat as the sole anti-partition candidate and in winning trebled his majority (to 806 votes).[39] However, following a further Unionist election petition Mitchell was again unseated and the seat awarded to his Unionist opponent Charles Beattie, who, as fate would have it, was in turn disqualified on a technical breach of parliamentary law.[40] A further by-election was scheduled for May 1956. On this occasion the local IAPL organisation took the decision to put forward Michael O'Neill as an anti-partitionist challenger to Sinn Féin.[41] When the Unionist Party declined to run a candidate on this occasion[42] it appeared that the contest would be a straight fight between O'Neill and Sinn Féin's re-nominated Tom Mitchell. However, the eleventh hour nomination of an unofficial Unionist candidate (George Forrest) made the possibility of a split nationalist vote, and a Unionist victory, appear a more likely outcome.[43] In this new scenario O'Neill attempted to focus his campaign on the contrast between the IAPL's loyalty to the Dáil and Sinn Féin's denial of its legitimacy: the election became 'a referendum of the people in support of the legitimate Irish Government'. By now O'Neill clearly felt that declarations of loyalty to Dublin had to be supplemented with a slightly more robust anti-partitionism, and this involved abandoning his pro-attendance policy at Westminster. O'Neill made it clear that if successful he would not regard his election as a mandate to take his seat.[44] This tactical manoeuvre notwithstanding, O'Neill's attempts to canvass the constituency were severely hampered by a campaign of disruption and physical assault perpetrated by Sinn Féin supporters; a campaign so intense that it led to the cancelation of all his eve-of-poll election meetings.[45]

The result of the second Mid Ulster by-election was a victory for the unofficial Unionist Forrest (28,605 votes) who took the seat on a split anti-partitionist vote – O'Neill coming in a very poor third place behind Mitchell (the votes received were Mitchell: 24,124; O'Neill: 6,421).[46] Shortly afterwards a downcast O'Neill visited the Department of External Affairs in Dublin where DEA officials found him in a recriminatory mood. Expressing regret that he had not backed out of the election when 'violent defeat was inevitable', O'Neill was strongly critical of the Irish government and the major southern political parties for failing to provide him with sufficient support, a charge he also made against the Catholic clergy in his constituency. Dramatically he pronounced that his defeat 'certainly meant the end of the Anti-Partition League'.[47] He had good cause for pessimism and his verdict on the immediate future of the IAPL was indeed prescient, but in his readiness to shift the blame for his derisory vote (and lost deposit) elsewhere O'Neill failed to grasp its more likely cause. This was perceptively accounted for in an *Irish Times* leader: 'What has happened is that the old nationalist Party, by its earlier willingness to efface itself for the sake of Sinn Féin, has paid the inevitable price. Its previous abstentions obviously have been interpreted by the electorate to mean that it has lost confidence in itself. How, then, could the voters be expected to demonstrate their confidence in it?'[48]

The question of how to rebuild this shattered confidence remained extant. It was not the case that the irresistible rise of Sinn Féin proved a major obstacle in the accomplishment of this task. In fact Sinn Féin showed remarkably poor political judgement in the wake of its electoral victories. At the Sinn Féin Ard Fheis, held in O'Connell Hall, Dublin, in October 1956, Sinn Féin president, Patrick McLogan, announced that the party would boycott future 'official elections' in the North[49] and, at the next Stormont general election, would instead hold an alternative unofficial election. This quixotic plan envisaged successful Sinn Féin candidates emerging out of the alternative election joining together with elected Sinn Féin candidates returned at the next general election in the South to 'constitute the lawful parliament of the Irish Republic'.[50] There was little here in the way of a serious political strategy. Republican instincts were not to build upon its electoral support but to pursue its objectives in an entirely different direction: namely to embark on 'Operation Harvest', the disastrous IRA border campaign that began in December 1956 only to peter out in 1962. While this campaign produced a number of republican martyrs (notably Sean South and Feargal O'Hanlon who died in an abortive attack on an RUC station in Co. Fermanagh in January 1957)[51] it was largely seen as an irrelevancy by most northern nationalists.[52] In the event, at the time of the next Stormont general election in March 1958, the holding of an alternative election proved beyond the capacities of Sinn Féin and they settled instead for an instruction to the Catholic electorate to write the name of Sinn Féin unofficial candidates on their ballot papers; thus inviting them to spoil their vote.[53] By this time the robust security action undertaken by Costello's government in the South, which had severely depleted the ranks of the IRA's leadership, had been further extended by de Valera's incoming Fianna Fáil government following the Republic's general election in March 1957. In office it introduced an internment policy which dealt a decisive blow to what remained of the IRA's organisation in the Republic.[54] And yet, despite the obvious political weakness of Sinn Féin and the IRA,[55] constitutional nationalists struggled to define a distinctive and dynamic programme with which to appeal to the nationalist electorate. As unemployment rose significantly in Northern Ireland, and as the unemployed and their families became increasingly reliant on state-provided social services, the IAPL (or at least its anti-abstentionist members) claimed that its attendance policy at Stormont would both expose Unionist bigotry and pro-tect Catholic educational and social security entitlements.[56] At the same time nationalist election committees, appealing to the more traditional communal instincts of Catholic politics, called for nationalist unity, particularly with the various strands of left nationalism in Belfast; an appeal which essentially called for Catholic solidarity rather than a synchronisation of policy between the IAPL and left-nationalist groups.[57] However, there was little new addition to the nationalist political lexicon here and the election messages broadcast to the Catholic electorate through the medium of the nationalist press bore the same familiar mix of millenarianism, and promise of incipient transformation of the political situation, as in the past. In the days before the election the editorial of the *Frontier Sentinel* opined:

> Political re-unity and independence must come to our land – and world events are bringing it much more speedily than is generally realised. In the meantime, the task of our people here is to hold on, to cling fast to whatever representation they can get, to hold on to the land in the confidence that the time is coming when their strength carefully maintained over many decades can tell.[58]

This was a statement could have been made at any time over the past three decades; indeed it had been made on many similar occasions. The party po-litical BBC radio broadcast made by Eddie McAteer and Senator Lennon on the evening of 12 March also rehearsed familiar nationalist tropes: for Lennon, Northern Ireland was a 'Puppet State … established as a result of anarchy treachery and disloyalty'[59] while McAteer, referring to the forthcoming election as 'farcical', declared that unionism 'rests firmly on a constant conspiracy to keep the Catholic minority in subjection'.[60] McAteer did take the opportunity to apprise his audience of the palpable unfairness of Derry's gerrymandered local government electoral system, however the effect of his exposé may well have been considerably weakened, among non-nationalists, by the somewhat irresolute tone of his comments on IRA violence,

> When everybody is busy calling the IRA names, remember that we have many times predicted that the frustration and cynicism of our political life here would inevitably lead to violence. Young men are being sentenced to centuries of imprisonment whilst

those who drove them to desperation are allowed off without a word of censure. Let no man condemn the effects without examining the causes.[61]

However, in the loosely constructed alliance that made up the Nationalist opposition in Northern Ireland it was inevitable that alternative strategies would emerge. That these called for a reappraisal of traditional positions was significant, and in many ways they were a harbinger of emerging currents of thought among a minority of nationalist activists. Of note here are the brothers Paddy and Tom Gormley,[62] both of whom could be described as being on the liberal-left wing of constitutional nationalism. Paddy Gormley had been elected for Mid Londonderry in the 1953 Stormont election as an Independent candidate running on a ticket that was sharply critical of the IAPL.[63] In 1958 he was returned as an unopposed candidate for the same constituency. In the same election his brother Tom ran in Mid Tyrone as an independent Farmers Candidate, contesting the seat against both Unionist and IAPL candidates; the seat was taken by the Unionist but with Tom Gormley comfortably outpolling the IAPL candidate.[64] The Gormley brothers' main innovation was to eschew, as far as possible, a sectional sectarian appeal in favour of a commitment to address the common economic grievances of Catholic and Protestant voters without distinction. Tom Gormley's election posters were notable for emphasising 'building bridges' and inter-communal cooperation and denouncing chapel-gate meetings.[65] This was an interesting development; but, as a perceptive post-election analysis by Desmond Fennell in the *Irish Times* observed, these tentative steps by the Gormleys were taken with a furtive glance over the shoulder at their nationalist critics, and this resulted in compromises. The brothers remained aloof from the type of sectarian sloganeering used by the successful IAPL candidate, R.H. O'Connor, in West Tyrone – 'Keep Tyrone Catholic' – but nonetheless Fennell noted that even the Gormley brothers' election addresses 'all ended up with rather extravagant references to "unity" and "national ideals" and "the invasion of Ireland"'.[66]

It was not only the younger, more liberal and moderate elements within nationalism that favoured a new approach. Fennell also identified the stalwart Cahir Healy, a man whose sedulous dedication to the nationalist cause could not be questioned, as being 'most alive to the new atmosphere and the new alignment'.[67] In support of this Fennell cited a speech that Healy had delivered on St Patrick's Day, three days before the election: 'he recognised that the old demand for a united nation was as much alive as ever in the hearts of the people, but "they (the Nationalist M.P.s) were realists and until a united Ireland emerged, they had to do their best for the people under existing circumstances. They had to live in Northern Ireland and carry on".'[68] In fact, Healy's 'realism' went far deeper than this snippet allows. The acuity of his reading of what Fennell termed the 'new atmosphere' in Northern Ireland was more fully revealed in a private letter sent to the Bishop of Cork, the Revd Dr Lucey, in April. In this Healy was outspokenly forthright in his recognition of the changed circumstances wrought by failed nationalist strategies and material developments:

> So far as we of the Six Counties are concerned we lived in an Ireland united prior to 1916, but now we live in a divided one. The insistence on a Republic and nothing but a Republic has left us Partition. Passing resolutions or even bombing disused huts or Customs Posts only hardens public opinion here. There is, indeed, no material lure to northern Nationalists now to go into a Republic. Our land is all de-rated, we get so many subsidies paid indirectly by England in order to make Partition work, that many who used to help the anti-Partition League now look upon the prospect with different eyes. The Catholic population in the Six Counties continues to increase.[69]

There is a perceptible tone of resignation and regret in Healy's letter. He still believed that 'Partition will go in time', but there was recognition that this would not happen any time soon, and there was concern that when it did eventually come 'the chief attraction will be of a sentimental nature'.[70] Nonetheless, Healy clearly felt that nationalist politics were approaching a significant moment, one that compelled him, at the age of eighty, to rescind his earlier announcement of retirement from active politics[71] and to accept the nomination for the South Fermanagh seat.[72]

Others were not so hopeful of, or resigned to, the 'new atmosphere'. Eddie McAteer was oblivious to its existence, or so Desmond Fennell thought. The tenor of McAteer's radio election broadcast defined his election campaign: he was a man of 'no compromise', one who would never 'fraternise'.[73] His electoral opponent in Derry at the 1958 Stormont election was a local trade union leader, Stephen McGonagle, a man of strong nationalist and socialist convictions who, along with other like-minded individuals, had quit the NILP in 1949 (in protest at its pro-Union stance) to join Jack Macgougan in his secular anti-partitionist Irish Labour Party. McGonagle and Macgougan had since parted company, a result it seems of personality rather than political differences,[74] and he ran in 1958 as an Independent Labour candidate. During the campaign Fennell noted the contrast between McGonagle's emphasis on the need to persuade the government to create jobs for the people of Derry and McAteer's prioritising of principle over policy. McAteer, he wrote, had 'rejoiced' at the closure of a Royal Navy base near Derry even though this resulted in unemployment for local Catholic workers.[75] Nor was McAteer shame-faced about this, he 'decried Mr McGonagle's softness, his "milk and water stuff"', while his supporters derisively referred to the practical policies of the Gormley brothers as 'spuds and yellow male in the place of politics'.[76] On polling day McAteer's election agents wore Tricolour button-holes, McGonagle's wore white ribbons (a non-sectarian gesture); McGonagle sent his electoral address to all electors in the constituency, McAteer sent his to Catholics, but not to Protestants. McAteer won the seat but McGonagle polled well (McAteer took 6,953 votes to McGonagle's 5,238, a margin of 1,715 votes). Fennell thought McAteer had secured the seat by the use of scare tactics: an announcement that Protestants were supporting McGonagle. In corroboration of this Eamonn McCann, the veteran Derry political activist, was later to recount his memory of loudspeaker cars touring the Bogside blaring the warning that '[t]he Protestants … are all voting for McGonagle'. [77] This tactic had, apparently, brought about a last-minute turn-out of Catholic voters. After the count, and the announcement of his victory, McAteer appeared to be in a more generous mood towards his Protestant constituents. Fennell cited the *Derry Journal* which reported McAteer as saying that it was 'a matter of common rejoicing that so many Unionists had found it possible to support an anti-partitionist candidate of some complexion' – which referred to Protestants who had voted for McGonagle. McAteer was also quoted as saying that this development would encourage him 'to continue his efforts at conversion' of unionists, and Fennell pressed him to elaborate on this. What efforts had he made to 'convert Unionist voters'? McAteer replied that the statement in the *Derry Journal* was only a 'wisecrack'.[78]

The 1958 election result brought few surprises, at least not for nationalists. Sitting abstentionists, such as Charles McGleenan in South Armagh and Liam Kelly in East Tyrone, boycotted the election.[79] Mid Tyrone was lost to a Unionist on a split nationalist vote.[80] Eight nationalist candidates were returned, standing under various Nationalist or Independent Nationalist labels;[81] an Independent, Dr Charles Stewart, took the seat normally won by a nationalist candidate at Queen's University (formerly held by Dr Eileen Hickey); meanwhile in Belfast Frank Hanna (Independent Labour) and Harry Diamond (Republican Labour) were returned for the Belfast Central and Falls seats respectively.[82] The notable major success of the election was the NILP's breakthrough in working-class constituencies in Belfast where, in a context of continually rising unemployment, it took four seats from the Unionist Party.

The issue now was what was to be the future policy of the elected Nationalist representatives? Here there was an early rift between those who were optimistic of, or resigned to, change and those who had no wish to 'fraternise'. Shortly after the election, on 31 March, a number of Nationalist MPs and Senators met in Belfast to consider nominations for the post of party leader and it was perhaps indicative of the IAPL's organisational malaise that not all eligible to attend did so. McAteer's supporters anticipated his assured election, but attempts to nominate him for the post were stymied by Cahir Healy whose preferred candidate, Joe Stewart, went forward as the sole nominee.[83] Following the nomination of Stewart it was announced to those present that Frank Hanna, Harry Diamond, Dr Charles Stewart and Senator Dr John Donaghy[84] were waiting in a separate room and wished 'to discuss common policy' with the assembled representatives. Upon being invited to address the meeting the four men then put forward two proposals; firstly, that the IAPL and the left-nationalist groups in the City come together to 'form a united party'; and secondly, that this united party should 'apply for recognition as the official opposition' at Stormont.[85] McAteer and his supporters instantly believed that this dramatic policy initiative had been deliberately sprung to catch them unawares and force them into a realignment that they had little enthusiasm for – indeed only days earlier one of McAteer's close supporters, Senator Patrick McGill, had made plain to Healy that he rejected any future liaison with the Belfast MPs ('Any form of Labour would only be a burden to us').[86] If this was indeed an attempt to railroad the IAPL in a bold new direction then it appeared successful, for when a vote was taken on the proposals they were accepted by eight votes to four.[87] McAteer's retort to the unfolding drama was to threaten his immediate resignation; but this move was unnecessary for McAteer's close associate and supporter, R.H. O'Connor, pressurised the chairman, Joe Stewart, into agreeing to a 24-hour embargo of any public statement on the unified party proposals; a delay which would allow the proposals to be put before a further meeting of all IAPL representatives without the presence of Hanna and Diamond.[88] In fact the details of the vote in favour of the proposals were leaked to the press 'within minutes'[89] of the conclusion of the 31 March meeting, very possibly in an attempt to influence the outcome of the IAPL meeting called for by Eddie McAteer and R.H. O'Connor which was scheduled for the following day. If this was the calculation then it proved ineffective; the proposals for a united party and official opposition status were put before the, more fully attended, reconvened IAPL meeting and rejected – O'Connor claimed the rejection was unanimous, although this was later challenged by Paddy Gormley.[90]

McAteer, meeting with DEA officials in Dublin some short time later, was anxious to pass this whole episode off as an unseemly and unprincipled affair. He insinuated that there were selfish financial motivations afoot and that Diamond coveted, and was primarily interested in, the £500 salary payable to an Opposition Chief Whip. Paddy Gormley was dismissed as a 'conspirator'. McAteer reconfirmed his own rather limited objectives in Stormont, which were to protect his 'own people' and to use parliament as a 'platform for publicity when the occasion arises', but he was also anxious to be seen as a man with dynamic ideas; ideas of renewal and action. Accordingly he now took the opportunity to disclose what 'he had been considering in his mind', and this was the abolition of the IAPL and the establishment of a Nationalist Party based on the elected attending IAPL representatives at Stormont. This, he thought, would free the parliamentarians from the stifling grip of the abstentionists ('pro-extremists') within the IAPL and allow for a 'more active and more vigorous opposition in Stormont',[91] although he was less forthcoming on the nature of this vigour. Conor Cruise O'Brien welcomed the winding up of the IAPL, he thought it could 'hardly be called an organisation at all: it is an invertebrate collectivity' which had 'an allegiance but no policy'. O'Brien was cautious about the prospects of a new party, he thought it possible it 'might suffer from many of the defects of the League', but it did 'afford at least an opportunity for making a fresh start' and this, he believed, was something positive.[92] However, Dublin attitudes to nationalist representatives in Northern Ireland were not about to undergo a sea change. In May a delegation, including McAteer, paid a visit to President de Valera; a report of the visit was compiled by Eoin MacWhite of the Department of External Affairs who recorded he thought the occasion 'went quite well', before adding, 'Of course, no business was discussed and the conversation was principally in the form of exchange and reminiscences.'[93] The 'Of course' was telling.

While some nationalist representatives reminisced in Dublin, others attempted a more cerebral, and challenging approach. A social studies conference at St MacNissi's College, Garron Tower, Co. Antrim, in August 1958, brought together those of a liberal inclination – clergy, politicians[94] and intellectuals – to reflect on the problems of Catholic isolation in Northern Ireland. Some of the participants advocated that Catholics should play a more active part in public life in the North, which, they thought, necessitated 'a *de facto* recognition of the Government and partition.'[95] Following on from this, in September, the southern barrister Donal Barrington addressing the Left Review Club in Belfast called upon Nationalists and Unionists to play a role in 'creating better relations'. Barrington, as he had done on previous occasions, made bold suggestions. He suggested that the Irish government should accept that it could not 'coerce' unionists into a united Ireland, and should not 'allow anyone else to do so'; he thought northern nationalists should 'respect the will of the Northern majority' and 'work constructively and persuasively, within the limits prescribed by the northern Constitution, to persuade the majority in Northern Ireland that a United Ireland would be a better place to live in than a partitioned one'; and he suggested that northern Protestants should demand 'an impartial inquiry into the complaints of ... Northern Catholics': complaints such as gerrymandering, property qualifications in municipal elections and discrimination in the allocation of housing and local authority appointments.[96] It was one thing, however, for well-meaning intellectuals and liberals to make these suggestions, the important question was – what would the politicians do? On this front there was little sign of a willingness to tamper with the existing political laagers. The response of both Unionists and Nationalists to the NILPs electoral breakthrough in 1958 was instructive here: Brian Faulkner, the Unionist Chief Whip, addressing the St, Anne's Unionist Association in February 1959, acknowledged the NILP's acceptance of Northern Ireland's constitutional status but pointed to the cross-community support which secured their success in the Belfast constituencies of Oldpark and Pottinger and concluded that 'their hands are tied because they have been returned by Nationalist votes'.[97] Cahir Healy, meanwhile, regarded the NILP as 'more Unionist than the Unionists'.[98]

But it was the decision by the Nationalist Party, as it was now called, not to contest the Westminster general election in October 1959 that indubitably pointed to the political diffidence and conservatism that the 'new' grouping had inherited from its predecessor. As in 1955 this decision left Sinn Féin as the unchallenged non-unionist contenders, and they again put forward convicted felons as candidates in the two winnable seats of Mid Ulster and Fermanagh and South Tyrone. Again this meant that if the Sinn Féin candidates were successfully returned in the election they would, as on previous occasions, be unseated under electoral law and their seats awarded to their Unionist challengers; in effect Catholic voters were being disenfranchised. The Special Correspondent of the *Irish Times* was baffled by the Nationalist Party's decision; the almost total lack of response to Sinn Féin's call for Catholic voters to spoil their votes in the recent Stormont election was seen as being indicative of the lack of support for militant republicanism and its unpopular and now faltering Border campaign. This therefore begged the question, 'why did the Nationalist Party not make a stand?' The correspondent thought the Nationalist Party's absence 'discredited' it and ignored a growing demand among Catholics to 'end the negative political outlook' of nationalist politics. The report concluded that it was possible the Nationalist Party 'may have decided their own fate' and that the election would 'mark the demise of this lethargic party'.[99] The election, on 8 October, saw the Sinn Féin vote collapse with all twelve Westminster seats going to the Unionist Party.[100] This outcome, however, did little to change negative unionist attitudes towards traditional constitutional nationalism; those on the right-wing of the Unionist Party, and those anti-liberal elements outside it (in the shape of Ian Paisley's Ulster Protestant Action movement),[101] felt vindicated in their suspicions that nationalism, in whatever hue it appeared, was unreliable and seditious.[102]

On the Nationalist Party side Joseph Stewart, the leader of the parliamentary party, also reflected on the result with a sense of vindication. In the face of the loss of Fermanagh and South Tyrone and Mid Ulster Stewart took the opportunity to castigate Sinn Féin, without a hint of irony, for not making 'the slightest semblance of a fight'.[103] The *Irish Times* Special Correspondent also reflected on the result, but with a sense of despair. He thought the belated post-election criticisms of Sinn Féin rang hollow and that only Joseph Connellan in South Down, who alone of all Nationalist MPs issued a pre-election condemnation of the use of force and urged Catholic voters not to vote Sinn Féin, emerged with any credibility.[104] He wondered what the eight Nationalist MPs at Stormont could achieve in their uncoordinated party ('still attending Parliament in an individual capacity, coming and going and voting … as they please') and he concluded, pessimistically, that for the Catholic minority the 1959 election 'has shown the hopelessness of their predicament'.[105]

Notes

1 In response to McAteer's suggestion that the IAPL should fight to hold their parliamentary seats the annual meeting of the Fermanagh branch of the IAPL expressed its 'general disapproval' at what was clearly regarded as an unwarranted interference. *Irish Times*, 15 April 1955.
2 Sinn Féin had in fact raised the prospect of standing in Westminster contests in 1952, some three years earlier. *Irish Independent*, 10 November 1952.
3 Mitchell was a 23-year-old bricklayer, Clarke a 21-year-old civil servant.
4 *Irish Times*, 19 April 1955.
5 *Irish Times*, 26 April 1955.
6 The composition of the conventions appears to have been made up of local notables – elected representatives (both national and local), journalists, lawyers, teachers, farmers, members of the clergy, those active in local community issues and those involved in political organisations – whose presence was determined by social position rather than democratic accountability.
7 *Irish Times Pictorial*, 14 May 1955.
8 E. Staunton, *The Nationalists of Northern Ireland 1918–1973* (Dublin, Columba Press, 2001), p. 196.
9 Tim Pat Coogan recounts how a young IRA associate of Clarke's, the barrister Seamus Sorahan, organised a letter of appeal to Maguire in support of Clarke's candidacy. The letter, which was signed by hundreds of students from University College Dublin (where Clarke had studied), stated, untruthfully, that Clarke had long admired Maguire as 'the leader of Nationalist thought in Occupied Ireland'. This sycophancy, plus a subsequent visit paid to Maguire by the loquacious Sorahan and a colleague – adorned with gold Fainnes and Pioneer Pins to demonstrate their Gaelic enthusiasm and Catholic piety – appear to have successfully secured the priest's support. See T.P. Coogan, *The IRA* (London, Fontana, 1970), p. 374.
10 *Irish Times Pictorial*, 14 May 1955.

11 *Irish Times*, 13 May 1955. These latent republican sympathies were later reflected in the ambivalence of some of the party's condemnations of the IRA during the 1956–62 Border Campaign which held IRA violence to be 'deplorable' but 'understandable' and which recognised 'the sincerity of those involved'. See *Irish Times*, 24 December 1956 and also the *Tribune*, 18 January 1957

12 C. Norton, 'The Irish Labour Party in Northern Ireland, 1949–1958', *Saothar* 21 (1996), p. 54.

13 *Irish Times*, 24 May 1955.

14 See the *Irish Times*, 12 May 1955.

15 See Aknefton, *Irish Times*, 21 May 1955.

16 *Irish Times*, 12 May 1955.

17 *Ibid.*

18 Staunton, *The Nationalists*, p. 197.

19 On the Christle group see J. Bowyer Bell, *The Secret Army: The IRA 1916–1979* (Dublin, Academic Press, 1983), p. 279, R. English, *Armed Struggle: A History of the IRA* (London, Macmillan, 2003), p. 72.

20 *Irish Times*, 18 April 1955.

21 *Irish Times*, 16 May 1955.

22 *Irish Times*, 17 May 1955.

23 *Irish Times*, 21 May 1955.

24 The result was Jack Beattie (Ir Lab) 16,050 (27.3 per cent), Eamonn Boyce (SF) 8,447 (14.4 per cent). www.ark.ac.uk/elections/dwb.htm, accessed 5 January 2012.

25 In 1951 O'Neill and Healy had majorities of 3,396 and 2, 635 respectively, on taking these seats in 1955 Mitchell had a majority of 260 and Clarke a majority of 261.

26 M. Farrell, *Northern Ireland: The Orange State* (London, Pluto Press, 1978), p. 209.

27 In 1951 Gerald Annesley, a protestant and owner of the Castlewellan Estate, stood as an Independent Nationalist candidate. See www.ark.ac.uk/elections/dsd.htm, accessed 5 January 2012.

28 In Londonderry the Sinn Féin candidate, Manus Canning, received 19,640 votes. There was no anti-partitionist candidate in 1951 but in the 1950 election Hugh McAteer, a senior IRA member standing as an Independent Republican, secured 21,880 votes. In 1945 a Nationalist candidate (Denis Cavanagh) ran in Londonderry and received 37,561 votes. In Armagh the Sinn Féin candidate (Tomás MacCurtain) received 21,363 votes in 1955; this seat was last contested by a Nationalist candidate (James O'Reilly) in a by-election in 1948, at which time O'Reilly received 24,422 votes.

29 *Irish Times*, 28 May 1955.

30 *Ibid.*

31 Also on display was Sinn Féin's inflexible attitude towards Unionism: 'If the Protestant population wished to fight with the British in the struggle they would be denounced as Quislings and treated as such', *Irish Times*, 6 June 1955.

32 John V. Kelleher, 'Can Ireland Unite?', *The Atlantic Monthly* 193: 4 (April 1954), pp. 58–62.

33 See M Kennedy, *Division and Consensus: The Politics of Cross-Border Relations in Ireland, 1925–1969* (Dublin, Institute of Public Administration, 2000), pp. 153–154.

34 *Ibid.*, pp. 158–159.
35 *Frontier Sentinel*, 30 July 1955.
36 The Unionist press (*Belfast Telegraph, Belfast Newsletter* and *Northern Whig*) collectively criticised the Taoiseach for what they regarded as his contradictory position; however, Eddie McAteer, while attributing responsibility for violence 'solely on the political pickpockets at Stormont', singled out Costello's anti-extradition stance for singular praise. See Parliamentary Debates Dáil Éireann, Volume 153, 30 November 1955, pp. 1347–1439; *Irish Times*, 2 December 1955.
37 Kennedy, *Division and Consensus*, p. 160.
38 Clarke was replaced by the previously defeated Unionist candidate Colonel Robert Grosvenor. Farrell, *Orange State*, p. 210.
39 *Irish Times*, 13 August 1955.
40 Beattie sat on National Insurance tribunals and thus was deemed to hold 'offices of profit under the Crown' which barred him from the role of parliamentary representative. *Irish Times*, 9 January 1956.
41 *Irish Times*, 16 January 1956. After Mitchell's disqualification following the first by-election Patrick McGill reported to Healy that 'The situation in the Border seats is now beyond remedy'. PRONI, D2991/B/24/26, McGill to Healy, 2 September 1955.
42 It was suggested – and denied – at the time that the Unionist Party's decision not to put forward a candidate was part of a 'gentlemen's agreement' with constitutional nationalists. See *Irish Times*, 8 May 1956.
43 *Irish Times*, 30 April 1956.
44 *Irish Times*, 7 May 1956.
45 *Ibid.*
46 Farrell, *The Orange State*, p. 211. Shortly after the election Senator Liam Kelly called for the unification of his Fianna Uladh with Sinn Féin. While regretting the loss of the seat to a Unionist, Kelly publicly applauded what he saw as the one positive to have come out of the election i.e. 'the almost total eclipse of the Anti-Partition League'. *Irish Times*, 11 May 1956.
47 NAI, DFA 305/14/2, E. McWhite to J. Belton, 19 May 1956.
48 *Irish Times*, 10 May 1956.
49 *Irish Times*, 3 October 1956.
50 *Irish Times*, 29 October 1956.
51 H. Patterson, *Ireland Since 1939: The Persistence of Conflict* (Dublin, Penguin Ireland, 2006), p. 135.
52 See D. Ferriter, *The Transformation of Ireland 1900–2000* (London, Profile Books, 2004), p. 460.
53 *Irish Times*, 28 February 1958.
54 Kennedy, *Division and Consensus*, p. 164.
55 Desmond Fennell, in a post-election review of the political scene in the North, produced a telling description of the contemporaneous state of Republicanism: 'The world of Republican diehardism in the hills of Tyrone and Armagh and in the backstreets of Belfast is partly quaint, partly weird and frightening'. See *Irish Times*, 9 May 1958.

56 See for example the election statements of Joseph Connellan (South Down) and Edward Richardson (South Armagh), *Frontier Sentinel*, 1 March 1958.

57 See for example the statement issued by the South Down Nationalist Election Committee in Newry, 'South Down's Call to Anti-Unionist Parties', *Frontier Sentinel*, 8 March 1958.

58 *Frontier Sentinel*, 15 March 1958.

59 *Ibid.*

60 *Ibid.*

61 *Ibid.*

62 For biographical details on the Paddy and Tom Gormley see B. Lynn, *Holding the Ground The Nationalist Party in Northern Ireland, 1945–72* (Aldershot, Ashgate, 1997), pp. 241–242.

63 See Chapter 5, n. 90.

64 Mid Tyrone 1958 election results, www.election.demon.co.uk/stormont/tyrone.html.

65 *Irish Times*, 10 May 1958.

66 *Ibid.*

67 *Ibid.*

68 *Ibid.*

69 PRONI, D2991/B/143/14, Cahir Healy papers, Healy to Rev Dr Lucey, Bishop of Cork, April 1958.

70 *Ibid.*

71 *Irish Times*, 28 February 1958.

72 *Irish Times*, 7 March 1958.

73 *Irish Times*, 10 May 1958.

74 On McGonagle see A Finlay, 'Stephen McGonagle' (Obituary), *Saothar* 27 (2002), pp. 10–12.

75 McAteer later reconfirmed this in a conversation with Dr Eoin MacWhite of the Irish government's Department of Foreign Affairs. Dr MacWhite related that McAteer ' said that he would do nothing to keep the naval base at Eglington even though its abandonment meant a lot of Catholic unemployment'. NAI, DFA 305/14/2/4, Dr MacWhite confidential note to C.C. O'Brien, 25 April 1958. Ironically the Unionist Prime Minister, Lord Brookeborough, campaigned vigorously to keep the naval base open. See Patterson, *Ireland*, p. 129.

76 *Irish Times*, 10 May 1958.

77 E. McCann, *War and an Irish Town* (London, Pluto Press, 1980), p. 12.

78 *Irish Times*, 10 May 1958.

79 McGleenan denounced IAPL candidates as 'political opportunists'. *Frontier Sentinel*, 15 March 1958. Kelly, whose term as a Senator in the Seanad ended in 1957, quit Irish politics in 1961and emigrated to the USA where he worked as a bus driver in New York. Kelly prospered in his new employment eventually rising to the position of assistant chief superintendent of the Metro Transit Authority. He died in New York on 6 June 2011. See obituary, *Irish News*, 18 June 2011.

80 See n. 64 above.

81 E.G. Richardson (Independent Nat.), South Armagh; E. McAteer (Nat.), Foyle; J. O'Reilly (Nat.), Down Mourne; J. Connellan (Nat.), South Down; C. Healy (Nat.),

South Fermanagh; P.J. Gormley (Nat.), Mid Londonderry; J. Stewart (Nat.), East Tyrone; R.H. O'Connor (Nat.), West Tyrone. www.election.demon.co.uk/stormont/stormont.html, accessed 7 January 2012.

82 Macgougan's secular anti-partitionist Irish Labour Party was now in free-fall. The final electoral annihilation of the party in Belfast came shortly afterwards in the municipal elections of May 1958 when all seven sitting IrLP councillors (some of whom had held office since 1949) lost their seats. A post-election statement issued by the party spoke ominously of an 'unwelcome feature of the election', the 'sectarian slant put forward … on the doorstep'. See Norton, 'The Irish Labour Party', p. 54.

83 Accounts of this meeting were later given to Dr Eoin MacWhite, of the Republic's Department of External Affairs, by McAteer and his close supporter R.H. O'Connor; they are therefore necessarily partial in their reading of events and conclusions drawn.

84 Dr Donaghy, who was consultant physician to the Mater Hospital, Belfast, and clinical lecturer in medicine at Queen's University, served in the Senate from 1953–69. See Obituary, *British Medical Journal* 295 (7 November 1987), p. 1215.

85 NAI, DFA 305/14/2/4, E. MacWhite, Confidential report, 3 April 1958.

86 PRONI, 2991/B/24/52, McGill to Healy, 27 March 1958.

87 For: H. Diamond, F. Hanna, Dr Steward, Senator Dr Donaghy, C. Healy, P. Gorman, Senator P.J. O'Hare, Senator J. McGlade. Against: E. McAteer, R.H. O'Connor, J. O'Reilly, Senator P. McGill.

88 O'Connor informed MacWhite that he had identified Joe Stewart as the 'weak link' and that his chosen strategy was to 'frighten Joe off the whole idea'. This he accomplished by warning Stewart that 'he would go to his grave like J. Campbell (who accepted a County Court judgeship) a discredited Nationalist and his children would bear the stigma of his actions to their dying day.' NAI, DFA 305/14/2/4, E. MacWhite, Confidential report, 3 April 1958.

89 *Frontier Sentinel*, 5 April 1958.

90 Lynn, *Holding the Ground*, p. 140.

91 NAI, DFA 305/14/2/4, E. MacWhite confidential note to C.C. O'Brien, 25 April 1958.

92 NAI, DFA 305/14/2/4, C.C. O'Brien to J.A. Belton, 1 May 1958.

93 NAI, DFA 305/14/2/4, E. MacWhite to J.A. Belton, 15 May 1958. These visits became something of a regular fete for the northern representatives. However, they were left in no doubt that these were very much 'courtesy' visits and were not occasions for exchanging ideas or tendering suggestions to the Irish government. Government officials went so far as to emphasise this to delegations in advance of their visit. See NIA, DFA 305/14/35, N. O'Nualláin to Con Cremin, Secretary, Department of External Affairs, 24 September 1959.

94 Cahir Healy and Joe Stewart attended.

95 Details of the conference were later published in a piece in the *Irish Times*, 30 December 1958.

96 *Irish Times*, 26 September 1958.

97 *Irish Times*, 28 September 1959.

98 *Ibid*.

99 *Irish Times*, 29 September 1959.

100 The Sinn Féin vote fell from 152,310 in 1955 to 63, 415 in 1959. Seven of the twelve Sinn Féin candidates lost their deposits. *Irish Times*, 12 October 1959.

101 H. Patterson and E. Kaufmann, *Unionism and Orangeism in Northern Ireland Since 1945: The Decline of the Loyal Family* (Manchester, Manchester University Press, 2007), p. 41.

102 Patterson, *Ireland Since 1939*, p. 184.

103 *Frontier Sentinel*, 17 October, 1959.

104 Connellan's statement was later praised by the victorious Unionist candidate, Captain Lawrence Orr, who thought it 'would go a long way towards creating goodwill, friendship and co-operation.' *Irish Times*, 13 October 1959.

105 *Ibid.*

7

National Unity: radicalism and renewal, 1959–64

For some nationalists the 1959 debacle provided an incentive to take action, and as the year ended a small group of like-minded individuals came together to form a new political movement in Northern Ireland: National Unity (NU). The leading figure in this initiative was a young Belfast secondary school teacher, Michael McKeown, who, along with about two dozen others, established National Unity not as an alternative political party but as a think-tank and sounding board through which fresh ideas and 'rational political analysis'[1] could be channelled into the existing nationalist parties. From the somewhat gloomier perspective of Northern Ireland in the mid-1980s McKeown was later to cast a jaundiced eye on his own role in this period;[2] but this should not detract from recognition that at the time the ideas and activities of McKeown and his associates were strikingly radical. Nowhere was this clearer than in National Unity's position on partition and the constitutional question. In December 1959 the policy statement of the nascent group announced an innovative stance; it was dedicated 'to the ideal of a united Ireland' but with the added proviso that this could only be achieved with 'the consent of the majority of the people of Northern Ireland'.[3] For National Unity the adoption of this principle – an explicit acceptance that the border could be removed only with the freely given consent of unionists – profoundly changed both the context and manner in which Catholic grievances were to be addressed. National Unity's emphasis was on securing effective and meaningful representation for Catholic interests in the Stormont parliament and this announced a far-reaching revision of those traditional nationalist strategies which rejected the North's political institutions as an agency through which reform and change would be effected. In addition, National Unity saw it as an imperative that nationalism, if it were to progress, would need to break free from the fetters of narrow sectional appeal and attempt to bridge the sectarian divide. This was a bold re-imagining of nationalism as a broader progressive movement which would aspire to 'advance the welfare of all sections of the community' both Catholic and Protestant.[4]

Such a departure from nationalist orthodoxy inevitably invited a critical response from those defending more established, and largely unchallenged, positions; and, as National Unity initially busied itself with disseminating new ideas through the press and open public forums, this response was not long in coming.[5] Addressing the Hibernians' St Patrick's Day demonstration in Dungannon in March 1960 Joseph Stewart, the Nationalist Party leader, rejected as 'utterly unacceptable' any suggestion that nationalists should accept the North's current constitutional position.[6] Speaking on the same platform Cahir Healy also concurred that any such acceptance of the constitutional status by what he called 'national opponents' would in effect 'be tantamount to saying they were traitors to their country'.[7] Enda Staunton, in his impressive study, suggests that these 'seemingly absolutist views' were in fact tempered by 'qualifications'.[8] He points out that in the course of both men's speeches more generous language was employed and more moderate positions outlined: Stewart declared himself 'in favour of good relations based upon a fair deal for every citizen', while Healy acknowledged that constitutional change could only come 'by persuasion and being friendly'.[9] However, there was little that was new in these 'qualifications'. Healy's advocacy of friendly 'persuasion' was premised on a very traditional view of Unionism as being ephemeral and of little substance. On this occasion, basing his analysis on a hypothetical assertion that the British government's economic subsidies to Northern Ireland would end in the near future, Healy argued that if the Southern government were able to develop the Irish Republic into a more economically attractive prospect then struggling 'Six Counties farmers' (meaning Protestant farmers) would awaken to the reality that 'Loyalty did not pay now-a-days',[10] and thus might be persuaded to abandon their support for the Union. However, as Healy also acknowledged that other social classes within the Unionist bloc would not be attracted to his imagined scenario ('engineers, railway men, teachers, doctors and even farm labourers … were getting or would soon get large increases in their incomes') his emphasis appeared to be more on fracturing and weakening unionism rather than on its friendly accommodation. Meanwhile, Stewart's entirely reasonable call on unionists to demonstrate their commitment to fair play and 'good relations' – by addressing the scandal of the gerrymander in Derry and the exclusion of Catholics from public positions in Fermanagh and Tyrone – was accompanied by a reminder of what he regarded to be the boundaries of acceptable political negotiation and 'good relations': 'We see no point in trying to come to terms with people utterly alien to their political outlook and so remote from the tradition of this nation. Whoever wishes to do so may try but no step involving permanent recognition of an imposed authority will be taken by us.'[11] The speeches therefore did not indicate a softening of traditional positions or strategies, instead they telegraphed the significant differences that existed between Nationalist Party orthodoxy and the new thinking of National Unity.

In fact on this occasion both Stewart and Healy misrepresented National Unity's revisionism on the constitutional question; this did not, as they suggested, amount to an unqualified acceptance of the permanence of North's constitutional status, instead National Unity regarded the existing constitutional position as an unavoidable fact that had to be recognised and accepted until such time as unionists could be persuaded of the advantages of, and give their consent to, any new constitutional arrangement. The tone of Stewart and Healy's response suggested a patrician impatience with younger dissenting voices within nationalism, but the froideur of party elders was also premised on their complacent reading of the current situation. This was visible in a letter from Senator Patrick McGill, the leader of the Nationalist Party in the Northern Ireland Senate, to Cahir Healy in August 1960. In this McGill struck an optimistic note on the party's immediate and future prospects. He reported that the high profile taken by Paddy Gormley in the protest against the decision of the Northern Ireland Minister of Home Affairs, Brian Faulkner, to allow an Orange parade to pass through the largely Catholic village of Dungiven in July – a decision which overturned a previous ban on the parade and which had resulted in two nights of rioting[12] – had 'enormously' increased 'the Party's stock in the Dungiven area and throughout Co. Derry'.[13] Furthermore, and building on this momentum, a meeting had been arranged to discuss the events at Dungiven with Denis Vosper, the joint Parliamentary Under-Secretary of State at the British Home Office, who was visiting Belfast.[14] Finally, he revealed, plans were in place to raise a private member's motion on 'Evil Literature' at Stormont, a matter, McGill conjectured, 'on which all sections [of the Nationalist Party] are united'.[15] The issue of provocative Orange parades and a motion on 'Evil Literature' appear incongruous, and indeed they were, but Nationalist Party representatives, unrestrained by party discipline, had a tendency to fly kites and the recent seizure by the RUC of a consignment of pornographic magazines in Belfast gave wind to a kite that McGill and some of his colleagues were determined to fly. The debate on 'Evil Literature' duly took place at Stormont in October. In moving the motion, James O'Reilly MP (Mourne), spoke of 'the serious threat to Christian morality, decency and public order presented by the objectionable immoral literature which is freely on sale in our cities and towns and in rural areas'.[16] His address made clear that the category of 'objectionable immoral literature' was extended beyond pornography to include *Lady Chatterley's Lover* (the unexpurgated edition of which had recently been published and was the subject of a famous obscenity trial in

London), British Sunday newspapers and children's comics (on the grounds that they 'show brutality and violence in their wildest forms'). In support of the motion Cahir Healy, expressing his concern that Sunday newspapers were a threat to the 'spiritual interests' of the young, read to the House, at length, extracts from the Sunday newspaper *The People* which had recently run an exposé detailing the priapic exploits of the legendary American film star Errol Flynn.[17] But what was perhaps most striking about the debate was the delivery by R.H. O'Connor, Nationalist MP for West Tyrone, of a paean to all that was positive and worthy in Northern Ireland; this included not just a celebration of a free press that was 'determined, energetic and forthright in [its] presentation of the news' but also a whole series of measures which had vastly improved conditions for the citizens of Northern Ireland:

> A lot of money has been spent on the health service. Vast amounts of money have been expended so that our people will receive first-class medical attention. Similar amounts have been expended in providing hospital accommodation. Dental attention has been stressed by everyone who is interested in the health of our people. A lot has been done in the way of education. Trained and skilled teachers have been provided and splendid schools have been erected … There are water and sewage schemes under way which will cost vast amounts of money and there are slum clearance programmes.[18]

The rationale behind O'Connor's speech was to point to the safeguards which guaranteed physical well-being in Northern Ireland in order to highlight the dangers posed to the young if similar safeguards were not in place to protect them from exposure to 'immoral filth' (which, for O'Connor, included the works of James Joyce).[19] However, the logical coherence of the Nationalist position (which emphasised the wholly negative experience of nationalists in the Northern Ireland state) was strained by his unreflective acknowledgement that material improvements, resulting from a prolonged period of post-war welfarism, had impacted in a highly generalised manner to the benefit of what he called 'our people'. The debate did not bear out McGill's sanguine assessment of a united party, it was in fact poorly attended by Nationalist Party members;[20] nor did the time devoted to an airing of the conservative moral values of an older generation (which were actually capable of greater flexibility than was displayed on this occasion)[21] demonstrate that the Nationalist Party was in touch with the outstanding economic and political issues of the day.

In contrast National Unity avoided platitudes, rhetorical hyperbole and logical inconsistencies. Working from the assumption that times had changed, and that changed times required new approaches, McKeown and his associates attempted to base their analysis of the current situation on something more tangible and concrete. This necessitated seeking out the views and opinions of ordinary Catholics: how did they feel about discrimination? What was their experience of social services? What role did they think the Nationalist Party should play in Stormont? To find answers to these questions National Unity conducted political polling surveys in nationalist areas of Belfast, a unique and innovative idea. These surveys may have been small-scale and rudimentary but they were an attempt to formulate political strategy based on relevant empirical data, and the results were revealing. One such survey, in the predominantly Catholic Markets district of Belfast, found that a majority of respondents believed that they enjoyed a higher standard of living than people in the Republic; less than half questioned reported they had experienced discrimination; many wished to see the border removed, but there were sizeable minorities who were either prepared to accept the status quo (interestingly this category included most of those who had reportedly experienced discrimination) or who had no definite position one way or the other; a majority had voted for the NILP in the last Westminster election, a tiny minority had voted for Sinn Féin; an overwhelming majority wanted to see a united Nationalist Party in Stormont which adopted constitutional tactics and supported left-of-centre social policies. All in all National Unity concluded that the picture was a complex one and that Nationalist politicians should take note of this complexity.[22]

Nor did National Unity hesitate to bring its observations and suggestions to a wider audience. In April 1961 at its first public meeting in the Republic (at the Shelbourne Hotel, Dublin), the platform speakers (Harry Diamond, Dr James Scott and Michael McKeown) addressing the theme 'Northern attitudes towards a United Ireland'[23] expressed opinions not normally associated by Dublin audiences with northern nationalists. Diamond, who now closely associated himself with National Unity,[24] acknowledged that the benefits derived from the Welfare State in Northern Ireland had brought about 'a substantial change in outlook' among nationalists living there; furthermore, he expressed the view that 'the regime in Northern Ireland was a fairly stable one' and that in responding to the IRA's border campaign the Northern Government 'had acted with considerable discretion'.[25] Dr James Scott, a Queen's University Belfast academic and founder member of National Unity, speaking on Irish nationalist attitudes to Ulster Unionism, pressed home the point that the 'North remained separate because the majority of its people desired separation'. Any change in Unionist attitudes, he argued, could only come through persuasion, which would require 'intelligence and patience, and above all a much deeper understanding of the North and the character of its people by those in the South'. Finally, Michael McKeown took the opportunity to share his vision of a rejuvenated and reinvigorated nationalism that was broad and accommodating. He regretted 'that people in the North were still clinging to the nationalism of

1916'; a nationalism which he thought 'had lost its dynamism' only to become a negative 'creed of "anti-something"'.[26]

While the members of National Unity may have been few (the Department of External Affairs in Dublin estimated that it had a membership of just over 100 in 1962)[27] the activism and articulacy of the group was not without impact on a Nationalist Party determined not to be outshone by the young usurpers. By early 1962 an increased vigour and seriousness in the performance of Nationalist Party MPs at Stormont was being noted,[28] and when in the run-up to the Stormont general election in May 1962, Cahir Healy was invited to write an opinion piece for the *Belfast Newsletter*, a Unionist daily newspaper, he used the opportunity to present the Nationalist Party (contra National Unity) as the real champions of social and economic progress in Northern Ireland.[29] Healy also used the opportunity to raise issues of Catholic grievance (gerrymandering and the unfair allocation of jobs and housing); however, he made it clear that these grievances could only be resolved through the ending of partition, which he described as the primary cause of 'unrest and unemployment on both sides of the Border'.[30] This was in essence a reiteration of the traditionalist nationalist position, albeit in a less acerbic language that usually characterised electoral pronouncements (both Unionist and Nationalist), and as such it was far from the constructive engagement with Protestants that National Unity aspired towards. In fact Healy had earlier toyed with the idea of including in his article details of interim federal arrangements which the Irish government would provide to Protestant unionists as a reassurance during an envisaged transitional process towards a united Ireland. He went so far as to contact Frank Aiken, the Minister of External Affairs, in Dublin for clarification of the federalist solution that de Valera had advocated from the late 1930s,[31] but Aiken thought that Healy was confusing de Valera's proposals (which involved the Stormont parliament retaining administrative responsibility over the six counties of Northern Ireland as a single unit within a federal Ireland) with those put forward by the Primate of all Ireland, Cardinal D'Alton, in an interview he gave to the *Observer* newspaper in 1957 (which envisaged Stormont retaining jurisdiction only over those counties with a Unionist majority).[32] In the event Healy left out any references to interim stages towards Irish unity or to safeguards and reassurances that would be on offer to unionists.

The Stormont general election in May saw only marginal changes in nationalist representation. The Nationalist Party returned the same candidates to the same safe seats as in 1958, with the one addition of Tom Gormley who, standing this time as the official Nationalist Party candidate, took back the seat in Mid Tyrone lost to a Unionist (as a result of a split nationalist vote) in the last general election.[33] With few exceptions there was little competition for the nationalist vote in the party's heartlands and many candidates were returned unopposed. In Derry Stephen McGonagle once again unsuccessfully challenged Eddie McAteer who characteristically offered a robust defence of his own 'traditional nationalism' as compared to the 'cringing, crawling type of nationalism' of McGonagle.[34] Meanwhile in Belfast, where Stewart, Diamond and Hanna were again returned, there was an additional gain when the populist and intuitive socialist Gerry Fitt was elected for Belfast Dock standing under the label of Dock Irish Labour Party. Impressively Fitt won the seat with the support of Protestant voters, a result of his energetic work as a local councillor for the area.[35]

Throughout this period National Unity attempted to maintain good relations with all political parties; however there were emerging tensions with the Nationalist Party, partly a result of an unguarded and critical comment McKeown had made (in a National Unity publication) on the competences of Nationalist MPs,[36] but also as a result of speculation (later confirmed to be true)[37] that National Unity were considering standing candidates in those Westminster seats that the Nationalist Party had conceded to Sinn Féin.[38] National Unity was also becoming increasingly sceptical about the political calculations of senior Nationalist Party members. When Senator James Lennon, addressing a Hibernian Order event on 15 August 1962, challenged the Grand Master of the Orange Order, Sir George Clark, to meet for talks, National Unity wished the Senator 'every success' with the venture; but they also observed it would be 'foolish to expect any spectacular results' from it. National Unity was not opposed to talks but it seemed to them that the remit of discussions between the Orange leadership and senior members of the Nationalist Party would prove restrictive. For this reason they hoped that Lennon's proposed leadership talks (which had been issued at the behest of Eddie McAteer) would merely be a precursor to more inclusive talks, 'at all levels of our divided community', which would go beyond discussing 'generalities' – something they clearly suspected – to 'deal with the concrete problems which are at the root of accusations of bigotry, discrimination and gerrymandering'.[39] Indeed, the Lennon/McAteer invitation to the Orange Order, while a novel idea, was not as far-reaching as it first appeared, for what it involved were essentially private talks outside of the normal channels of political debate and away from the glare of public scrutiny; a strategy far removed from National Unity's preference for talks 'at all levels' and in open public forums. There were also serious questions as to what the proposed Orange–Green talks, as they were dubbed by the press, could actually achieve, as well as serious doubts as to the commitment of the parties involved. For his part Clark feared that refusal to talk would perpetuate an image of the Orange Order as innately bigoted, an image which he wished to correct. At the same time he was also wary of the more intransigent elements within the Order and mindful of incurring their displeasure to the detriment of Orange unity.[40] To placate the intransigents Clark announced in advance of the first meeting (which took place in October) that he hoped there would be Nationalist Party recognition of Northern Ireland's constitutional status; a move which, although not set as a precondition for talks to take place, was suspected by some to be a hurdle designed to wreck them.[41] On the Nationalist Party side a press report quoted a 'prominent Nationalist leader' as saying that the recognition issue "will give us a way of dropping out of the talks", which implied that this was to be welcomed rather than regretted; however, it also observed that there were 'many influential members of the party' (very likely Paddy and Tommy Gormley) who disagreed that constitutional recognition should be a non-negotiable principle.[42] It was perhaps to offset intra-party discussion on this sensitive question that a decision was made to compartmentalise the Orange–Green exchange: Senator Lennon announced that a further round of talks planned to take place in February 1963 would not 'directly involve' the Nationalist Party but would be led by a committee comprised of himself, Eddie McAteer and Cahir Healy.[43] If this was meant to stifle internal party dissent then it did not succeed. Paddy Gormley was emphatic in his publicly declared support for democratic dialogue between political parties, but he was insistent that this should be conducted free from 'the interference of a Klu Klux Klan organisation'.[44] Gormley left little doubt that he thought the Orange–Green talks a distraction from the more substantive party political engagements which he favoured; and, in visibly distancing himself from such senior conservative party luminaries as Lennon, McAteer and Healy, he also signalled the beginnings of an inner-party tussle over its future direction.

National Unity, meanwhile, pushing ever further the boundaries of nationalist orthodoxy, now suggested that the Irish government should recognise the Northern Ireland government's right to exist, a recognition which, they held, would not prevent nationalists in the North from working towards 'a peaceful … and … eventual political integration with the rest of Ireland'.[45] On this very topic National Unity organised a public debate in Dublin, in March 1963, at which Ernest Blythe spoke in favour of the motion 'That the Government of Northern Ireland should be recognised', and Eddie McAteer opposed. In his contribution Blythe made a number of concrete proposals to improve cross-border relations; he suggested the Irish government could advance diplomatic ties by the appointment of an Irish consul-general in Belfast and by agreeing to the extradition of 'political prisoners' to the North. He was also highly critical of the irredentist claims of the Irish Constitution and by what he believed was the needless affront caused to unionists by the refusal to recognise the symbols and emblems of the northern state. Eddie McAteer, for his part, argued along more familiar lines; in the North, he declared, '[s]ins of discrimination were practised against the minority daily' and unionists were 'ingrained in evil and discrimination'. He also suggested that history had placed inviolable restrictions on political accommodation; the nationalist minority were the 'caretakers for the beliefs of so many Irishmen who fought down through the ages' and these Irishmen would 'turn in their graves if this generation gave up the fight' for these beliefs.[46]

The distance between Blythe and McAteer was an unbridgeable gulf, but the distance between McAteer and National Unity (who themselves thought that Blythe went too far in abandoning the aspiration for national unity)[47] was also considerable.[48] Nonetheless, despite these differences National Unity continued in its attempts to maintain fraternal relations with the Nationalist Party and hosted Nationalist Party members at its meetings and events. It also invited Irish government Ministers to attend, but they declined. Jack Lynch, the Minister for Industry and Commerce, was one such invitee (to National Unity's St Patrick Day dinner in the Wellington Park Hotel, Belfast, on 17 March 1963), however, officials in the Department of External Affairs advised Lynch against accepting the invitation on the grounds that 'the status and importance of the organisation was not such as to warrant his attendance'.[49] George Colley TD went instead as his replacement. Members of the Unionist Party also declined to speak at National Unity meetings, although members of the NILP and the small Liberal Party did so.[50] And yet, even if some refused their invitations, Michael McKeown was upbeat; he detected an 'easing of tensions' in Northern Ireland, a 'more moderate tone' in political discourse, a 'more sympathetic awareness' on behalf of the Irish government in relation to northern concerns (particularly economic ones), and the development of 'more cordial relationships' between the Irish and British Governments'.[51] There was of course some truth to all this; as Henry Patterson has pointed out the Irish Taoiseach, Sean Lemass, who had succeeded the ageing de Valera in 1959, was at this time pursuing a more cooperative strategy in relation to the Unionist government, while Capt. Terence O'Neill, the new Unionist prime minister who replaced Brookeborough in March 1963, had adopted a liberal and modernising rhetoric that emphasised economic and social renewal within Northern Ireland. However, Patterson also points to the very real limitations of these strategies and hence their limited potential to displace the more traditionally entrenched and regressive positions of Irish Nationalism and Ulster Unionism. As Lemass was faced with the dual concerns of placating the anti-partitionist wing of his party while at the same time steering his minority Fianna Fáil government towards abandoning de Valera's economic nationalism, his recognition of the legitimacy of the Northern government was actually less compelling and more limited and ambiguous than McKeown realised. O'Neill, on the other hand, prioritised winning back the support of Protestant working-class voters who had defected to the NILP and maintaining Unionist Party unity and this was pursued at the expense of addressing Catholic grievances.[52]

In hindsight these were hardly conducive circumstances to realise the hopes of McKeown and his colleagues, and even at the time there were indicators that questioned McKeown's exuberance. As the Orange–Green talks stumbled into 1963 a motion passed at the NILP's annual conference in April – calling on the participants in the talks to set up a joint tribunal to examine cases of alleged religious discrimination, and a joint working party to work out rules for a points system to ensure the fair allocation of housing[53] – must have struck the leaders of National Unity as being both more timely and apposite than anything suggested so far by Senator Lennon and his colleagues. Significantly, when, in June 1963, McAteer and Lennon announced that the Orange–Green talks would continue[54] they declined to give details of any progress made to date; however, Healy had earlier already privately confided his view that the talks were of no use[55] while other voices opined that they had in fact 'failed miserably before they got much off the ground'.[56] These pessimistic assessments proved to be accurate; the talks had become bogged down on the constitutional question and by the end of 1963 were abandoned with no perceptible achievement made. The Nationalist Party now turned its attention to cultivating direct contacts with senior political figures in Britain and, in January 1964, McAteer, Lennon and McGill announced that a delegation would travel to London to meet with the leaders of all the main British political parties to discuss the issue of Catholic discrimination. They were to be disappointed; the Prime Minister, Sir Alec Douglas-Home, refused to meet with them,[57] so too did Harold Wilson, the Leader of the Opposition – both on the grounds that the matter they wished to discuss was the responsibility of the government of Northern Ireland.[58] The delegation went ahead anyway and met with Joe Grimond MP (leader of the Liberal Party) and his colleague Jeremy Thorpe MP, plus a number of Labour Party representatives including Fenner Brockway MP, Hugh Delargy MP and Lord Longford. The only member of the Conservative Party they met with was the maverick MP for Brighton Pavilion, the Catholic and Dublin-born Sir William Teeling. Afterwards the delegation announced that their visit had been 'very successful'.[59] In support of this assessment Michael Kennedy points to a motion on Religious Intolerance in Northern Ireland, calling for the appointment of a Royal Commission to investigate religious discrimination in 'housing, employment and other spheres in Northern Ireland', which was put before parliament by Fenner Brockway – with the support of fifty-two Labour

MPs – shortly after the delegation's visit.[60] This was success of a kind, however the motion was not actually debated in parliament (the Leader of the House, Selwyn Lloyd, ruling there was insufficient time)[61] and its brief raising at Westminster must have had limited impact on a nationalist audience in Northern Ireland. Indeed, in the North, impatience with the performance of Nationalist Party parliamentary representatives was growing.

Notes

1 M. McKeown, *The Greening of a Nationalist* (Lucan, Murlough Press, 1986), p. 17.
2 *Ibid.*
3 *Irish Times*, 29 December 1959. See also McKeown, *The Greening*, p. 19.
4 *Irish Times*, 29 December 1959. See also C. McCluskey, *Up Off Their Knees* (Galway, Conn McCluskey & Associates, 1989), p. 62.
5 National Unity organised its first public event, a lecture delivered by the Ballymena born distinguished scientist, Michael A. MacConaill, Professor of Anatomy at University College Cork, at the Wellington Park Hotel in Belfast in February 1960. The purpose of this and other NU events was not to promote a particular blueprint for the future but to provide a platform to those who advanced a variety of solutions to Ireland's divisions. See McKeown, *The Greening*, p. 19 also *Irish Independent*, 8 February 1960; *Irish Press*, 8 February 1960.
6 *Frontier Sentinel*, 26 March 1960.
7 *Ibid.*
8 E. Staunton, *The Nationalists of Northern Ireland 1918–1973* (Dublin, Columba Press, 2001), p. 230.
9 *Ibid.*
10 *Frontier Sentinel*, 26 March 1960.
11 *Ibid.*
12 H. Patterson, *Ireland Since 1939: The Persistence of Conflict* (Dublin, Penguin Ireland, 2006), p. 184.
13 PRONI, D2991/B/24/37, Cahir Healy papers, McGill to Healy, 9 August 1960.
14 *Irish Times*, 10 August 1960. In fact the meeting with Vosper produced nothing of substance. See B. Lynn, *Holding the Ground: The Nationalist Party in Northern Ireland, 1945–72* (Aldershot, Ashgate, 1997), p. 150.
15 PRONI, D2991/B/24/37, Cahir Healy papers, McGill to Healy, 9 August 1960.
16 House of Commons (Northern Ireland) Debates, Volume 47 (1960/61), p. 325, also *Frontier Sentinel*, 19 November 1960.
17 House of Commons (Northern Ireland) Debates, Volume 47 (1960/61), pp. 333–336.
18 *Ibid.*, p. 340.
19 House of Commons (Northern Ireland) Debates, Volume 47 (1960/61), p. 342.
20 The motion was heavily defeated.
21 There was an unfortunate denouement to the main issue of debate some years later. In 1964, at the behest of The Most Revd Eugene O'Callaghan, Bishop of Clogher, Cahir Healy arranged a private meeting with the Attorney General for Northern Ireland,

Edward Warburton Jones MP, to discuss the case of a Catholic priest who was implicated in a pornography ring. Healy reported to the Bishop that Jones, who had not yet decided whether to proceed with a prosecution, was 'sympathetic' to the delicacy of the situation. However, Healy cautioned that in the event that Jones did decide on a prosecution, 'I think the wiser way for our friend would be to be outside the jurisdiction'. Bishop O'Callaghan acted upon Healy's advice and the priest was moved over the border into the Republic. A prosecution did not go ahead and the Bishop (who assumed the guilt of the recalcitrant priest), relieved to have avoided 'a terrible scandal' and the adverse reaction of 'our people' who 'would have been horrified that such a priest would be engaged in the sordid business', wrote in thanks, 'I know that it was chiefly through your mediation and influence that the Attorney General decided not to prosecute'. See PRONI, D2991/B/143/17, Cahir Healy papers, Healy to Bishop O'Callaghan, 17 September 1964; PRONI, D2991/B/143/18, Jones to Healy, 15 September 1964; PRONI, D2991/B/143/24 Bishop O'Callaghan to Healy, 25 September 1964; PRONI, D2991/B/143/19 Bishop O'Callaghan to Healy, 9 October 1944.

22 Details of this survey are contained in M. McKeown, 'Northern Nationalist Attitudes', *Hibernia*, April 1961.

23 *Irish Times*, 12 April 1961. See also McKeown, *The Greening*, p. 21.

24 This was much to the consternation of Republicans. At a National Unity public meeting in Belfast, in March 1961, they accused Diamond of having made use of the Republican movement to further his political career in the 1930s and of now being a 'Stormont Catholic'. Diamond's reply to his erstwhile allies was that while his goals remained the same his methods had changed. See PRONI, HA/32/1/1361, Cahir Healy papers, RUC Crime Special Branch Report, 14 March 1961.

25 *Irish Times*, 12 April 1961.

26 *Ibid.*

27 NAI, DFA 305/14/325, Report on National Unity, April 1963.

28 In their sustained opposition to the Electoral Law Bill – which restricted the voting rights of southern Irish immigrants resident in the North – the Nationalists took up all of the sixty-four hours that had been allocated for debate of this measure. See G. Walker, *A History of the Ulster Unionist Party: Protest, Pragmatism and Pessimism* (Manchester, Manchester University Press, 2004), p. 146.

29 *Belfast Newsletter*, 28 May 1963.

30 *Ibid.*

31 NAI, DFA 305/14/341, Healy to Frank Aiken, 12 May 1962.

32 NAI, DFA 305/14/341, Aiken to Sean Lemass, 18 May 1962.

33 McCluskey, *Up Off Their Knees*, p. 63.

34 *Irish News*, 28 May 1962, cited in Lynn, *Holding the Ground*, p.155.

35 See M.A. Murphy, *Gerry Fitt: Political Chameleon* (Cork, Mercier Press, 2007), pp. 64–65.

36 These were contained in a National Unity pamphlet, 'Unity: New Approaches to Old Problems'. In this McKeown opined that 'the calibre of Nationalist MPs was that of adequate County Councillors'. In retrospect this was an entirely fair, if impolitic, comment. See McKeown, *The Greening*, p. 23.

37 PRONI, D2991/B/44, Cahir Healy papers, National Unity Bulletin, October 1962; see also Lynn, *Holding the Ground*, p. 164.

38 *Irish Times*, 9 March 1962.

39 *Irish Times*, 18 September 1962.

40 H. Patterson and E. Kaufman, *Unionism and Orangeism in Northern Ireland Since 1945: The Decline of the Loyal Family* (Manchester, Manchester University Press, 2007), p. 43.

41 *Irish Times*, 18 December 1962.

42 *Ibid.*

43 *Irish Times*, 7 January 1963.

44 *Irish Times*, 26 January 1963.

45 *Irish News*, 4 February 1963.

46 *Irish Press*, 13 March 1963, see also *Irish Times*, 13 March 1963.

47 See PRONI, D2991/B/44/1, Cahir Healy papers, *National Unity Bulletin*, No. 2, October 1963.

48 In the National Unity pamphlet, 'Unity: New Approaches to Old Problems' Michael McKeown had specifically criticised the tendency of the Nationalist Party to become stuck in the mire of mourning the 'martyred dead' at the expense of the concerns of the living unemployed. See H. Patterson, 'Seán Lemass and the Ulster Question, 1959–65', *Journal of Contemporary History* 34: 145 (1999), p. 149.

49 NAI, DFA 305/14/325 Report on National Unity, April 1963.

50 *Irish News*, 8 April 1963.

51 *Ibid.*

52 Patterson, *Ireland*, pp. 155–157, 185–193.

53 *Irish Times*, 17 April 1963.

54 *Irish Times*, 17 June 1963.

55 PRONI, D2991, Cahir Healy papers, Healy to McCool, 13 March 1963 cited in Staunton, *The Nationalists*, p. 235.

56 *Irish Times*, 19 June 1963.

57 *Irish Times*, 13 January 1964.

58 *Irish Times*, 17 January 1964.

59 *Irish Times*, 1 February 1964.

60 M. Kennedy, *Division and Consensus: The Politics of Cross-Border Relations in Ireland, 1925–1968* (Dublin, Institute of Public Administration, 2000), p. 219.

61 House of Commons (Hansard) Debates, 13 February 1964, vol. 689 c558.

8

Nationalist Party: division and decline, 1964–70

Dr Conn McCluskey, a Dungannon GP and a founder of the civil rights group the Campaign for Social Justice, was later to locate the 'nemesis' of the Nationalist Party to a televised debate between James O'Reilly MP and Brian Faulkner, the Unionist Minister of Home Affairs, that took place in February 1964. The subject of the debate was discrimination but O'Reilly was ill-prepared and hopelessly 'out of his depth' against the urbane Faulkner.[1] When Faulkner challenged O'Reilly to produce any evidence to substantiate his charges of anti-Catholic discrimination in Northern Ireland the hapless O'Reilly, unable to do so, feebly countered that he was not an encyclopaedia with facts at hand.[2] The ill-judged debate, and O'Reilly's televised humiliation, became something of a rallying point for nationalist liberals. Paddy Gormley, speaking in Enniskillen, declared that the time was now right for the political re-organisation of the Nationalist Party and the formulation of a new policy that would appeal across sectarian boundaries.[3] Michael McKeown too was convinced, not only of the urgency of establishing a 'properly organized nationalist political machine' but also of the necessity for National Unity to step from the sidelines and 'intervene directly … in electoral politics'.[4] This intervention came on 19 April, when National Unity hosted a meeting – of some 300-plus delegates – at Mackle's Hotel in the small village of Maghery on the shores of Lough Neagh; the purpose of the meeting, which became known as the Maghery Convention, was to set in motion the establishment of a new 'united Nationalist political organization'.[5] The following day the *Irish News* published a positive assessment of the day's deliberations. It announced that the convention had resulted in the formation of a 'new challenging political unit', provisionally titled the National Political Front (NPF), which was representative of the broad spectrum of constitutional nationalist opinion present on the day.[6] It was further reported that agreement had been reached that the NPF would undertake the task of 'creating the machinery of a normal political party'. Eddie McAteer was described as being enthusiastic about the outcome of the day's proceedings, of which, he was quoted as saying, the 'keynote was unity'.[7] The *Irish News* account, however, exaggerated both the mood of the convention and its level of success. In fact the convention, far from being a united gathering, had some notable absentees; Francis Hanna and Gerry Fitt, both deeply sceptical as to whether the majority of Nationalist Party MPs actually supported the idea of a united and modernised party machine, stayed away.[8] Their scepticism was not without foundation. Some days earlier the Nationalist Party was report-ed as giving the proposal to host the convention a 'cool reception' and Eddie McAteer had made known that his presence in Maghery would only be 'as a matter of courtesy'.[9] When he and his supporters did attend they appeared to some delegates to do so as an 'organised opposition'[10] and it became clear from the outset that their intention was to strongly oppose the establishment of a new Nationalist Party.[11] McAteer's address to the delegates was negative and uncompromising; described as creating 'general unease' among many[12] it was suspected that his sole purpose on the day was to disrupt and 'discredit the motives' of the convention.[13] The fractious and heated atmosphere of the day is further corroborated by Michael McKeown's account in which he de-scribes National Unity supporter Gerry Quigley delivering an 'impassioned' rebuttal of Nationalist Party coat-trailing on the main issue of the day (party re-organisation) which 'brought the house down' and had the assembled audi-ence 'baying for blood'.[14] And yet, despite this high drama, at the conclusion of the day a compromise was brokered by Senator Lennon who was anxious to see the convention conclude with some semblance of unity. The statement announcing the formation of the NPF, and the establishment of a Provisional Council tasked with moving forward proposals to create a united and modern-ised party machine, was that compromise.[15] What emerged from Maghery was therefore perplexing to observers; there appeared to be some movement but at the same time there was an absence of agreement between many delegates and senior Nationalist Party figures on the main objective of the convention, i.e. the establishment of a new political party representative of all strands of na-tionalist opinion. To the *Irish Independent* the outcome appeared 'exiting' while at the same time 'vague and rather muddled'.[16] The tensions of the day were further exacerbated when, on leaving the meeting, McAteer presented himself to the media as representing the general consensus of the convention and, os-tensibly, the new leader of the NPF; a display of political manoeuvring which 'alarmed' many of the delegates.[17] McAteer's self-proclaimed titular leadership was however brief. On 5 May the inaugural meeting of the NPF Provisional Council (which was made up of all existing nationalist MPs and Senators plus twelve lay delegates elected by the convention) appointed the more amenable Joseph Connellan as chairman with Harry Diamond and Joseph McMullan, of

Ardglass, as vice-chairmen. Both Hanna and Fitt were present at this meeting, which concluded with the issue of a statement announcing agreement to 'promote the integration of all existing political parties which support the national ideal into a unified political party'.[18]

The question now was which of the existing parties would be willing to unite and what would be the strategy of any resulting new party? In fact there was continued strong resistance to the whole venture from senior Nationalist Party MPs. Cahir Healy, responding directly to Dr James Scott of National Unity, decried 'splinter groups' and professed that he did not see 'anything seriously wrong' with the Nationalist Party.[19] He pointed to the election of the youthful Austin Currie, at a Stormont by-election in East Tyrone in June 1964 – following the death in May of the sitting member, and Nationalist Party parliamentary leader, Joseph Stewart – as evidence of the Nationalist Party's continued vibrancy. Currie – young, radical and energetic – epitomised all that National Unity looked for in a political representative and he had received their strong and active support during his successful campaign, but he was also careful to reach out to the more conservative elements within nationalism[20]and thus Healy was equally enamoured by his abilities. The *Derry Journal*, which generally reflected Eddie McAteer's outlook, sought to redefine the Maghery unity proposal as something amorphous and meaningless, claiming that, 'it did not propound a scheme on such closely-knit lines as to imply elimination or absorption of this existing nationalist element or that'.[21] However, it was the vacancy of the party leadership, following Joseph Stewart's death, that now presented McAteer with the opportunity of stymieing the kind of developments in nationalist politics envisaged by more liberal elements such as Paddy and Tommy Gormley and National Unity. In the ensuing positioning for the leadership position McAteer took steps to marginalise Paddy Gormley by seizing on a passing comment the latter had made in a recent interview with the *Irish Times*. In a characteristic display of his liberal and non-sectarian standpoint Gormley revealed in the course of the interview that when attending a recent official function at Stormont he was 'not unduly troubled about standing for the British National Anthem or drinking the Royal toast'.[22] Claiming that such views 'were not shared by many others describing themselves as Nationalists' McAteer set out his own position: 'I welcome and encourage cooperation, but not at the expense of Nationalist principles. No concessions to Unionist attitudes has yet been made and I cannot understand why we must surrender ground.'[23] There were those who did share Gormley's outlook and a young Derry teacher, John Hume, writing in the *Irish Times*, applauded his 'realistic attitude'; although Hume was also acutely aware that Gormley's position was a minority one within nationalism and that the task of changing traditionalist perspectives would be a long process.[24] The *Irish Times* too came to Paddy Gormley's defence. It thought that McAteer's inflexibility on Gormley's display of courtesy was somewhat disingenuous considering that Nationalist Party MPs swore the Oath of Allegiance to the Crown as a condition of taking their seats in parliament; it also pointed out that when Nationalist Party representatives had been presented to Queen Elizabeth the Queen Mother during her visit to Omagh the previous year they had not been similarly admonished.[25]

Although it was assumed that the rift between McAteer and Gormley would announce the start of a 'struggle' for the party leadership[26] these assumptions failed to take into account the pressures on the party to show a united face. Gormley made no public response to McAteer's criticisms of him and in June McAteer was unanimously elected as leader by his parliamentary colleagues.[27] However, this outcome had all the appearance of a compromise within the parliamentary party. Eddie McAteer had been proposed as party leader by Joseph Connellan, who was seen as sympathetic to Gormley's conciliatory approach,[28] and seconded by James O'Reilly (Mourne), a traditionalist on the right of the party. In turn Connellan, who was elected as Deputy Leader, had been proposed for the position by Edward Richardson (South Armagh), who was also associated with Gormley, and seconded by R.H. O'Connor, again on the traditionalist wing of the party.[29] At the close of the election Connellan was at pains to distance himself from 'highly distasteful' press reports associating him with splits within the party.[30]

The divisions within the Nationalist Party were, however, only temporarily resolved and the strains within the party, and between the party and the NPF, were soon telegraphed by James O'Reilly in a lengthy *Irish News* article in which he defended the Nationalist Party's 'traditional policy', derided any 'watered-down' form of nationalism and dismissed Paddy Gormley's advocacy of a left-of-centre policy for a new united party as 'so much clap trap'.[31] But it was the announcement by Sinn Féin, in August, that they again intended to contest all twelve Northern Ireland seats in the upcoming Westminster general election in October[32] that stretched these strains to breaking point. The corollary of the announcement was the decision by the Nationalist Party convention for Fermanagh-South Tyrone, which met in Enniskillen on 1 September, not to contest the seat 'in the interests of unity'.[33] Cahir Healy, who had organised the convention, and Senator Lennon, who presided over it, were both strongly in favour of contesting the seat, but as the convention was 'unanimous' in its decision not to put forward a candidate they obviously held little sway over its proceedings. Their position was, however, undoubtedly weakened by those within the Nationalist Party who maintained an antagonistic attitude towards the NPF. This appears to have been the stance of Eddie McAteer who, as Patrick McGill later revealed to Cahir Healy, was 'adamant' that there was to be no 'Political Front Chairman and no PF observers' in Enniskillen.[34] The response of National Unity to the convention's decision to abandon the seat to Sinn Féin was one of fury and in a press release they rounded on it as 'an act of gross political irresponsibility'.[35] The following day the Council of the NPF, meeting in Belfast, also condemned the Fermanagh-South Tyrone convention's unilateral decision; it was, they argued, a 'repudiation' of the programme that had been agreed to at Maghery.[36] McAteer's response to this was to announce that the NPF had 'crumbled', that the 'materials' which comprised the organisation were 'incompatible', and that it would now 'require rebuilding from the foundation'.[37]

McAteer's decision to marginalise potential allies was injudicious. His own preference was in fact to contest the Westminster elections, and yet the decision to exclude the NPF effectively conceded the constituency nomination to Sinn Féin and in so doing exposed the Nationalist Party's political impotence. Even after the Fermanagh-South Tyrone decision McAteer still hoped that the party would stand in Mid Ulster, but again he was to be disappointed by the Mid Ulster local convention's decision to let Sinn Féin have a free run.[38] Frustrated that his leadership of the party conferred so little influence, McAteer now contemplated some form of party reorganisation, though this was to be of a minimal sort (he considered 'a rigid organisation pattern … unsuited to our people').[39] He also toyed with the idea of putting himself forward for the Mid Ulster constituency and proposed this in a letter to Healy;[40] but while Healy favoured contesting the seat it seems that he now resigned himself to the belief that Sinn Féin's candidate, Tom Mitchell, would in all likelihood outpoll an official Nationalist Party candidate.[41] In the end nothing came of McAteer's suggestion.

At the Westminster general election of 15 October 1964 Sinn Féin, now in their post-militarist phase after the end of the IRA's border campaign in 1962,[42] fared slightly better in Fermanagh-South Tyrone and Mid Ulster than they had in the previous 1959 Westminster contest. However, they returned no candidates, had a string of lost deposits and overall received 50,000 fewer votes than in the 1955 Westminster election.[43] The election period itself was marred by the emergence of serous rioting in West Belfast – the Divis Street riots – sparked by an RUC attempt to remove the Irish tricolour flag from the Sinn Féin office in Divis Street; a precipitate and ill-advised action which O'Neill had sanctioned under pressure from the voluble Protestant fundamentalist clergyman Revd Ian Paisley, who viewed O'Neill's rhetorical reformism as an unacceptable capitulation to the enemies of Protestant unionism.[44] The election also witnessed yet another low turn-out of the Catholic electorate, and this left little room for Nationalist Party complacency. McAteer was now spurred to respond to a depressingly familiar situation. Shortly after the election he wrote to the four Belfast MPs (Diamond, Fitt, Hanna and Stewart) proposing a merger of all anti-partitionist parties and elected representatives; suggesting the title 'United Nationalist' for this new party.[45] Observers were pessimistic about the likelihood of a possible merger and suspected that McAteer's action was a response to pressures from a new generation of articulate middle-class Catholics who were critical of the election fiasco and who expected more active and constructive political engagement from the Nationalist Party.[46] The response from the Belfast MPs was a cautious one. A stumbling-block towards unity was the question of whether any new merged party would take on the role of official Opposition at Stormont, which was the preference of the Belfast MPs. [47] Revealingly, this was an issue McAteer side-stepped when announcing a 'dynamic new-look' 39-point Nationalist Party policy statement at a press conference in Belfast on 20 November. When asked under what conditions the Nationalist Party would accept the role of official Opposition McAteer remained deliberately vague, referring enigmatically to possible future 'close and official consultations with the government in Dublin to find out how far we would be prepared to go to get a settlement'.[48] Brendan Lynn, in his important study of the Nationalist Party, argues that the 39-point policy statement unveiled at the press conference – a wide-ranging politically left-of centre document covering political, economic and social issues – provided the party with 'a programme which could be presented as part of its continuing effort to be at the forefront of attempts to secure unity amongst the various opposition groupings'.[49] He is certainly correct that the policy statement was intended to secure unity, for as McAteer was to later admit, its origins lay in the collective efforts of the short-lived NPF sub-committee which arose from Maghery.[50] But that experiment in party building was now at an end and this raised doubts as to the continued relevance of the policy; indeed some pointed to its 'general – even nebulous – terms'[51] and McAteer himself openly admitted that it was, to a large extent, 'platitudinous'. [52] Undoubtedly the 'conciliatory' language of the policy document, with its shift in focus away from the constitutional question and towards civil rights and unemployment issues, won support from the liberal wing of the Nationalist Party; certainly Paddy Gormley thought that on the basis of the document the party could 'transcend religious barriers'.[53] However, there were serious doubts as to whether it provided the means to reconcile the Nationalist Party's own internal divisions and both nationalist and unionist commentators remained sceptical that the policy statement could pave the way to a new united nationalist party. [54] There were good grounds for this scepticism. On 6 December Harry Diamond and Gerry Fitt, who had combined their political organisations at the end of 1963 to create the Republican Labour Party (RLP),[55] announced that there would be no immediate merger between themselves and the Nationalist Party; a decision which was met with some dissent within the RLP and led to the Party secretary, Councillor Sean McGivern, standing down from his post. Publicly McAteer took a magnanimous position on the rebuff declaring that although he was disappointed 'one must not expect overnight miracles';[56] the *Derry Journal*, less diplomatically, called it 'vexatious to the point of being sickening'.[57]

These inter-nationalist wrangles were, however, about to be eclipsed by what appeared at the time as a political event of unparalleled significance. The unannounced visit of Sean Lemass to meet his counterpart, Capt. Terence O'Neill, at Stormont on 14 January 1965, long described with the epithet 'historic', was to have a profound though nuanced impact on the Nationalist Party, and nationalist politics generally. The initial response of the Nationalist Party to the meeting appeared positive, Patrick Gormley was swift to applaud O'Neill for meeting Lemass ('a bold decision')[58] and McAteer welcomed it as 'a significant step forward'.[59] However, Lemass had not informed McAteer of the meeting in advance and the latter deferred any announcement on his party's future strategy until after discussions with Lemass in Dublin. Despite the apparent cordiality of their meeting and the appearance of agreement on the issue of the Nationalist Party assuming the role of Official Opposition at Stormont,[60] McAteer later revealed that his meeting with the Taoiseach was in fact an uncomfortable affair which left him feeling 'more worried than ever'.[61] He found Lemass unsympathetic to the 'oppressed Irish minority in the six Counties' and the Taoiseach's opinion that 'Catholics in the North were just as intractable as Protestants' clearly unsettled McAteer, who departed Dublin fearing that 'the Northern Irish were very much on their own'.[62]

The announcement by McAteer that the Nationalist Party would accept the role of official Opposition came on 2 February 1965. The Dublin *Evening Press* noted that the decision had 'been made easier' by a more traditional anti-partitionist speech Lemass had recently delivered in Dun Laoghaire in which he reaffirmed his government's 'ultimate object of achieving National unity'.[63] In his statement announcing the Nationalist Party's new departure McAteer appeared to downplay what some at the time were calling a 'revolutionary transformation'.[64] He was at pains to present the situation as a transitional step towards a united Ireland and he emphasised that the Nationalist Party's new role would necessarily operate within a specific timeframe determined by the temporary nature of Northern Ireland's constitutional status ('Stormont must be seen as a federal or regional Irish parliament to continue in existence until fears of an all-Ireland parliament are finally resolved');[65] he also claimed that

assuming the role of official Opposition would '[f]or all practical purposes …
mean little change in existing practice'.[66]

Despite this low-key response the exceptionality of the moment reignited
the efforts of those who remained committed to the united nationalist party
objective of the Maghery Convention. Within days of McAteer's announcement Councillor Sean McGivern, the former RLP secretary, along with the
entire Andersonstown branch of the RLP, resigned from the party en masse
and made known their intention to seek a closer alignment with the Nationalist
Party.[67] Some days later a new political organisation, provisionally titled the
National Party, was launched at a meeting in Belfast attended by 200 'invited
delegates', including Eddie McAteer and Senator Lennon.[68] Gerry Quigley, the
former NPF member who had been so vocal in his criticism of the Nationalist
Party at Maghery, was named as chairman of the new party with Councillor
McGivern as secretary.[69] Although this latest addition to the nationalist canon
was clearly left-of-centre in its political outlook (its founding policy document
has been described as 'nominally socialist'),[70] Quigley announced that there
were no areas of disagreement between the new group and the Nationalist Party
and spoke of his hopes of a 'full association' between them in the future.[71]
Quigley was undoubtedly exaggerating the extent of agreement between his
group and the Nationalist Party (or certainly its right wing) but if he held out
hopes of strengthening the left of the party then he underestimated those senior
figures in the Nationalist Party who remained strongly opposed to any political
merger. Patrick McGill in particular was highly dismissive of what he deroga-
tively called the 'Quigleyites' and warned McAteer of his suspicions that their
objective was 'takeover' and not some kind of fusion as they claimed.[72]

In the Stormont general election of November 1965 the National Party –
renamed the National Democratic Party (NDP) in June – secured what was
to be its only parliamentary success when it took Frank Hanna's seat of Belfast
Central (following his retirement from politics).[73] The Nationalist Party, contesting its first ever election as an official opposition, held its nine safe seats with
some minor change in personnel: Cahir Healy finally retired from active politics, at the age of eighty-seven, and in his absence John Carron was returned
(unopposed) to Healy's seat in South Fermanagh.[74] A major blow to the party,
however, was an almost fatal car accident involving Paddy Gormley in Co.
Monaghan, just two days before the election. As he lay critically ill in hospital
Gormley was returned unopposed to his Mid Derry seat, however, although
he was later to resume his political career the severity of his injuries were such
that he never fully recovered from them.[75] Paddy Gormley was a significant
figure in nationalist politics in that he possessed qualities of political tolerance and generosity of spirit that won him the respect and admiration of his

political opponents – as he lay grievously ill in Drogheda hospital, in the Irish Republic, he was visited by the Unionist Prime Minister Capt. Terence O'Neill. He also won praise from the liberal Unionist newspaper the *Belfast Telegraph* for his preparedness to 'seek a social accommodation' in Northern Ireland.[76] This did not mean that Gormley shied away from vigorously raising Catholic grievances; however, he saw the alleviation of these grievances as being inti- mately connected to adverse economic and social conditions which impacted on both Protestants and Catholics. The key to lessening ethno-religious ten- sions, therefore, lay in dealing with the common grievances of unemployment and economic marginalisation (urban and rural) which fed sectarian divisions in Northern Ireland. For Gormley this meant moving away from a ghettoised politics fixated on the constitutional question and he saw Lemass and O'Neill meeting as heralding the possibility of just such a development. He was not the only one enthused with optimism by the new political diplomacy. In a letter to Jack Sawyers, the editor of the *Belfast Telegraph,* in February 1965, Cardinal William Conway, the head of the Catholic Church in Ireland, spoke of his belief 'that the atmosphere has lightened in the past year in a way that we would not have dared hope for'.[77] And yet traditional nationalist gestur- al politics were very much still in evidence during the election campaign. In Derry Eddie McAteer's opponent Seamus Quinn, a local trade union official standing as an Independent Labour candidate, joined a deputation to London to petition the British government to reverse its decision to close the Sea Eagle naval base in Derry which would result in the loss of 500 local jobs. McAteer, however, while expressing regret that jobs would be lost, refused to oppose the closure of the base on the grounds that Derry men should not be dependent on work provided by the British navy.[78] After the election McAteer, in an apparent continuation of the 'existing practice' he was reluctant to move beyond, refused to attend the state opening of Stormont in December stating that 'too much importance was attached to attendance'.[79]

The Nationalist Party now entered an uneasy and uncertain period of re- adjustment to its new role at Stormont. With a Westminster general election scheduled to take place in March 1966 McAteer took steps to sharpen the party's image as a disciplined and coherent opposition capable of overcoming the debilitating factionalism of the past. At a constituency delegate meeting in Belfast, in February, he announced measures that were intended to demon- strate that the Nationalist Party was taking the necessary steps to secure this goal: it was revealed that the party had adopted the 39-point policy charter published in 1964, that it would hold its first ever annual conference in May, and that a complete reorganisation of the party, from the branch level upwards, would be undertaken.[80] Reorganisation was however a long-term prospect and there was still little internal agreement between liberals and the traditionalists as to the future direction the party should take. In the enforced absence of Paddy Gormley, still recovering from his injuries, it was Austin Currie who now emerged as the most vocal advocate of moving the party towards the left and away from its 'Green Tory' image; a position supported by the National Democratic Party, which maintained its position of being open to discuss 'any reasonable proposal' for amalgamation with the Nationalist Party.[81] On the traditionalist side James O'Reilly (described in one press report as 'a sort of Nationalist Enoch Powell'),[82] remained resolute that the party should remain 'uncontaminated and undiluted' in its ideological outlook.[83] However, McAteer astutely recognised that the changed political circumstances in which he found himself necessitated a new proactive approach with the Unionist government. He now made it known that he was looking to that government for 'some token … that they are going to normalise conditions in the Six Counties'[84] and, not unreasonably, he warned O'Neill against 'resting on his laurels' when it came to reforms addressing Catholic grievances.[85] There was also a noticeable moderation of McAteer's tone in the run-up to the Westminster election. In a departure from his earlier emphasis on the maximalist goal of achieving Irish unity McAteer now suggested that the Nationalist Party concentrate its efforts on achieving civil rights within Northern Ireland and he called on nationalists to 'open our eyes' and accept the need to work towards 'peaceful negotiation' within the Stormont parliament which, he acknowledged, would be 'a fairly long time surviving'.[86]

The Nationalist Party's chances of capitalising on its changed circumstances by consolidating its position at the Westminster election were, yet again, to be obstructed by the continued autonomy of the constituency conventions responsible for selecting parliamentary candidates; as in the past the decisions of the conventions continued to frustrate Nationalist Party hopes of contesting the Westminster election as the sole representatives of the Catholic elector-ate. In Mid Ulster Thomas Mitchell again went forward for Sinn Féin as the only anti-partitionist candidate. In Fermanagh-South Tyrone, meanwhile, an attempt to propose an agreed Unity candidate – the Enniskillen businessman J.J. Donnelly[87] – failed to win the support of Sinn Féin who stood their own man, Rory Brady (Ruairí Ó Brádaigh) against Donnelly, which ensured that the seat went to the Unionist candidate.[88] In the election, as in the previous Westminster election in 1964, the Sinn Féin vote continued to slide and none of their candidates were returned.[89] Nonetheless, Sinn Féin were able to stand candidates in five constituencies[90] while the Nationalist Party in comparison put forward only one – the still ailing Paddy Gormley who stood in the safe Unionist constituency of Londonderry (where he achieved a creditable vote).[91]

The Unionist Party almost achieved a clean sweep in the election; however, there was one gain for a nationalist candidate; Gerry Fitt took West Belfast for the RLP, his victory aided both by the announcement of support for his candidature from all the Nationalist Party Stormont MPs and by the NDP's decision (under pressure from Fitt and the Nationalist Party) not to stand against him.[92] Fitt stood as the only nationalist candidate in the constituency.[93]

For the Nationalist Party the setback of the election was shortly to be compounded by a general deterioration in the political climate (and in communal relations) resulting from a series of event, held in April 1966 to commemorate the 50th anniversary of the 1916 Easter Rising. The Nationalist Party had little involvement in these commemorative events, which did attract appreciable levels of nationalist support across Northern Ireland.[94] Sinn Féin, on the other hand, played a substantial role and, although the Republican movement was in transit on its journey towards the Marxist left, a number of senior republicans (all of whom were to become founder members of the Provisionals) took the opportunity to publicly criticise the Nationalist Party's moderate stance and to issue veiled (and direct) calls for physical force solutions to partition.[95] The Unionist government, which had prior fears that the commemoration could be the occasion for a resurgence of IRA activity, had put in place security precautions to respond to this eventuality; however, O'Neill was anxious not to be seen by the new Labour premier, Harold Wilson, to be over-reacting to the situation and so he decided to allow the commemorative rallies and marches to go ahead with little restriction. This decision was much to the ire of Ian Paisley and his Protestant ultra supporters who, provocatively branding liberal Unionists as 'Papists', accused O'Neill of 'capitulating to the rebels'.[96] Even more disturbingly the loyalist paramilitary gang, the Ulster Volunteer Force (UVF), taking advantage of unionist hysteria in some quarters, embarked on a terror campaign which involved targeting and killing Catholics.[97] Here was the delicacy of the situation: O'Neill was coming under increasing pressure from the unionist right for conceding too much to nationalism, while at the same time the Nationalist Party were accused of weakly capitulating to unionism by republicans.

McAteer was alive to the problems his party faced but by the time of the Nationalist Party conference in May he had little to show in the way of the hoped for 'tokens' from the Unionist government. It appears that greater access to British politicians continued to sustain McAteer's 'cautious optimism' of the potential for positive political developments in Northern Ireland – in August he travelled to London to meet with the British Home Secretary, Roy Jenkins, and the Conservative spokesman on Home Affairs, Quintin Hogg.[98] Certainly, the energetic campaigning of the 'indefatigable' Gerry Fitt at Westminster (where he enjoyed the support of the 100-strong Labour back-bench group the Campaign for Democracy in Ulster)[99] supported an impression that the nationalist viewpoint was now being taken seriously by the major British political parties.[100] However, both Jenkins and Hogg entertained a sanguine view of O'Neill's capacity for progressive reform and they too resorted to the Westminster convention of not interfering in matters that were claimed to be the responsibility of the Stormont parliament. In the North O'Neill faced resistance from unionists who saw the whole question of reform as a zero sum game in which one side's gain must inevitably mean another's loss. In response to a joint memorandum presented to the Unionist government by the NILP and the Irish Congress of Trades Unions, in September 1966 – calling for an overhaul of the local government franchise, fair boundaries in local elections, measures to end discrimination in housing and employment, fair representation for the minority on public boards and the appointment of an ombudsman – the Unionist Attorney General, E. W. Jones, counselled O'Neill and his Cabinet against concessions which, he warned, could result in the North's 'destruction as a political entity'.[101] McAteer's erstwhile optimism was short-lived. In early December he warned that if the Queen's Speech opening the new parliamentary session at Stormont did not indicate new measures to deal with religious discrimination and electoral reform then the Nationalist Party would surrender their role of official Opposition.[102] His warning also contained the following ill-guarded passage: 'History has shown that people who pin their hopes for improvement on constitutional methods, and are continually frustrated, eventually turn to other means to achieve their aims. I would not really be surprised if frustration led to a resurgence of the bomb-and-bullet boys.'[103] This return to the less conciliatory language of the past brought swift condemnation from some of McAteer's party colleagues and he was forced to clarify that his comments were made in a personal capacity and not as party leader.[104] In the event McAteer's threat to withdraw his party from official Opposition was not carried out, however all Nationalist Party and RLP MPs did boycott the Queen's Speech which, while announcing a commission to review the boundaries of parliamentary constituencies in Northern Ireland, made no specific reference to electoral reform or discrimination.[105]

On the eve of the Nationalist Party's second annual conference, in July 1967,[106] Austin Currie, writing in the *Irish Times*, provided a pessimistic assessment of the situation as he saw it. He pointed out that the decision to accept the role of official Opposition in 1965 'had not been an easy decision to take' and that the decision was 'not popular' amongst a 'sizeable proportion' of the party membership; nevertheless, they had gone down that road and in doing so they had made 'no hard and fast demands' on the Unionist government. However, he felt that after two-and-a-half years as official Opposition the Nationalist Party now found themselves 'bitterly disappointed with Unionist intransigence and lack of cooperation' and disillusioned with 'Captain O'Neill's "Brave New Ulster"'. Currie was of the opinion that the Unionist government's response had been indifferent and 'had not been followed up with action'. He gave specific examples to illustrate his disappointment: the Leader of the Opposition and his Shadow Ministers had been given no right to any form of consultation with the government, 'even on non controversial matters'; the Leader of the Opposition was denied a salary, or even allowances; and, the government had dragged its feet over the reorganisation of local government. Currie wondered 'for how much longer must there be one way traffic'.[107] A *Belfast Newsletter* editorial thought that Currie exaggerated his case somewhat; it admitted the response of the government to the Nationalist Party had not been 'wholehearted', but it pointed out that the Nationalist Party attitude to their new role had also been 'grudging'.[108] The paper, however, went on to make much of the emollient tone of McAteer's address to the conference which, it was assumed, pointed the way 'towards that ideal of better community relations to which the present administration is committed'.[109] This seriously misread both the malign effects of the government's failure to introduce meaningful, or even symbolic, reforms (of the type highlighted by Currie) and the rapidly reducing options, and credibility, of the Nationalist Party.

At the party conference speaker after speaker rose to detail a litany of unresolved Catholic grievances: the lack of industry and employment in Catholic areas, unreformed local government electoral laws, etc. The issue for the party now was how to address these grievances by pushing forward with a civil rights agenda. There is evidence that McAteer had moved towards prioritising the attainment of civil rights in Northern Ireland above the goal of Irish unity (this was his stated position at a meeting with British officials in November 1968)[110] but, in his party leader's speech to the delegates, McAteer singularly failed to establish an authoritative position as to the way forward. He acknowledged that there was 'some little impatience' among Nationalist Party supporters but he urged them to 'be realistic' and recognise that they 'had little room for manoeuvre'. However, what he did offer the delegates – the prospect that 'in the future there will be closer co-operation and liaison between ourselves and the Government in Dublin'[111] – suggested a return to the nationalist *attentisme* of old. In response the *Belfast Telegraph*, while praising McAteer's moderation and pragmatism, cautioned against looking to Dublin for 'salvation'; the Irish government, it noted, had given nationalists 'little enough encouragement' to do this.[112] These comments in the *Belfast Telegraph* editorial leader were picked up by an official of the Department of External Affairs in Dublin, who observed, in a note to his superior Brendan Nolan, that northern nationalist calls for further contacts with Dublin had become more pronounced in recent weeks. The official had some sympathy with these calls, he considered that 'a general weakening of the link [with the Nationalist Party] through neglect or over-cautiousness on our part might be detrimental to the long term interests of Irish unity' and he suggested that 'rather than leave our friends "out in the cold" we should ... seek to cultivate their friendship in the furtherance of our common aims'.[113] Enda Staunton has commented that 'Unfortunately for the nationalists, there was no recorded follow-up to this rare spasm of bad conscience.'[114] But there was a follow-up. Nolan did indeed acknowledge the possible benefits that could ensue from closer contacts between political parties in the Republic and northern nationalists, it could, he thought, lead to 'a new identity of purpose ... which would have greater appeal for the younger electorate';[115] but nonetheless he counselled: 'This would appear ... to be impracticable at the present time and be unlikely in the future. It is not therefore clear whether any purpose would be served in suggesting at the present time that the political parties here should tackle the question.'[116] He also recognised that such a policy of inaction would have consequences, 'inevitably ... the gap between the Nationalists in the North and the people here will grow wider in the future',[117] but significantly Nolan thought that would have a long-term beneficial outcome: 'This development will of course force the Nationalists to adopt policies which are fully in keeping with their status in the Six Counties itself and which will offer some hope of attracting support from those who are present committed to the Unionist Party.'[118]

This reluctance on the part of the Irish government apparently was not unknown to the Nationalist Party leadership; in later years McAteer revealed that he was only too aware of Dublin's 'less than enthusiasm to get involved' in the North.[119] Nonetheless, this did not prevent an outburst of outraged incredulity in response to a speech delivered by Sean Lemass at Queen's University Belfast, in October 1967, in which he blamed politicians on both sides of the political divide in Northern Ireland for 'perpetuating the politico-religious cleavage' and called upon nationalists to seek to 'promote the prosperity of the North and the efficiency of its administration'.[120] The *Derry Journal* called Lemass's comments 'astonishing',[121] for Gerry Fitt they were 'amazing',[122] while McAteer held that in departing so radically from the historic narrative of nationalist grievances (in which any notion of equivalency of responsibility was an anathema) Lemass 'had goofed' while shamelessly 'ingratiating himself with the Unionists by tarring everybody with the same brush'.[123] Lemass had spoken at Queen's University as an ex-Taoiseach, having resigned his position in November 1966 to be replaced by Jack Lynch, but his views undoubtedly reflected a widely held attitude amongst a significant section of political opinion in the South. This did not imply indifference to or a lack of sympathy with nationalists in the North. There was awareness that O'Neill's rhetorical moderation and conciliatory gestures had not gone far enough and that they had not brought any 'significant material improvement' to Catholics;[124] but empathy did not override hard-headed realism. Commenting on Lemass's speech, and its 'traumatic effect', the *Irish Independent* pointed to what it regarded as an inescapable fact: 'The trouble is that no one can really deny the truth of Mr Lemass's charge. Most of the attacks on him amount to an admission of guilt and a plea of extenuating circumstances.'[125] The *Irish Times* starkly summed up what it believed would likely be the Irish government response to any future requests Eddie McAteer might make for assistance: 'Don't ask us to do anything.'[126]

If McAteer's leadership appeared to stall at this time there were other strategies that now came to the forefront. The Northern Ireland Civil Rights Association (NICRA), founded in January 1967[127] as an umbrella organisation bringing together existing campaigning groups and radical political organisations and parties, gathered pace as the vehicle articulating the demand that Catholic grievances should be addressed. The way forward for NICRA was not to be a series of appeals to Dublin or London but a campaign of activism and protest. In August 1968 Austin Currie, who had been prominent in highlighting discriminatory practices in the allocation of local authority housing in Tyrone, proposed that NICRA hold a march from Coalisland to Dungannon to protest against anti-Catholic discrimination in the county. The march went ahead, although ultra-loyalist opposition and a police cordon prevented the holding of a rally at the end of the march.[128] Currie was enthused with the result and his enthusiasm was expressed with a passionate and unrestrained rhetoric: 'O'Neill and those Orange bigots behind him [will] realise once and for all that we are on our way forward. We will keep going with disobedience and anything else that is necessary to achieve our aims.'[129] The Dungannon march was nonetheless a peaceful affair.[130] A further march was held in Derry, on 5 October, but on this occasion the Stormont Minister of Home Affairs, William Craig, banned the march (not outright but from certain areas of the city)[131] and the RUC were tasked with preventing its progress. In this they performed poorly and the over-reaction of the RUC officers, to what was in fact a very small and low-level demonstration, spectacularly, and fatefully, escalated into two days of rioting between Catholic youths and the RUC.[132] McAteer, whose presence on 5 October was a reluctant one, and who had attempted to restrain those marchers engaging in confrontation with the RUC[133] (both he and Gerry Fitt were struck by police batons), now had to respond to unfolding events, and his response, announced on 15 October, was that the Nationalist Party would withdraw from their role as official Opposition at Stormont.[134]

This was not the only response to the tumultuous events in Derry. On 18 December 1968 Paddy Gormley rose to speak in Stormont, the first time he had spoken in the House since his almost fatal car accident in November 1965. In his address Gormley referred back to a speech he had delivered in his constituency shortly before his accident, in which he had called upon the nationalist Opposition to abandon old verities and adopt radical new positions ('to forget past ideologies and accept facts'),[135] and he thought now, as he did then, that this was still required and 'what the people at large want'. He then turned his attention to the current situation:

> I have stressed to my constituents the fact that while there are civil rights which they want there are civil duties which go along with those rights. I am very conscious of this. During the past few months I have heard nobody talk about civil duties; all the talk has been about civil rights. If we are to have a united community every man will have to be prepared to do his duty. Excuses and electrifying speeches are no good. As I have said, people will have to accept facts even if they are unpleasant. It is not necessary to accept them in defeat; they can be accepted and then changed. One cannot close a door if one does not see it. It is as simple as that.[136]

Gormley's comments came shortly after O'Neill's televised 'Ulster at the Crossroads' speech, broadcast on 9 December, in which O'Neill had committed himself to a reforming civil rights programme, while at the same time reassuring unionists that this would not amount to a diminution of the Unionist Party's parliamentary dominance.[137] The content and tenor of Gormley's contribution was therefore of significance; for while being a response to O'Neill's speech, and the initial popular support that it received, it also indicated a radical reappraisal of nationalism's political relationship to, and engagement with, the Northern Ireland state. Gormley saw 'civil duties' and 'civil rights' as being inextricably linked within a democratic system. He believed that a genuine reform process in Northern Ireland required both governmental even-handedness and an acceptance, by nationalists, of their civic responsibilities within that polity; this did not, in his mind, pre-determine any particular outcome but clearly he felt that a 'united community' and adherence to democratic principles were an essential in arriving at any political settlement. This was politics premised on Paddy Gormley's incisive moderation and his commitment to democratic practices; however, his influence already severely weakened by his enforced absence, was soon to be over-shadowed by the rapidly deteriorating conditions arising from the 'long march' (from Belfast to Derry) organised by the leftist People's Democracy group in January 1969. The marchers (mainly student radicals), ignoring the advice of NICRA not to march and inflame an already febrile situation, were viciously attacked en route by militant loyalists; the failure of the police in preventing the assaults on the marchers confirmed in the minds of many nationalists the complicity of the Unionist government.[138] The event was to trigger days of intensive rioting between the RUC and residents in nationalist districts of Derry and Belfast. The exhilaration of the ensuing political maelstrom which followed led some to believe that progressive, even revolutionary, changes would ensue,[139] but instead there was only a tragic re-emergence of bitter ethno-religious animosities; an eventuality that Paddy Gormley had hoped to avoid, the door that he had hoped to close. His own political marginalisation was to be brusquely demonstrated at the 1969 Stormont general election in February when he lost his Mid Derry seat (coming in third) to the civil rights campaigner Ivan Cooper (standing as an Independent). Gormley was not the Nationalist Party's only electoral fatality to the rising civil rights activists; Edward Richardson lost his seat in South Armagh (to Paddy O'Hanlon) and, more spectacularly, Eddie McAteer lost his Foyle seat to John Hume.[140] New faces did not, however, automatically guarantee new panaceas; in a rapidly deteriorating and unstable political situation some of the new Stormont MPs were overwhelmed by the unfolding sectarian conflagration in Belfast and in August 1969 three MPs – Paddy O'Hanlon, Paddy Kennedy and Paddy Devlin[141] – rushed to the office of the DEA in Dublin to deliver an emotive plea for arms to protect Catholic districts; a plea that was declined.[142]

Tensions within the Nationalist Party could now no longer be contained. There was speculation before the party's annual conference, in November 1969, about the continued membership of Tom Gormley and Austin Currie.[143] In the event Tom Gormley resigned from the party prior to the conference while Currie did not attend; Tom Gormley later became an early member of the non-sectarian Alliance Party[144] while Currie gravitated towards those civil rights activists who were soon to form the Social Democratic and Labour Party (SDLP). At the conference, party chairman James Doherty spoke disparagingly of the 'few rats who are running away from what they think is a sinking ship'.[145] And yet, despite his angry words, Doherty's outlook was essentially reforming and moderate, in fact not so distant from that of the Gormley brothers.[146] In his chairman's address Doherty criticised Michael Farrell, the leader of People's Democracy, whom, he alleged, was more interested in 'chaos, anarchy and disorder' than civil rights. He also went on to call for 'practical measures' – he suggested economic development in areas West of the Bann and in South Down and South Armagh – to deal with underlying grievances, and he pointedly stressed that the Nationalist Party's immediate objective should be 'right policies' and 'good ideas' rather than unachievable political goals.[147] Noticeably, in the absence of Paddy and Tom Gormley the resolutions before the conference were weighted heavily towards 'the re-unification of the country',[148] which reflected Eddie McAteer's own return to a nationalism that restored the immediacy of Irish territorial unity as its strategic desiderata.[149] Doherty, in contrast, took it upon himself to point out to delegates that the existing economic and social disparities between the two states in Ireland meant that nationalists in the North 'saw re-union as a challenge to the stark actuality of their standard of living'. He expressed his hope that Dublin would direct its efforts toward 'levelling-up the two economies' and, with this in mind, he supported a motion calling on the Irish government 'to set up a working party to examine in detail the social, economic and other problems that are obstacles to the realisation of national unity'.[150] However, from the vantage of its remove the Irish government could see the writing on the wall more clearly than those on the ground; DEA officials noted that moves to set up the SDLP were advancing[151] and observed that the Nationalist Party was 'in a state of disarray … and may even disappear as a significant influence in the North within a foreseeable time'. When, in February 1970, the Executive of the Nationalist Party forwarded a request to the Irish government to establish a working party 'to keep the situation in the Six Counties under constant review',[152] the response was an emphatic no. The only issue of concern for the DEA was how the Taoiseach's reply to the Nationalist Party Executive 'might be softened'.[153]

The decision of the Irish government to distance itself from the Nationalist Party was undoubtedly damaging, even though relations with Dublin had hardly been close. It was, however, the party's own internal disagreements that were to prove fatally divisive. Throughout 1969 rioting and sectarian confrontation had intensified on the streets of Belfast and Derry and by 1970 republicans (and loyalists) were engaged in armed actions, the impact of which was to only further inflame an already incendiary situation. In October 1970 the party chairman, James Doherty, along with the party treasurer, Eugene O'Hare, and Tom McDonnell, the chairman of the Derry branch of the party – voicing the concerns of what Doherty would later call a 'large minority' in the party[154] – jointly announced their resignation from the Nationalist Party over what they claimed was the Derry branch's 'serious abdication of political responsibility' in failing to condemn recent violence in the city.[155] As in Belfast rioting in Derry had escalated and was supplemented by the growing activities of the IRA.[156] Doherty and his colleagues, in their letter of resignation, wrote of their unease that by not openly and unambiguously condemning all acts violence in the city the party position might be construed to be one of 'neutrality or apathy'. In his reply Eddie McAteer regretted the loss of 'three of the strongest pillars of the Party', but while taking note of their concerns his comment that 'there might be equal need to condemn the authorities for failure to deal with the causes of violence'[157] appeared to suggest the very 'neutrality' that Doherty, O'Hare and McDonnell found so unacceptable. Their constitutional nationalism entailed a rejection of undemocratic means which was transparent and unequivocal, certainly a laudable and principled position. The loss of these men, some of the most able and dynamic members of the Nationalist Party, sealed the fate of that party: without the support of its 'strongest pillars' its decline was inevitable.

Notes

1 C. McCluskey, *Up Off Their Knees* (Galway, Conn McClusky & Associates, 1989), p. 63, see also M. McKeown, *The Greening of a Nationalist* (Lucan, Murlough Press, 1986), p. 25.
2 See John Hume's account of the exchange, *Irish Times*, 18 May 1964. McCluskey recalled that, in response to O'Reilly's discomfiture, he 'squirmed' in his seat in embarrassment. McCluskey, *Up Off Their Knees*, p. 63.
3 For an account of this speech see *The Kerryman*, 6 June 1964.
4 McKeown, *The Greening*, p. 25.
5 *Ibid*. On the background to the organisation of the Maghery Convention see *Irish Times*, 29 May 1964.
6 *Irish News*, 20 April 1964.
7 *Ibid*.
8 *Irish Independent*, 27 April 1964.
9 *Irish Times*, 28 April 1964.
10 *Ibid*.
11 *Ibid*., and *Irish Times*, 29 May 1964.
12 *Dungannon Observer*, 25 April 1964.
13 *Ibid*., see also McCluskey, *Up Off Their Knees*, p. 65.
14 McKeown, *The Greening*, p. 26.
15 *Ibid*.
16 *Irish Independent*, 27 April 1964.
17 *Irish Times*, 28 April 1964.
18 *Irish Independent*, 6 May 1964.
19 PRONI, D2991/B/13/13, Cahir Healy papers, Cahir Healy, 'There is Nothing Wrong With the Nationalist Party: A Reply to Professor Scott', 1964.
20 B. Purdie, *Politics in the Streets: The Origins of the Civil Rights Movement in Northern Ireland* (Belfast, The Blackstaff Press, 1990), p. 53.
21 *Derry Journal*, 24 April 1964.
22 *Irish Times*, 8 May 1964.
23 *Irish Times*, 13 May 1964.
24 *Irish Times*, 19 May 1964, see also *Irish Times*, 18 May 1964.
25 *Irish Times*, 29 May 1964.
26 *Irish Times*, 13 May 1964.
27 *Irish Times*, 3 June 1964.
28 *Irish Times*, 29 May 1964.

29 *Ibid.*

30 *Irish News*, 3 June 1964.

31 *Irish News*, 24 July 1964.

32 *Irish Times*, 3 August, 1964.

33 *Irish Times*, 2 September 1964.

34 PRONI, D2991/B/24/56, Cahir Healy papers, McGill to Healy, n.d.

35 *Irish Times*, 8 September 1964.

36 *Irish News*, 9 September 1964.

37 *Ibid.*

38 PRONI, D2991/B, Cahir Healy papers, McAteer to Healy, 19 September 1964.

39 PRONI, D2991/B/21/4, Cahir Healy papers, McAteer to Healy, 28 September 1964.

40 *Ibid.*

41 E. Staunton, *The Nationalists of Northern Ireland 1918–1973* (Dublin, Columba Press, 2001), p. 246.

42 The IRA had officially abandoned the campaign in February 1962. See R. English, *Armed Struggle: A History of the IRA* (London, Macmillan, 2003), p. 75.

43 S. Prince and G. Warner, *Belfast and Derry in Revolt: A New History of the Start of the Troubles* (Dublin, Irish Academic Press, 2012), p. 58.

44 On the Divis Street riots see *Ibid.*, pp. 51–62.

45 PRONI, D2991/B/21/5, Cahir Healy papers, McAteer to Healy, copy of letter sent to H. Diamond, C. Stewart, F. Hanna and G. Fitt, 29 October 1964.

46 *Irish Independent*, 16 November 1964.

47 *Derry Journal*, 3 November 1964.

48 *Irish News*, 21 November 1964.

49 B. Lynn, *Holding the Ground: The Nationalist Party in Northern Ireland, 1945–72* (Aldershot, Ashgate, 1997), p. 180.

50 *Ibid.*

51 *Irish Independent*, 23 November 1964.

52 *Ibid.*

53 *Ibid.*

54 See the article by Proinsias Mac Aonghusa in the *Kilkenny People*, 27 November 1964 and the editorial of the *Belfast Newsletter*, 4 December 1964.

55 M. Murphy, *Gerry Fitt: Political Chameleon* (Cork, Mercier Press, 2007), p. 68.

56 *Irish News*, 7 December 1964.

57 *Derry Journal*, 8 December 1964.

58 *Irish Times*, 19 January 1965.

59 M. Kennedy, *Division and Consensus: The Politics of Cross-Border Relations in Ireland, 1925–1969* (Dublin, Institute of Public Administration, 2000), p. 237.

60 *Ibid.*

61 Frank Curran, *Derry: Countdown to Disaster* (Dublin, Gill & MacMillan, 1986), pp. 37–38.

62 *Ibid.* On Lemass's attitude towards northern nationalists see also H Patterson, 'Seán Lemass and the Ulster Question, 1959–65', *Journal of Contemporary History* 34: 145, p. 148.

63 *Evening Press*, 2 February 1965.

64 *Irish Times*, 3 February 1965.

65 *Ibid.*

66 *Ibid.*

67 *Irish News*, 5 February 1965.

68 *Irish News*, 8 February 1965.

69 *Irish Press*, 8 February 1965.

70 I. McAllister, 'Political Opposition in Northern Ireland: The National Democratic Party, 1965–1970', *Economic and Social Review* 6 (1975), p. 361.

71 *Irish Weekly*, 13 February 1965.

72 McGill to McAteer, 30 November 1965, cited in Staunton, *The Nationalists*, p. 253.

73 Hanna had condemned Quigley's group as belonging to the 'same narrow sectarian opposition conclave' as the Nationalist Party (*Irish News*, 26 February 1965) and yet it was a former member of Hanna's Independent Labour Group (John Brennan) who took his vacated seat.

74 Carron was no newcomer to Nationalist politics, he had been vice chairman of the IAPL in 1946 and was fifty-six years old at the time of his election.

75 See Paddy Gormley's obituary, *Belfast Telegraph*, 3 September 2001.

76 *Belfast Telegraph*, 8 December 1965.

77 Cardinal Conway to Sawyers, 6 February 1965, cited in A Gailey, *Crying in the Wilderness Jack Sawyers: A Liberal Editor in Ulster, 1939–69* (Belfast, The Institute of Irish Studies, 1995), p. 93.

78 *Irish Times*, 25 November 1965.

79 *Irish Times*, 13 December 1965.

80 *Irish Press*, 15 February 1966.

81 *Ibid.*

82 *Irish Independent*, 14 February 1966.

83 *Ibid.*

84 *Belfast Newsletter*, 8 February 1966.

85 *Irish News*, 12 February 1966.

86 *Frontier Sentinel*, 19 March 1966, cited in M. O'Callaghan, 'From Casement Park to Toomebridge – The Commemoration of the Easter Rising in Northern Ireland in 1966', in M.E. Daly and M. O'Callaghan (eds), *1916 in 1966 Commemorating the Easter Rising* (Dublin, Royal Irish Academy, 2007), p. 127.

87 *The Fermanagh Herald*, 19 March 1966.

88 Donnelly out-polled Ó Brádaigh.

89 In percentage terms the Sinn Féin vote fell from 15.9 per cent in 1964 to 10.5 per cent in 1966. For details see www.ark.ac.uk/elections/fw64.htm and www.ark.ac.uk/elections/fw66.htm, accessed 13 March 2012.

90 Armagh, South Down, Fermanagh-South Tyrone, Mid Ulster and Londonderry

91 And even here McAteer's statement, 'We do not particularly wish to send people to Westminster but it is essential to send Paddy Gormley at this moment', appeared to give somewhat half-hearted support to Gormley. *Derry Journal*, 25 March 1966, cited in M. O'Callaghan, 'From Casement Park to Toomebridge', p. 135.

92 Purdie, *Politics in the Streets*, p. 60.

93 Murphy, *Gerry Fitt*, pp. 80–81.

94 The largest event was a march in West Belfast for which the *Irish News* estimated a figure of 70,000-plus. The *Belfast Newsletter* estimate was less than half of that but nonetheless it was clearly a large turnout. See O'Callaghan, 'From Casement Park to Toomebridge', p. 144 fn. 80 and C. O'Donnell, 'Pragmatism Versus Unity: The Stormont Government and the 1966 Easter Commemoration', in Daly and O'Callaghan (eds), *1916 in 1966*, p. 269 fn. 57.

95 Ruairí Ó Brádaigh in Dungannon, Sean MacStiofáin in Armagh and Seán Keenan in Derry. See O'Callaghan, 'From Casement Park to Toomebridge', pp. 113, 118, 129.

96 O'Donnell, 'Pragmatism Versus Unity', pp. 256–257.

97 M. O'Callaghan, 'From Casement Park to Toomebridge', p. 109; see also Prince and Warner, *Belfast and Derry*, pp. 72–74.

98 *Irish Independent*, 11 August 1966.

99 See Murphy, *Gerry Fitt*, p. 42; Patterson, *Ireland*, p. 197.

100 *Derry Journal*, 16 August 1966.

101 Cited in Eamon Phoenix, 'O'Neill cabinet dismissed claims of discrimination', *Irish Times*, 2 January 1997.

102 *Irish Times*, 11 December 1966.

103 *Irish Times*, 13 December 1966.

104 *Ibid.*

105 *Evening Press*, 13 December 1966.

106 The conference went ahead without the presence of Joseph Connellan who died on 11 April 1967. See *Frontier Sentinel*, 15 April 1967. That he was still the sitting MP for South Down in the golden years of his life was not a cause of celebration for Connellan himself; at the time of the 1965 election he had written to Cahir Healy expressing envy at Healy's retirement ('Sitting by your fireside and enjoying your books in peace') and regretting that his own South Down constituents had 'failed to produce an acceptable successor'. Connellan was very much alive to the negative side of his candidacy, 'This reliance on the old workhorses is bad and reflects poorly on the Nationalists at a time when they should be more progressive and far seeing.' PRONI, D2991/B/6/2, Cahir Healy papers, Connellan to Healy, 21 December 1965.

107 *Irish Times*, 1 July 1967.

108 *Belfast Newsletter*, 3 July 1967. The lack of 'substance' to the Nationalist Party's performance at Stormont had been earlier noted by the liberal *Belfast Telegraph* which unfavourably compared the Nationalist Opposition at Stormont with the more rigorous unofficial Opposition of their NILP predecessors. See *Belfast Telegraph*, 23 February 1966.

109 *Belfast Newsletter*, 3 July 1967.

110 Prince and Warner, *Belfast and Derry*, p. 168.

111 *Irish Times*, 3 July 1967.

112 *Belfast Telegraph*, 3 July 1967.

113 NAI, DFA 345/297/2 hand-written note by P. McCabe to B. Nolan, 5 July 1967.

114 Staunton, *The Nationalists*, p. 253.

115 NAI, DFA 345/297/1, B. Nolan to O'Sullivan, 6 July 1967.

116 *Ibid.*

117 *Ibid.*

118 *Ibid.*
119 See J. Horgan, *Seán Lemass: The Enigmatic Patriot* (Dublin, Gill & Macmillan, 1997), p. 288.
120 *Irish Independent*, 6 November 1967.
121 *Derry Journal*, 27 November 1967.
122 *Irish Independent*, 30 October 1967.
123 *Sunday Independent*, 29 October 1967.
124 *Irish Times*, 2 November 1967.
125 *Irish Independent*, 6 November 1967. It also pointed out that British politicians, who were not favourably disposed to the Unionist Party, held similarly critical views of northern Nationalism. Those mentioned were Roy Jenkins, the British Home Secretary; Jeremy Thorpe, the leader of the Liberal Party; and Geoffrey Bing MP, who was cited as recently having remarked on the 'tribalism of society' in the North.
126 *Irish Times*, 2 November 1967.
127 Purdie, *Politics in the Streets*, p. 132 gives the date as 29 January 1967. Other accounts give the founding date as 1 February 1967.
128 P. Bew and G. Gillespie, *Northern Ireland: A Chronology of the Troubles 1968–1993* (Dublin, Gill and Macmillan, 1993), p. 3.
129 Cited in Purdie, *Politics in the Streets*, p. 136.
130 S. Prince, '5 October 1968 and the Beginning of the Troubles: Flashpoints, Riots and Memory', *Irish Political Studies* 27: 3 (2012), p. 396.
131 Prince and Warner, *Belfast and Derry*, p. 88.
132 *Ibid.*, pp. 94–95.
133 S. Prince, '5 October 1968', p. 401.
134 Bew and Gillespie, *Northern Ireland*, pp. 3–4.
135 House of Commons (Northern Ireland) Debates, Volume 71 (1968, 69, 78), pp. 59–60.
136 *Ibid.*
137 Patterson, *Ireland*, p. 206.
138 Bew and Gillespie, *Northern Ireland*, p. 12.
139 See S. Prince, 'The Global Revolt of 1968 and Northern Ireland', *The Historical Journal* 49: 3 (2006), 851–875.
140 Those Nationalist Party MPs who retained their seats were James O'Reilly (Mourne), M.J. Keogh (South Down), J. Carron (South Fermanagh), A. Currie (East Tyrone), Thomas Gormley (Mid Tyrone) and R.H. O'Connor (West Tyrone). In Belfast Gerry Fitt retained his seat in Dock. See W.D. Flackes, *Northern Ireland: A Political Directory 1968–83* (London, British Broadcasting Corporation, 1980), pp. 258–263.
141 Paddy Kennedy of the Republican Labour Party (RLP) was MP for Belfast Central, a seat previously held by J. Brennan (NDP); Paddy Devlin (NILP) was MP for Belfast Falls, previously held by Harry Diamond.
142 'Stormont MPs asked Lynch for arms "to stop massacre"', *Irish Independent*, 10 January 2000.
143 *Irish Times*, 21 November 1969.
144 The Alliance Party was established in April 1970.
145 NAI, DFA, Note on Mr James Doherty, 14 May 1970.

146 Like the Gormley brothers Doherty, who held a seat on Derry City Council, had a past record of putting the material welfare of Catholics above that of nationalist dogmas. In the 1960s he supported the work of the Northern Ireland Housing Trust in its efforts to improve housing quality in the Bogside district of Derry. As the Trust was a quasi-government organisation its activities were viewed with distrust by other Nationalists who suspected that its brief was to ghettoise Catholics in certain electoral districts. See Gerald McSheffrey, *Planning Derry: Planning and Politics in Northern Ireland* (Liverpool, Liverpool University Press, 2000), pp. 42, 44.

147 NAI DFA, Note on Mr James Doherty 14 May 1970.

148 *Belfast Telegraph*, 18 November 1969.

149 See Prince and Warner, *Belfast and Derry*, p. 191.

150 NAI, DFA, Note on Mr James Doherty, 14 May 1970.

151 The SDLP was established in August 1970.

152 NAI, DFA, Gallagher to Holmes, 23 February 1970.

153 NAI, DFA, hand-written note 23 February 1970.

154 Interview transcript with James Doherty, 4 June 2010, *Civic Voices: An International Democracy Memory Bank Project*, p. 7, www.civicvoices.org/UserFiles/james%20 doherty%20edited%20formatted%20(2)1.pdf, accesed 15 March 2012.

155 *Irish Times*, 16 October 1970.

156 In June three members of the IRA had died when the bomb they were assembling prematurely exploded; two young girls aged four and nine, the daughters of one of the bomb makers also perished in the explosion. See Martin Melaugh, *A Chronology of the Conflict – 1970*, http://cain.ulst.ac.uk/othelem/chron/ch70.htm.

157 *Irish Times*, 16 October 1970.

Conclusion

What was the legacy that constitutional nationalism of the period 1932–70 left behind? It was, as we have seen, a diverse rather than a homogenous entity; it encompassed both a conservative Catholic communalism and a left-nationalism, which itself had both Catholic communalist and secular variants. On the whole, left-nationalists adopted a policy of participation when it came to representing the interests of their (predominantly Catholic) constituents in British parliamentary institutions (Stormont and Westminster); many conservative nationalists, on the other hand, favoured abstentionism. However, there were no hard and fast rules here; some conservative nationalists viewed abstention not as a principle but as a tactic which was to be adopted or discarded, depending on the political context. Nonetheless, regardless of ideological orientation or context, it is difficult not to see the consequences of abstentionism as having been other than negative and unproductive (especially in regard to alleviating Catholic grievances). For much of the time up until the 1960s many conservative constitutional nationalists focused on the primacy of securing the national ideal of territorial unity above all else (although there were notable exceptions, like Joe Devlin and T.J. Campbell in Belfast). And while this undoubtedly had an emotional and popular appeal, the effect of its non-delivery was to create a sense of hopelessness and encourage a general disengagement from politics amongst many Catholics. Also, the elevation of anti-partitionism as a nationalist panacea invariably resulted in precious little time, or thought, being devoted to just how northern unionists would fit into a newly envisioned united Ireland. Even those on the secular nationalist left, like Jack Macgougan, were guilty of this omission; his belief that the unionism of the Protestant working class was based on economic privilege, and was thus relatively superficial, shared many of the same assumptions as the conservatives who felt that accommodating unionists was an unnecessary distraction. This took Macgougan further away from any hope of achieving the working-class unity he aspired towards. At times some constitutional nationalists displayed (what appeared to unionists to be) a disturbingly ambiguous attitude towards those who used violence to secure their goal of Irish unity; this did not mean that these constitutionalists themselves supported such methods, they did not. But, there was insensitivity as to how their perceived ambiguity was received, and when greater restraint and consideration was called for, particularly in times of heightened communal tensions, these were sometimes regrettably absent. There was also a dogged tendency among constitutional nationalists, of all hues, to look towards Dublin to provide the solution to what a future Irish government minister would vividly call the 'nationalist nightmare' in Northern Ireland.[1] This phraseology suggests an intensity of concern for northern nationalists which rarely surfaced in Dublin in the period under review. Expectations that Dublin (or London) could be called upon to end partition by imposing a settlement on unionists proved to be a mixture of wishful thinking, naivety, and, in the case of elected representatives, quite often an abdication of responsibilities to their constituents. The resulting inactivity, not to say passivity, led to a propensity for northern nationalists to espouse a 'rhetoric of victimhood',[2] which further compounded their sense of hopelessness. Perhaps one of the most damaging effects of this was that, for a long time, it prevented any meaningful self-criticism; a major and debilitating weakness for any politics.

However, the picture is not all irredeemably gloomy. From the late 1950s there were those, both in the Nationalist Party and on the fringes of nationalist politics, who confronted this difficult task of self-criticism with vigour and purpose. They concluded that by abandoning the political millenarianism of nationalist orthodoxy and by throwing themselves into the hitherto largely untested waters of political activism they could take the first steps towards creating a modernised, reinvigorated nationalism free from ethnic labels and historical baggage: a pluralist nationalism in fact. There was undoubtedly an element of utopianism here but it was mixed with a determination to move beyond the inertia of sectarian confrontation and a prudent acknowledgement that consent and agreement must lie at the heart of any future settlement between Nationalism and Unionism. Even though this project failed it is difficult not to admire the audacity and vision of these self-critical reformers. Indeed, they have been so acknowledged. A recent authoritative work points to these visionaries, and their ideas, as an early influence on John Hume, by far the most prominent constitutional nationalist figure to have emerged since 1970.[3] It argues that the revisionism on National Unity and the National Democratic Party (NDP) was 'hugely influential' on Hume, that it provided the platform on which he built his own revision of Irish nationalism – even if this did (quite quickly) depart in many respects from the more conciliatory revisionism of the visionaries of the late 1950s and 1960s. Hume's revisionism is said to have eventually allowed him to 'share some common ground' with the leader of Sinn Féin, Gerry Adams, and through a circuitous route (passing by Hume–Adams before arriving at the Downing Street Declaration) is said to have finally led to the triumph of the Peace Process (which also, of course, led to the triumph of Sinn Féin over Hume's party the SDLP). The substance of Hume's revision of Irish nationalism has come in for more critical scrutiny.[4] Nonetheless, it is certainly true that Hume was influenced by National Unity and the NDP. We know this because Hume wrote about his admiration of them in his *Irish Times* article of 1964, the same article in which, as we have seen, he applauded Paddy Gormley's 'realistic attitude' in making his conciliatory gestures towards Unionists; gestures which, at the time, Eddie McAteer criticised while declaring his own unflinching fealty to 'Nationalist principles', principles that prevented him making concessions which might 'surrender ground'. And yet, while the visionaries of National Unity and the NDP are occasionally remembered in academic treatises, if only in passing, others, like Paddy and Tommy Gormley, have faded from public memory. This does seem to be a significant historical oversight, for these men were not outsiders on the fringes of nationalist politics, they were very much on the inside; elected as Nationalist Party representatives; even – in Paddy Gormley's case – a potential party leader. Furthermore, their revisionism was in many ways as far-reaching as that of those younger radicals who did operate on the fringes. It was, after all, Paddy Gormley who, in his speech at Stormont, responding to the escalating street violence in 1968, spoke of the need to close the door on the sacrosanct beliefs of the past; who prioritised uniting communities; who called for civil rights, and of the need for all, unionists and nationalists, to accept also their civil duties and responsibilities. In short, this was a nationalist revisionism couched in an uncomplicated language of toleration, moderation and compromise. One is struck by the relevance and currency of such ideas, but at the time they struggled to be heard, and, as Northern Ireland sank into a slough of sectarianism and violence, it seemed that there was a shrinking constituency for them. Did these ideas belong to a specific moment? Perhaps they did. Even so, they resulted from a period of disillusionment with past orthodoxies which enabled some to imagine the development of a more pluralist politics in the future, one that held out the possibility of moving beyond the politics of grievance to embrace reconciliation. For this reason alone, that vision and those individuals deserve to be recorded in history.

Notes

1 This term was used in 1984 by the Irish Government Minister for Foreign Affairs, Peter Barry.
2 P. Bew, *Ireland: The Politics of Emnity 1789–2006* (Oxford, Oxford University Press, 2007), p. 578.
3 P.J. McLoughlin, *John Hume and the revision of Irish nationalism* (Manchester, Manchester University Press, 2010).
4 See for example John Paul McCarthy, '"Hume-Adams" is not the elixir of political life', *Sunday Independent*, 6 October 2011.

Bibliography

Public collections

Public Records Office of Northern Ireland (PRONI)
Cahir Healy papers
Denis Ireland papers
Jack Macgougan papers
Patrick McGill papers
A.J. Mulvey papers
Ministry of Home Affairs papers

National Archive of Ireland (NAI)
Department of Foreign Affairs papers
Department of the Taoiseach papers

UK National Archives
Home Office papers

Parliamentary records

House of Commons (Hansard) Debates
House of Commons (Northern Ireland) Debates
Dáil Éireann Debates

Newspapers

Belfast Newsletter
Belfast Telegraph
Derry Journal
Dungannon Observer
Evening Press

Fermanagh Herald
Frontier Sentinel
Hibernia
Irish Examiner
Irish Independent
Irish News
Irish Press
Irish Times
Irish Times Pictorial
Irish Weekly
Kerryman
Kilkenny People
Northern Star
Northern Whig
Saoirse – Irish Freedom
Sunday Express
Sunday Independent
Tribune
Ulster Herald
United Irishman

Books and articles

Bartlett, T. and Jeffrey, K., *A Military History of Ireland* (Cambridge, Cambridge University Press, 1996)

Barton, B., *Brookborough: The Making of a Prime Minister* (Belfast, Institute of Irish Studies, 1988)

Barton, B., *Northern Ireland in the Second World War* (Belfast, Ulster Historical Foundation, 1995)

Bew, P., *Ireland: The Politics of Emnity 1789–2006* (Oxford, Oxford University Press, 2007)

Bew, P., *The Memoir of David Gray: A Yankee in De Valera's Ireland* (Dublin, Royal Irish Academy, 2012)

Bew, P., Darwin, K. and Gillespie, G., *Passion and Prejudice: Nationalist-Unionist Conflict in Ulster in the 1930s and the Founding of the Irish Association* (Belfast, Institute of Irish Studies, 1993)

Bew, P., Gibbon, P. and Patterson, H., *Northern Ireland 1921–1994: Political Forces and Social Classes* (London, Serif, 1995)

Bew, P. and Gillespie, G., *Northern Ireland: A Chronology of the Troubles 1968–1993* (Dublin, Gill & Macmillan, 1993)

Bowman, J., *De Valera and the Ulster Question 1917–1973* (Oxford, Oxford University Press, 1982)

Bowyer Bell, J., *The Secret Army: The IRA 1916–1979* (Dublin, The Academy, 1983)

Bruckner, P., *The Tyranny of Guilt: An Essay on Western Masochism* (Princeton, NJ, Princeton University Press, 2010)

Buckland, P., *The Factory of Grievances: Devolved Government in Northern Ireland 1921–3* (Dublin, Gill & Macmillan, 1979)

Buckland, P., *James Craig* (Dublin, Gill & Macmillan, 1980)

Carroll, A.J., *Northern Ireland: The Background to the Conflict* (Belfast, The Appletree Press, 1983)

Coogan, T.P., *De Valera: Long Fellow, Long Shadow* (London, Hutchinson, 1993)

Coogan, T.P., *The IRA* (London, Palgrave Macmillan, 2002)

Cradden, T., *Trade Unionism, Socialism and Partition: The Labour Movement in Northern Ireland 1939–1953* (Belfast, December Publications, 1993)

Cunningham, M.J., *British Government Policy in Northern Ireland 1969–2000* (Manchester, Manchester University Press, 2001)

Curran, F., *Derry: Countdown to Disaster* (Dublin, Gill & Macmillan, 1986)

Daly, M.E. and O'Callaghan, M. (eds), *1916 in 1966: Commemorating the Easter Rising* (Dublin, Royal Irish Academy, 2007)

Delaney, E., 'Political Catholicism in Post-War Ireland: The Revd Denis Fahey and Maria Duce, 1945–54', *Journal of Ecclesiastical History* 52: 3 (July 2001)

Devlin, P., *Straight Left: An Autobiography* (Belfast, Blackstaff, 1993)

Dolan, A., *Commemorating the Irish Civil War: History and Memory, 1923–2000* (Cambridge, Cambridge University Press, 2006)

Douglas, R.M., 'The Pro-Axis Underground in Ireland, 1939–1943', *The Historical Journal*, 49: 4 (2006)

Duggan, G.C., *Northern Ireland: success or failure* (Dublin, Irish Times, 1950)

Duggan, J., *Neutral Ireland and the Third Reich* (Dublin, Lilliput Press, 1989)

Dunphy, R., *The Making of Fianna Fail Power in Ireland 1923–1948* (Oxford, Oxford University Press, 1995)

Edwards, A., *A History of the Northern Ireland Labour Party: Democratic Socialism and Sectarianism* (Manchester, Manchester University Press, 2009)

Elliott, M., *The Catholics of Ulster: A History* (London, Allen Lane, 2000)

Elliott, S., *Northern Ireland Parliamentary Election Results 1921–72* (Chichester, Political Reference Publications, 1973)

English, R., *Armed Struggle: A History of the IRA* (London, Macmillan, 2003)

Farrell, M., *Northern Ireland: The Orange State* (London, Pluto Press, 1978)

Ferriter, D., *The Transformation of Ireland 1900–2000* (London, Profile Books, 2004)

Finlay, A., 'Stephen McGonagle' (Obituary), *Saothar* 27 (2002)

Fisk, R., *In Time of War: Ireland, Ulster and the Price of Neutrality 1939–45* (Dublin, Gill & Macmillan, 1983)

Fitzpatrick, D., *The Two Irelands 1912–1939* (Oxford, Oxford University Press, 1998)

Flackes, W.D., *Northern Ireland: A Political Directory 1968–83* (London, British Broadcasting Corporation, 1980)

Gailey, A., *Crying in the Wilderness Jack Sawyers: A Liberal Editor in Ulster, 1939–69* (Belfast, The Institute of Irish Studies, 1995)

Girvin, B., *The Emergency: Neutral Ireland 1939–45* (London, Pan Books, 2007)

Gray, J. (ed.), *Thomas Carnduff: Life and Writings* (Belfast, 1994)

Hanley, B., '"Oh Here's to Adolph Hitler" the IRA and the Nazis', *History Ireland* 13: 3 (May/June 2005)

Harkness, D., *Northern Ireland Since 1920* (Dublin, Criterion Press, 1983)

Harris, M., *The Catholic Church and the Foundation of the Northern Irish State* (Cork, Cork University Press, 1993)

Harris, M., 'The Catholic Church, Minority Rights and the Founding of the Northern Irish state', in D. Keogh and M. Haltzel (eds), *Northern Ireland and the Politics of Reconciliation* (Cambridge, Cambridge University Press, 1994)

Harris, M., 'Religious Divisions, Discrimination and the Struggle for Dominance in Northern Ireland', in G. Hálfdanarson (ed.), *Racial Discrimination and Ethnicity in European History* (Pisa, Pisa University Press, 2003)

Hart, P., *The IRA and its Enemies: Violence and Community in Cork 1916–1923* (Oxford, Oxford University Press, 2009)

Healy, C., *The Mutilation of a Nation: The Story of the Partition of Ireland* (Derry, The Derry Journal Ltd, 1945)

Hennessey, T., *A History of Northern Ireland 1920–1996* (Dublin, Gill & Macmillan, 1997)

Hepburn, A.C., *A Past Apart: Studies in the History of Catholic Belfast 1850–1950* (Belfast, Ulster Historical Foundation, 1996)

Hepburn, A.C., *Catholic Belfast and Nationalist Ireland in the Era of Joe Devlin 1871–1934* (Oxford, Oxford University Press, 2008)

Hinsley, F.H. and Simpkins, C.A.G., *British Intelligence in the Second World War* (Cambridge, Cambridge University Press, 1990)

Horgan, J., *Seán Lemass: The Enigmatic Patriot* (Dublin, Gill & Macmillan, 1997)

Jackson, A., *Ireland 1798–1998: Politics and War* (Oxford, Blackwell, 1999)

Johnson, D.S., 'The Northern Ireland Economy, 1914–39', in L. Kennedy and P. Ollerenshaw (eds), *An Economic History of Ulster 1820–1939* (Manchester, Manchester University Press, 1985)

Keane, E., *An Irish Statesman and Revolutionary: The Nationalist and Internationalist Politics of Sean MacBride* (London, I.B. Tauris, 2006)

Kelleher, J.V., 'Can Ireland Unite?', *The Atlantic Monthly* 193: 4 (April 1954)

Kelly, J., *Bonfires on the Hillside: An Eyewitness Account of Political Upheaval in Northern Ireland* (Belfast, Fountain Publishing, 1995)

Kennedy, D., 'Catholics in Northern Ireland 1926–1939', in F. McManus (ed.), *The Years of the Great Test 1926–39* (Dublin, Mercier Press, 1978)

Kennedy, K., Giblin, T. and McHugh, D., *The Economic Development of Ireland in the Twentieth Century* (London, Routledge, 1989)

Kennedy, M., *Division and Consensus: The Politics of Cross-Border Relations in Ireland, 1925–1969* (Dublin, Institute of Public Administration, 2000)

Keogh, D., *Twentieth-Century Ireland: Nation and State* (Dublin, Gill & Macmillan, 1994)

Lee, J., *Ireland 1912–1985* (Cambridge, Cambridge University Press, 1989)

Livingstone, P., *The Fermanagh Story* (Enniskillen, Cumann Seanchais Chlochair, 1969)

Lynch, R., *The Northern IRA and the Early Years of Partition, 1920–1922* (Dublin, Irish Academic Press, 2006)

Lynn, B., *Holding the Ground: The Nationalist Party in Northern Ireland, 1945–72* (Aldershot, Ashgate, 1997)

Lynn, B., 'The Irish Anti-Partition League and the Political Realities of Partition, 1945–9', *Irish Historical Studies* xxxiv: 135 (May 2000)

Mac an Aili, C., 'Uniting Ireland: Violence or Non Violence', *Hibernia* (January 1962), p. 15.

MacDermott E., *Clann na Poblachta* (Cork, Cork University Press, 1998)

Maguire, J., 'Internment, the IRA and the Lawless Case in Ireland: 1957–61', *Journal of the Oxford University History Society* (Michaelmas 2004)

McAllister, I., 'Political Opposition in Northern Ireland: The National Democratic Party, 1965–1970', *Economic and Social Review* 6 (1975)

McAteer, E., *Irish Action: New Thoughts on an Old Subject* (Ballyshannon, Donegal Democrat, October 1948), reprint (Belfast, Athol Books, 1979)

McCann, E., *War and an Irish Town* (London, Pluto Press, 1980)

McCluskey, C., *Up Off Their Knees* (Galway, Conn McCluskey & Associates, 1989)

McCracken, J.L., 'The Political Scene in Northern Ireland, 1926–1937', in F. McManus (ed.), *The Years of the Great Test 1926–39* (Dublin, Mercier Press, 1978)

McKeown, M., *The Greening of a Nationalist* (Lucan, Murlough Press, 1986)

McLoughlin, P.J., *John Hume and the Revision of Irish Nationalism* (Manchester, Manchester University Press, 2010)

McSheffrey, G., *Planning Derry: Planning and Politics in Northern Ireland* (Liverpool, Liverpool University Press, 2000)

Mulholland, M., 'Why Did Unionists Discriminate?', in Sabine Wichert (ed.), *From the United Irishmen to Twentieth-Century Unionism: Essays in Honour of A.T.Q. Stewart* (Dublin, Four Courts Press, 2004)

Munck, R. and Rolston, B., *Belfast in the Thirties: An Oral History* (Belfast, Blackstaff Press, 1987)

Murphy, M.A., *Gerry Fitt: Political Chameleon* (Cork, Mercier Press, 2007)

Norton, C., 'The Left in Northern Ireland 1921–1932', *Labour History Review* 60: 1 (Spring 1995)

Norton, C., 'The Irish Labour Party in Northern Ireland, 1949–1958', *Saothar* 21 (1996)

Norton, C., 'An Earnest Endeavour for Peace? Unionist Opinion and the Craig/Collins Peace Pact of 30 March 1922', *Études Irlandaises* 32: 1 (2007)

Norton, C, 'The Internment of Cahir Healy M.P., Brixton Prison, July 1941–December 1942', *Twentieth Century British History* 18: 2 (2007)

Norton, C., 'Jack Macgougan (1913–1998)', in K. Gildart and D. Howell (eds), *Dictionary of Labour Biography Volume XIII* (London, Palgrave Macmillan, 2010)

O'Brien, C. C., *States of Ireland* (London, Panther Books, 1974)

O'Brien, C.C., *Ancestral Voices: Religion and Nationalism in Ireland* (Dublin, Poolbeg Press, 1994)

O'Brien, C.C., *Memoir: My Life and Themes* (Dublin, Poolbeg Press, 1998)

Ó Corráin, D., "Ireland in his Heart North and South': The Contribution of Ernest Blythe to The Partition Question', *Irish Historical Studies* XXXV: 137 (May 2006)

Ó Corráin, D., *Rendering to God and Caesar: The Irish Churches and the Two States in Ireland, 1949–73* (Manchester University Press, Manchester, 2006)

O'Donoghue, D., *The Devil's Deal: The IRA, Nazi Germany and the Double Life of Jim O'Donovan* (Dublin, New Island Books, 2010)

Parkinson, A.F,. *Belfast's Unholy War: The Troubles of the 1920s* (Dublin, Four Courts Press, 2004)

Paseta, S., 'Northern Ireland and the Second World War', in *Northern Ireland: A Divided Community, 1921–1972* (Gale Digital Collection, n.d.), www.gale.com/ DigitalCollections

Patterson, H., *The Politics of Illusion: A Political History of the IRA* (London, Serif, 1997)

Patterson, H., 'Party versus Order: Ulster Unionism and the Flags and Emblems Act', *Contemporary British History* 13:4 (Winter 1999)

Patterson, H., 'Seán Lemass and the Ulster Question, 1959–65', *Journal of Contemporary History*, 34: 145 (1999)

Patterson, H., *Ireland Since 1939: The Persistence of Conflict* (Dublin, Penguin Ireland, 2006)

Patterson, H. and Kaufman E., *Unionism and Orangeism in Northern Ireland since 1945: The Decline of the Loyal Family* (Manchester, Manchester University Press, 2007)

Phoenix, E., *Northern Nationalism: Nationalist Politics, Partition and the Catholic Minority in Northern Ireland 1890–1940* (Belfast, Ulster Historical Foundation, 1994)

Prince, S., 'The Global Revolt of 1968 and Northern Ireland', *The Historical Journal* 49: 3 (2006)

Prince, S., *Northern Ireland's '68: Civil Rights, Global Revolt and the Origins of the Troubles* (Dublin, Irish Academic Press, 2007)

Prince, S., '5 October 1968 and the Beginning of the Troubles: Flashpoints, Riots and Memory', *Irish Political Studies* 27: 3 (2012)

Prince, S. and Warner, G., *Belfast and Derry in Revolt: A New History of the Start of the Troubles* (Dublin, Irish Academic Press, 2012)

Purdie, B., 'The Friends of Ireland: British Labour and Irish Nationalism, 1945–49', in T. Gallagher and J. O'Connell (eds), *Contemporary Irish Studies* (Manchester, Manchester University Press, 1983)

Purdie, B., *Politics in the Streets: The Origins of the Civil Rights Movement in Northern Ireland* (Belfast, Blackstaff Press, 1990)

Rafferty, O., *Catholicism in Ulster 1603–1983: An Interpretative History* (Dublin, Gill & Macmillan, 1994)

Read, C., 'Protestant Challenges to the "Protestant State": Ulster Unionism and Independent Unionism in Northern Ireland, 1921–39', *Twentieth Century British History* 19: 4 (2008)

Rees, R., *Labour and the Northern Ireland Problem 1945–51: The Missed Opportunity* (Dublin, Irish Academic Press, 2009)

Simpson, A.W.B., *In the Highest Degree Odious: Detention Without Trial in Wartime Britain* (Oxford, Clarendon Press, 1992)

Sinnott, R., *Irish Voters Decide: Voting Behaviour in Elections and Referendums Since 1918* (Manchester, Manchester University Press, 1995)

Smyth, S., 'In Defence of Ulster: The Visit of Sir Basil Brooke to North America, Spring 1950', *The Canadian Journal of Irish Studies* 33: 2 (Fall 2007)

Staunton, E., *The Nationalists of Northern Ireland 1918–1973* (Dublin, Columba Press, 2001)

Swan, S., *Official Irish Republicanism, 1962 to 1972* (Lulu.com, 2008)

Ultach, 'The Persecution of Catholics in Northern Ireland', *Capuchin Annual*, 1943 (reprint Athol Books, Belfast, 1995)

Walker, G., *The Politics of Frustration: Harry Midgley and the Failure of Labour in Northern Ireland* (Manchester, Manchester University Press, 1985)

Walker, G., '"Protestantism before Party!": The Ulster Protestant League in the 1930s', *Historical Journal* 28:4 (1985)

Walker, G., *Intimate Strangers: Political and Cultural Interaction between Scotland and Ulster in Modern Times* (Edinburgh, John Donald Publishers, 1995)

Walker, G., *A History of the Ulster Unionist Party: Protest, pragmatism and pessimism* (Manchester, Manchester University Press, 2004)

Whyte, J., *Interpreting Northern Ireland* (Oxford, Clarendon Press, 1991)

Theses

Harbinson, J., 'A History of the Northern Ireland Labour Party', unpublished M.Sc. thesis, Queen's University Belfast (1966)

McKeever, P., 'The Discourse of Nationalists in Northern Ireland 1921–1991', unpublished Ph.D. thesis, Queen's University Belfast (1993)

Websites

http://cain.ulst.ac.uk/othelem

www.civicvoices.org

Index